T0330011

The Economic Institutions of Higher Education

We are forever grateful for the understanding and support of our families during the course of writing this book. Thank you Judy and Patrick; Marilyn, Colby, Amelia, Danni, Bill and William Edward.

The Economic Institutions of Higher Education

Economic Theories of University Behavior

J. Patrick Raines

Professor of Economics and F. Carlyle Tiller Chair in Business
University of Richmond, USA

Charles G. Leathers

Professor of Economics
University of Alabama, USA

Edward Elgar
Cheltenham, UK • Northampton, MA, USA

Published by
Edward Elgar Publishing Limited
Glensanda House
Montpellier Parade
Cheltenham
Glos GL50 1UA
UK

Edward Elgar Publishing, Inc.
136 West Street
Suite 202
Northampton
Massachusetts 01060
USA

A catalogue record for this book
is available from the British Library

Library of Congress Cataloguing in Publication Data

Raines, J. Patrick, 1951-
 The economic institutions of higher education : economic theories of university behaviour
  /J. Patrick Raines, Charles G. Leathers.
   p. cm.
  Includes bibliographical references (p.) and index.
   1. Education, higher – Economic aspects. 2. Universities and colleges – Administration. 3. Universities and colleges – Sociological aspects. I. Leathers, Charles G., 1940- II. Title.

LC67.6.R35 2003
338.4'3378 – dc21

                                                         2003045755

ISBN 1-84064-991-7

Printed and bound in Great Britain by MPG Books Ltd, Bodmin, Cornwall

Contents

1. Introduction   **1**

The Applicability of Economic Analysis   3
Economics of Higher Education: Recent Studies   4
Economic Perspectives on Universities' Behavior   5
Modeling Universities' Decision-making Processes   6
The Foundational Work of Adam Smith and Thorstein Veblen   7
Organization of the Book   10

2. Historical Development of Universities   **15**

Medieval Universities   17
The English Universities   21
The Scottish Universities   30
The New German Universities   40
The Emergence of Modern American Universities   44

3. Adam Smith on Failures of English Universities   **54**

The Institutional Nature of Universities   57
Smith's Criticism of Universities   59
Proposals for Reform   68
Incompleteness, Weaknesses, and Contradictions   69

4. John Stuart Mill on Universities   **74**

The Special Social Functions of Universities   75
Why the English Universities Were Failing   78
Mill's Economic Analysis of Universities' Failures   80
Government Schools vs. Private Schools   85

5. Veblen on Failures of American Universities   **90**

The Social Importance of Knowledge   92
The Social Functions of Universities   94
Universities and the Principle of Institutional Specialization   94
Evolutionary Development of Modern 'University Corporations'   96
Institutional Failures of American Universities   102
Transitional Statement   119

6. Veblen's Economic 'Model' of University Behavior   **120**

Universities as Non-Profit Corporations   121
Endowed Institutions   122
Identities and Motives of Discretionary Officials   123

Modeling Institutional Behavior   134
Institutional Drift and 'Proposals' for Reform   138

7. Riesman on Veblen and Modern Universities   **144**

Riesman's Critique of Veblen and the Higher Learning   145
Riesman on Modern Universities: An Era of Faculty Dominance   151
Riesman's 'Era of Rising Student Consumerism'   158

8. The Buchanan–Devletoglou Economic Model of Universities   **163**

The Taxpayers' Representatives: Governing Boards   171
Students as Consumers Who Do Not Pay   172
Control of Universities by Faculties Who Do Not Sell   173
The Nature and Causes of Universities' Failures   175
Lack of Competition   180
The Crisis on Campuses   181

9. Recent Economic Models of Higher Education   **186**

Economic Models of Non-Profit Institutions   187
Garvin's Economic Model of University Behavior   189
The University as an Organization: The Prestige Objective   191
Garvin's Formal Model   201

10. Meeting the Challenge: Explaining the Emergence of 'Entrepreneurial Universities' and 'Academic Capitalism'   **210**

First Phase   210
Second Phase   212
The Challenge for Economic Models of Universities' Behavior   213
Overview   213
The Emergence of 'Entrepreneurial Universities'   214
The Consequences of 'Entrepreneurial' Research by Universities   215
An Alternative View   218
The 'Commoditization of Instruction'   219
Explaining the Emergence of 'Entrepreneurial Universities'   222
A Veblenian Perspective   224
Smith and Veblen on 'Entrepreneurial Universities'   227

Bibliography   **231**

Index   **239**

1. Introduction

A substantial part of economic theory and analysis seeks to explain the behavior of economic organizations. Profit-seeking business firms and the markets in which they operate have received the bulk of attention. But in recognition of the large and growing social importance of public and non-profit organizations, economists have increasingly turned their attention to explaining the behavior of these institutions. Within that broad group, universities would be expected to hold special interest for economists for several reasons. Most immediately, universities are the institutional habitat of most economists. They received their training and professional certification from doctoral degree-granting universities and the majority are employed as faculty members by colleges and universities. As intellectually curious and self-interested people, economists would naturally be interested in understanding the behavioral tendencies of those institutions, especially in relation to how their own work and welfare tend to be affected.

As social scientists, economists have ample professional reasons for applying their analytical tools to the behavior of universities. Universities are important institutions in all societies, and are especially prominent in both the cultural and economic systems of the United States. From a budgetary perspective alone, their economic impacts command serious attention. In the aggregate, universities have huge revenues and expenditures, and provide employment for large numbers of professionals of many varieties and even larger numbers of operational support and staff people. More importantly, as institutions of post-secondary and post-graduate education, universities are viewed as serving special social purposes through their academic functions of teaching and research. That largely accounts for the fact that most are either public or private/non-profit institutions. The elite private universities and some of the major state universities are endowed with extremely large assets (Harvard University has an endowment exceeding $19 billion). But most institutions of higher education, private as well as public, are substantially supported, either directly or indirectly, by public funding.

Modern universities are complex multi-purpose institutions that engage in a number of activities that have little or nothing to do with traditional academic work of teaching and research. Some of those activities can easily be categorized as providing public service, applying specialized knowledge to solving social problems and giving informed guidance to those in business, manufacturing, agriculture, government, the professions, and consumers. Major universities have become important elements in the industrial development and recruitment strategies of states and local economic areas. These service activities may be termed academic-related. Hence, universities often claim that their missions are teaching, research, and service.

But universities also engage in a growing number of non-academic activities whose social purposes are obscure, to say the least. Examples are athletic programs, quasi-commercial enterprises on campuses that go beyond providing basic support for student life, contract research, for-profit commercial operations, property developments that are often in the form of joint-ventures with private enterprises, and financial management of large portfolios of assets. The most recent development of this nature has been research aimed at producing intellectual properties that have high commercial value, which the universities intend to market for profit. Indeed, there is considerable descriptive truth in the critics' claim that the four E's of higher education are Employment, Entertainment, Enterprise, and Education.

In virtually all of their activities, whether the purely academic, academic-related, or non-academic, universities are competitive institutions. That behavioral characteristic would lead economists to ask a number of questions. Why do universities compete? How do they develop and implement their competitive strategies? What are the key elements in those strategies? What are the social and institutional consequences of a competitive environment? In the market economy, competition is expected to promote consumer welfare. Does the type of competition in which universities engage lead them to pursue their special social functions with greater efficiency and effectiveness? Or does competition result in a diversion of resources toward other activities and programs?

The substantial public interest in the performances of universities invites normative analyses of what society expects universities to do. But evaluations of whether universities can be expected to accomplish their assigned social purposes require positive analyses that explain how universities determine institutional goals and objectives. Subsequent positive analyses are required to explain how universities make decisions on operational missions, academic policies, non-academic activities, and internal resource allocations within the constraints that are imposed by such factors as institutional charters, legal rules affecting non-profit organizations, governmentally-mandated requirements, and revenues from legislative appropriations, tuition, fees, endowments, grants and contracts, and profits from commercial operations.

From a public policy perspective, economists' interest in understanding universities' behavioral tendencies has been particularly stimulated by two general perceptions. The first is that universities tend to experience institutional failures. From an economic perspective, that means that universities fail to efficiently and effectively pursue those particular functions that society has assigned to them as specialized institutions. The second is that universities are continuing to experience evolutionary institutional changes, which may be altering their nature and character. This is especially true for the large complex research universities, to which the term 'university' generally applies in modern economic analyses. From the late Middle Ages to the first half of the 20th century, universities evolved from being institutions whose primary function was to teach and train for professions to institutions that allowed scientists and scholars to pursue pure research. Currently, large research universities are undergoing another transformation, becoming 'entrepreneurial universities' engaging in research aimed at generating intellectual properties with considerable market value and seeking to commercially exploit their ownership of those properties.

THE APPLICABILITY OF ECONOMIC ANALYSIS

A legitimate question is to what extent economic analysis may provide insights into the institutional behavior of universities. Conventional economic analyses rely on principles of property rights and rational pursuit of self-interest by individuals to explain resource allocations that are directed by the price mechanism under the market forces of competitive supply and demand. Supply functions are assumed to fully reflect information about the opportunity costs of inputs. Demand functions are assumed to reflect the true values of the outputs to the consumers. How applicable are the conventional economic tools in explaining the determination of universities' institutional goals and missions, academic policies, programs and activities, and internal resource allocations? To what extent can universities be viewed as economic institutions that purposely attempt to organize production functions to maximize definable objective functions? To what degree do they respond to and are disciplined by market forces?

An economist writing about the 'awkward economics of higher education' has stated that 'Higher education is a business: it produces and sells educational services to customers for a price and it buys inputs with which to make that product. Costs and revenues discipline decisions and determine the long-run viability of a college or university' (Winston 1999, p. 13). But he quickly noted that, in important ways, institutions of higher education function differently from commercial businesses that operate on a for-profit basis. What can conventional tools of economic analysis tell us about the behavior of the institutions engaged in the 'business' of higher education?

Modern universities have evolved from institutions established centuries ago, and they continue to experience further institutional evolutionary changes. A particular challenge for analysts is to explain the processes that initiate and guide that evolutionary change, as well as the consequences on the behavioral tendencies of the institutions. Conventional micro-economic theory and analysis largely deals with given institutional structures. But institutional economics and the growing field of socio-economics seek to explain how evolutionary development and change occurs and its consequences for behavioral tendencies. How applicable are the methodologies of these branches of economics in analyzing evolutionary changes in universities' behavior?

ECONOMICS OF HIGHER EDUCATION: RECENT STUDIES

Partly in response to the enormous expansion in student enrollments and physical facilities in higher education in the post-World War II era, economists have increasingly applied their analytical tools to various aspects of higher education. In the earlier studies, the focus was largely on post-secondary education as investment in human capital (see, e.g., Schultz 1968 and McMahan 1974), with relatively little analytical attention to the behavioral tendencies of the institutions that provided that education. In 1988, McCormick and Meiners perceived 'a surprising dearth of analysis by economists of their institutional environment, the university' (1988, p. 423), although they were able to cite a number of exceptions.

That situation quickly changed. In 1989, the National Bureau of Economic Research began a program of research on the economics of higher education which resulted in the publication of two books edited by Clotfelter and others: *Economic Challenges in Higher Education* (1991) and *Studies of Supply and Demand in Higher Education* (1993). In 1990, a collection of papers edited by Hoenack and Collins was published as *The Economics of American Universities*. The second and third parts of *The Academy in Crisis*, edited by Sommer (1995), consisted of papers dealing with the political economy of higher education and university research. In 1993, Rothschild and White were able to observe that 'The application of economic principles to the behavior of colleges and universities is a topic of substantial interest and importance. The literature on various aspects of the economics of higher education is now large and growing rapidly' (p. 11). In 1999, papers from a symposium on the economics of higher education were published in the *Journal of Economic Perspectives* (Clotfelter 1999).

A wide range of topics has been investigated in this growing literature on the economics of higher education, as indicated by the following representative examples. Production and cost functions have been analyzed by Getz and Siegried (1991), Hopkins (1990), Brinkman (1990a), and Hoenack (1990). Demand functions for the different services of higher education were analyzed by Becker (1990), while demand for undergraduate education was analyzed by Clotfelter (1991). The supply of faculty was analyzed by Ehrenberg (1991), and Green (1993). The pricing of university education was examined by Tollison and Willett (1976). University research has been analyzed by Dresch (1995), Lindsay (1995), and Balderston (1990).

Quality changes have been modeled by Smyth (1991). Academic labor markets, with particular attention to tenure, have been analyzed by Brown (1997) and Carmichael (1988). Human capital and social benefits of higher education have been analyzed by West (1995). Financial aspects have been examined by Brinkman (1990b), Ehrenberg, et al. (1993), Kimberling (1995), Merton (1993), Froomkin (1990), and Creedy (1995). College athletics have been examined by Koch (1983), Fleisher, et al. (1992), Brown (1993), Pacey and Wickham (1985), and McCormick and Tinsley (1987 and 1990). Rothschild and White (1993) have dealt with the market context of higher education in terms of whether and how universities compete and the consequences of that competition on input, production, pricing, and output decisions.

ECONOMIC PERSPECTIVES ON UNIVERSITIES' BEHAVIOR

All of those who have studied universities from an economic perspective have explicitly noted the complex institutional nature of universities and the difficulty of ascertaining – conceptually, quantitatively, and qualitatively – their actual outputs. In each of the above-cited studies, universities were recognized as being rather peculiar not-for-profit organizations. That applies to large state (public) universities, which have major features of non-profit institutions, e.g., functioning as autonomous institutions under boards of trustees, collecting substantial portions of their revenues from students fees, and depending heavily on private-sector donors and research grants from both governments and businesses. Universities are vested with a large sense of public purpose, operate internally under non-hierarchical governance structures in which multiple interested parties, including students, have some ability to influence institutional decisions, and function in economic environments in which market forces play relatively weak roles. External forces, most noticeably state and federal governments and academic accreditation agencies, mandate that universities behave in certain ways. But even in many of those cases, universities have some discretionary range in choosing how they comply with those requirements.

MODELING UNIVERSITIES' DECISION-MAKING PROCESSES

Some economists have focused their efforts primarily on developing and testing hypotheses on how universities determine their institutional goals, academic policies, and internal resource allocation decisions. In these analyses, critical attention has been given to the internal processes of decisionmaking involved in the effective governance structure of universities. Recent papers that analyzed university governance include Brennan and Tollison (1980), Brown (1997), McCormick and Meiners (1988), Meiners and Staaf (1995), Tuckman and Chang (1990), James (1990), and Manne (1978). In formal modeling, the most definitive work was done by Garvin (1980). These models of universities' behavior are specialized versions of the more general models of non-profit organizations that have been applied also to hospitals (see, in particular, Newhouse 1970; and also Lee 1971). In these investigations, the basic economic principle of self-interested behavior of individuals has been applied to explain institutional decisions as reflecting at the first level the relative influence of the members of the governing boards, administrators, faculty, students, and alumni. At a deeper level, the analyses have focused on the personal utility functions that define the motives of the individuals in each groups, in conjunction with the incentives provided and constraints imposed by universities' internal institutional structures and external economic environments in which they function.

For the most part, these studies have tended to produce static models, which give little attention to how the decision-making processes under scrutiny may be involved with internal processes that initiate and guide evolutionary institutional change. Some researchers, however, have sensed that evolutionary changes in universities' behavior have quickened in recent time, especially in response to changing sources of revenues. In particular, investigations by Noll (1998), Powell and Owen-Smith (1998), and Slaughter and Leslie (1997) have noted the extent to which research universities as non-profit/public organizations are undergoing transformation to commercial enterprises. While these studies have been rather narrowly focused, they point to the much larger fact that modern universities have not only evolved from past institutions but are continuing to evolve.

THE FOUNDATIONAL WORK OF ADAM SMITH AND THORSTEIN VEBLEN

Ehrenberg (1999) stated that academic economists began using utility-maximizing models to explain universities' behavior after Garvin's investigative work was published in *The Economics of University Behavior* (1980). In a formal modeling sense, that is true. But the economic approach of seeking explanations of universities' institutional behavior in the pursuit of self-interest by individuals in positions to influence decisions relating to goals, academic policies, funding, and internal resource allocations actually has deep roots in the development of economic theory. The purpose of this book is to develop an historical survey of economic perspectives on universities' behavioral tendencies, showing how aspects of earlier works remain relevant to efforts to understand the behavioral tendencies of modern universities that are experiencing new forces of evolutionary change.

Particular attention is paid to the foundational work by Adam Smith in *Wealth of Nations*, published in 1776, and Thorstein Veblen in *The Higher Learning in America*, published in 1918. In the latter book, Veblen presented normative views on the social functions of universities and how they would operate in their ideal institutional form. Unfortunately, the heavily satirical nature of his exposition and the provocative nature of his basic thesis, as suggested in the subtitle *A Memorandum on the Conduct of Universities by Business Men*, may have caused many of his readers to overlook the serious economic analysis of universities' behavior that was presented. In typical fashion, Veblen denied any personal views on the subject, contending instead that the normative perspective being applied was that held by society at large, which he explained as rooted in a psychology of instincts and a theory of evolutionary institutional change. (Scholars, of course, have attributed much of Veblen's normative analysis to his personal experiences as a faculty member at the University of Chicago and Stanford University.) But intertwined with his normative commentary, Veblen developed a positive analysis that explained how institutional behavior of American universities was determined and why they were failing to function as true universities as defined in his normative analysis. Characteristically, he offered no serious recommendations for reform.

Nearly a century and a half earlier, Smith had presented an equally critical commentary on the behavior of English universities in Book V of *Wealth of Nations*. He too expressed normative views on what universities should be doing that clearly reflected his own personal views, and presented a positive analysis that explained why English universities were failing to function as they should in that regard. Unlike Veblen, Smith's normative analysis clearly reflected his own personal views, and he noted the reforms that would be needed if those failures were to be corrected. Scholars have also recognized that Smith's normative views reflected his unhappy experiences as a student at Oxford University and his more pleasant experiences as a student, faculty member, and administrator at Glasgow University. But his positive analysis represented an application of his general economic theory to what today would be termed 'non-profit' institutions.

The earlier analyses of universities' behavioral tendencies by Smith and Veblen merit special attention because each, in his own unique way, developed an economic perspective on universities' behavior that anticipated the more recent economic models as exemplified by Garvin (1980). An additional feature found in both Smith's and Veblen's analyses of the behavior of the universities of their respective eras was the explicit attention given to how those institutions had evolved from the medieval European universities. While Smith gave no real indication that evolutionary change was continuing, that was an integral element in the basic framework of Veblen's analysis of American universities.

The relationships between Smith's and Veblen's analyses of university behavior and institutional failures are complex. There were remarkable similarities in their positive analyses. Both explained institutional goals, academic policies, and internal resource allocations in terms of pursuit of self-interest on part of individuals in positions to influence universities' decisions. Both analyses focused on the incentives provided and the constraints imposed on individuals' pursuit of self-interest by the special features of universities as non-profit organizations. But there were important differences, especially in the connections between their positive analyses of behavioral tendencies and the normative implications of those analyses. From a political economy perspective, their normative analyses were guided by virtually polar opposite views on how responsive universities should be to market forces. Smith argued that the English universities should function more like competitive suppliers in a market ruled by student-consumer sovereignty. In contrast, Veblen blamed the failures of American universities primarily on the intrusive influence of competitive business enterprise. To a substantial degree, Veblen attributed the failures of American universities to the institutional practices and arrangements that Smith had recommended as solutions to the failures of the English universities.

Smith's and Veblen's economic perspectives on university behavior have more than just historical interest. Both continue to be recognized as having considerable relevance to problems and possible reforms of universities. For example, Meiners (1995) declared that 'Adam Smith's discussion of higher education in *Wealth of Nations* provides as insightful view of college teachers and students as any that has ever been written. The American system of higher education is the same in some fundamental ways as that observed by Smith over two centuries ago' (p. 21). Ortmann (1997) declared that Smith offered advice for today's colleges and universities on how to survive in 'post-industrial' environments. In a survey of universities, *The Economist* (1997) lauded Smith's argument that university teachers would be more diligent if their incomes were dependent upon student fees, and lamented that today's campuses have 'few Adam Smith's with a strong pecuniary incentive to heed their students' real wants' (p. 12).

Similarly, Barber (1988) observed that 'the issues Veblen raised in *The Higher Learning in America* continue to generate lively discussion among commentators on American education' (p. 424). Sowell (1969) commented that the 1918 book reads as if it had just been published (p. 73). Hayden and Stephenson (1992) argued that Veblen's maxim on university administrators and boards of trustees have substantial explanatory power when applied to modern state universities. Lucas (1994) observed that many of the critiques of American higher education in the 1990s 'were strikingly reminiscent of Thorstein Veblen's indictment in *The Higher Learning in America*' (p. 281). Lucas recognized, but without elaboration, that Veblen was presenting a model of university behavior. Ehrenberg (1999) criticized the utility-maximizing model of university behavior as describing 'fairly well the behavior of small liberal arts colleges, which typically lack separate centers of power' (p. 101). He argued that 'bargaining models' were more applicable in the cases of large complex universities with multiple units, each motivated by its own self-interests (p. 103). Smith's analysis of the behavior of the 18th century English universities fits the former, while Veblen's analysis of the behavior of the early 20th century American universities fits the latter.

But while Smith and Veblen continue to be cited, little critical attention has been given to the complexity of their analyses, the internal contradictions that exist, and the areas in which those analyses are incomplete. This is especially true in the case of Veblen. Citations of his work tend to refer to his normative assessments, to be couched in negative terms and not infrequently, to be either incorrect or misleading. For example, in a special report on universities, *The Economist* (1997) noted the aspirations of teaching colleges to become prestigious research universities. The article stated that Veblen's view that the university by doing any undergraduate training at all was 'in danger of becoming a body of secondary-school teachers masquerading as something much grander' continues to have its sting (p. 10). In citing Veblen's characterization of universities as bodies of mature scholars and scientists, Meiners and Staaf (1995) incorrectly stated that 'Veblen's view . . . fails to mention either the existence of administration or of students in a university' (p. 26). And even though Smith has generally received more approving citations, there has been a marked tendency for those citations to refer to only certain elements in his discussion of universities, in particular his argument for making faculty incomes dependent upon student fees.

The themes and issues that appeared the economic perspectives on universities' behavior in *Wealth of Nations* and *The Higher Learning in America* continued to resonate in studies of universities in the post-World War II era, when the great expansions in the number of institutions of higher education and the number of students enrolled in those institutions occurred. Issues that were addressed by Smith and Veblen continue to be contentious issues in the modern economic studies of universities' behavior. And the range of normative views on the social functions of universities expressed between Smith and Veblen still appear prominently within the range of views expressed by the various parties in modern debates. In addition, the evolutionary approach that Veblen incorporated in his critical analysis of American universities has special relevance to the current institutional changes that are occurring in large research universities.

ORGANIZATION OF THE BOOK

In the following chapters, modern economic perspectives on universities' behavior are shown to have pursued themes, identified concepts, and employed methodological approaches that appeared in either (or both) *Wealth of Nations* or *The Higher Learning in America*. Those include: identifying the social functions of universities as unique institutions characterized by such features as the absence of proprietary claimants and hence of the profit motive; non-hierarchical forms of governance, and multiple-parties involved in universities' decision making; explaining universities' choices of goals, academic policies, and resource allocations in terms of the motives, incentives, and degree of influence over institutional decision making of members of those parties; analyzing the behavior of universities in terms of competitive environments, with particular emphasis on the importance of reputation and prestige and the impact of external and internal environments on universities' behavior; and the importance of heavy dependence on endowments.

Chapter Overviews

The term 'university' has been applied to a number of different institutions of higher education. It is important to understand the nature of the institutions whose behavior was being analyzed by economists in different historical periods with different socio-cultural systems. That facilitates separating out aspects of the economic analyses that applied to unique features of universities in particular time periods and those that applied to features common to the universities of the 18th, 19th, and 20th centuries. For that purpose, Chapter Two reviews the historical evolution of universities, with particular attention to the English universities observed by Smith and the American universities observed by Veblen. The focus is primarily on the evolutionary development of those characteristics and features that are most relevant to behavioral tendencies of universities, namely, the organizational structures, systems of government, and sources and methods of financing.

In Chapter Three, we examine Adam Smith's analysis and criticism of the behavior of the English universities in the 18th century. We note not only his arguments but also areas in which there were contradictions or incompleteness.

In Chapter Four, we examine John Stuart Mill's views on the social functions of universities and his critique of universities' behavior in the first half of the 19th century. Mill's views position him as something of a transition figure between Smith and Veblen. His economic analysis followed the essential lines of Smith's, reaffirming much of what Smith had earlier argued. But there are important differences which reflected Mill's own thinking, particularly on the viability of the economic principles of competitive markets to education at all levels. At the same time, Mill's views on the social functions of universities, including what they should not be doing, were much more in line with Veblen's views.

The next two chapters are then devoted to Veblen's critical analysis of the behavior of American universities in the early 1900s. Our intent is look past Veblen's sarcastic commentaries to focus on his serious analytical work in *The Higher Learning in America*. In Chapter Five, we examine his normative analysis of the social functions of universities. Veblen drew upon his evolutionary social theory and psychology of human instincts to identify the ideal university as a seminary of the higher learning, devoted to the advancement and diffusion of knowledge through science and scholarship. Within that normative framework, he discussed the institutional nature of 'modern' universities as they had evolved in Europe and the United States, and explained how they were failing to function as true universities.

In Chapter Six, we focus on Veblen's positive analysis of the micro-structure of universities' governance system, which essentially sketched the framework of an economic model of universities that explained institutional behavior in terms of the 'motives' of the 'discretionary officials.' The 'discretionary officials' definitely included members of the governing boards and the administrators. But faculty members were not entirely excluded from being 'discretionary officials,' although their presence in that group tended to be very limited. While this positive analysis largely anticipated the modern economic models of universities, it was also much more complex. Veblen's normative and positive analyses were not only evolutionary in nature but were inter-twining. In particular, Veblen related the 'motives' of the discretionary officials and how those motives manifested into forms of behavior to underlying sets of values, which in turn were related to evolutionary institutional conditioning.

In relation to that interpretation, we note the differences between what he wrote about the higher learning in the last chapter of *The Theory of the Leisure Class*, published in 1899, and in *The Higher Learning in America*.

We then move forward to the modern (post-World War II) era. In Chapter Seven, we make an exception to dealing with economists' perspectives on the institutional behavior of universities to critically examine the criticism of Veblen by lawyer-turned-sociologist David Riesman and to compare his views on universities with those of Veblen and Smith. In *Thorstein Veblen: A Critical Interpretation* (1953), Riesman bitterly criticized Veblen's analysis of university behavior, especially his scathing treatment of the role of trustees and administrators. In *The Academic Revolution* (1968), Riesman and co-author Jencks argued that universities were effectively governed by faculties, who had achieved a 'hegemony.' In conjunction with that view, we detour to examine John Kenneth Galbraith's argument in *The New Industrial State* (1971) that universities and their faculties had achieved a position of great importance to modern large corporate enterprise. In Riesman's later book, *On Higher Education: The Academic Enterprise in the Age of Rising Student Consumerism* (1980), he did an about-face, arguing that faculty hegemony was quickly giving way to the rising power of student-consumers. We note that despite Riesman's criticism of Veblen, his various analyses of the parties who influence university decision-making followed Veblen's approach of explaining institutional goals, policies, and resource allocations in terms of the interests of 'discretionary officials.' Where Riesman differed from Veblen was largely in his perception of the parties that constituted the more powerful group of such officials.

The presentation of students as consumers of universities' services in Riesman's later book had several implications. One was to make his portrayal of the manner in which universities were functioning in 1980 very relevant to Adam Smith's argument that universities should be responsive to student demand. Curiously, Riesman made no mention of Smith's views on student-consumer sovereignty. A second implication was that students might behave in a radical manner. Disruptive actions by students, in actual occurrence or in threatened form, and the negative effects on universities' behavior had earlier been addressed by Nobel laureate James Buchanan and his co-author, Nicos E. Devletoglou. In *Academia in Anarchy: An Economic Diagnosis* (1970), they developed a general economic analysis and critique of the institutional structures that determine universities' behavior, which they then applied to explain the campus unrest and sometimes violently disruptive behavior of college students during the Viet Nam War era. We examine the Buchanan–Devletoglou economic model of universities and the normative critique they presented in Chapter Eight. Here is where Smith's earlier analysis is most captured in a modern model.

In Chapter Eight, we also note Joseph Schumpeter's views on the social effects of expansions in the number of people attending institutions of higher education. Schumpeter argued that an excess supply of university-educated persons had resulted in under-employment or unemployment. These frustrated alienated individuals become disaffected intellectuals who instigate hostility toward the capitalist system and aligned themselves with the various social/political groups, e.g., labor, advocating anti-capitalist policies. In light of Adam Smith's discussion of endowments that allowed a number of individuals to attend universities and the consequences for the incomes of 'men of letters' and public teachers, this offers an interesting contrast. We note that there is something of a Schumpeterian normative view of 'radical intellectuals' present in the Buchanan–Devletoglou critique of universities in the era of campus protests.

In Chapter Nine, we review recent economic models that predict how universities behave as non-profit institutions. These models are much more technically specified than Veblen's loosely sketched behavioral model. But they essentially follow his approach of explaining choices of institutional goals, academic policies, and activities in terms of the motives, incentives, and constraints for those individuals who are in positions to have some influence in the internal processes of institutional decision-making. As in Veblen's 'model,' the modern models postulate that this process leads universities to seek to maximize institutional prestige. In the first part of the chapter, a general economic model of non-profit institutions is examined, with the Veblenian antecedents noted. Then Garvin's model of research universities is examined as a representative version of the modern economic models of universities' behavior. These models, however, became disconnected from Veblen's evolutionary analysis.

2. Historical Development of Universities

Studies in which the behavior of modern universities is analyzed from an economic perspective have focused primarily, although not exclusively, on the large multi-purpose and organizationally complex research or doctoral universities. Differences between those universities and the various other institutions of post-secondary education (e.g., non-doctoral universities, liberal arts colleges, teachers colleges, community colleges, and technical institutes) reflect a long process of evolutionary development and change that traces back to the medieval universities in the late Middle Ages in Europe. Many of the changes (perhaps most) occurred as unplanned adaptations and modifications in response to various internal and external pressures. The long history of the English universities provides numerous examples of evolutionary institutional development of that form. But as exemplified by the new German universities of the 19th century, major developments sometimes resulted from planned innovations that were intended to implement a particular vision of higher education.

The emergence of the doctoral degree-granting American universities in the late 19th century involved both types of institutional development. The colleges established in colonial America were modeled after the English residential colleges of Oxford and Cambridge. But in the graduate programs leading to doctoral degrees that appeared in the post-American Civil War period, American higher education borrowed heavily from the newer German universities. In a few cases, new universities were established to offer programs of advanced scientific and scholarly studies. Johns Hopkins, Clark, and Chicago are the classic examples. In other cases, graduate programs in arts and sciences were simply added to private colleges, e.g., Yale University, and public post-secondary institutions, e.g., the universities of Michigan, Wisconsin, and California. But even the new doctoral-degree universities retained the characteristic features and programs of the older, undergraduate colleges, and added professional schools such as law, engineering, and medicine.

In the brief review of the historical development of universities that follows, particular attention is paid to the English and Scottish universities of Smith's 18th century, and the American universities of Veblen's early

19th century. In many respects, the universities observed by Smith and Veblen were different institutions, existing in different socio-cultural systems in different historical stages of economic development. The 19th century English universities that J. S. Mill criticized were the same universities that Smith had described as failing, although some institutional changes were beginning to occur by mid-century. The research/doctoral universities whose behavioral tendencies have been modeled by modern economists are essentially of the same institutional type as Veblen's American universities. Indeed, the universities that Veblen attended as a graduate student (Johns Hopkins and Yale) and those that employed him as a faculty member (Chicago and Stanford) rank among the most prominent research universities today. While American universities have experienced substantial institutional changes since Veblen wrote *The Higher Learning in America*, especially during the post-World War II era, the basic organizational structures have remained largely unchanged. In that regard, the 19th century German universities also merit attention because of their influence on the American universities.

Yet, despite their differences, all the universities in question had common origins in the universities that emerged in Europe in the late Middle Ages, and they all exhibited (as modern universities continue to do) characteristic features acquired in earlier periods. Virtually always being in a state of slow but continuous process of evolutionary development and change, universities have never been (and probably never will be) fully compatible with the particular cultural values and institutional norms of their periods and places. For better or worse, they retained institutional elements of earlier times, and acquired reputations for being resistant to institutional change. At the same time, the intellectual processes that form the essential core of universities as academic centers of inquiry have led to forward-looking searches for knowledge and critiques of existing knowledge and institutions. Hence, the institutional nature of universities has always been (and probably will continue to be) an often frustrating, and occasionally highly volatile, institutional mixture of the archaic past and impulses toward futuristic changes within one corporate organization. Critics have frequently lamented universities' archaic features. But often when institutional changes occurred, some have viewed the new developments and trends as no better, or even worse, than the past.

In the historical review that follows, the focus tends to be on internal features that played significant roles in determining institutional behavior – the general organizational and governance structures, the characteristics of the faculty and students, and the sources of finance. But it is also important to note the links between the internal systems of the universities and external sources of influence. In a time-line, the most important external influences were the Church and the Crown, and then later democratically-elected governments. But in nearly all stages, private donors were also important in founding colleges, libraries, and professorships, as well as providing endowments for more general purposes.

MEDIEVAL UNIVERSITIES

During the early Middle Ages, the higher education was carried on in monastic and cathedral schools, with the curriculum limited to the seven liberal arts – grammar, rhetoric, logic, arithmetic (in Roman numerals), astronomy, geometry, and music. But in the 12th century, Western Europe experienced an influx of new knowledge, partly through Italy and Sicily where Roman institutions and law had never completely disappeared, but chiefly through the Arab scholars in Spain. The new knowledge included the works of the Greek philosophers and physicians, the new arithmetic using Arabic numerals, and the texts of Roman law. That early intellectual renaissance gave rise to the learned profession, and those who developed reputations for teaching their specialized knowledge drew students from throughout Europe. The medieval universities emerged from that beginning to take over the higher learning from the monastic and cathedral schools.

Scholars have incomplete records of the exact manner in which medieval universities became organized in the 12th and 13th centuries. But by the end of the Middle Ages, at least 80 universities had been established in different parts of Europe, some of which (e.g., University of Paris, University of Oxford) have survived to modern times. All of the medieval universities belonged to the universe of Latin Christianity rather than to nations or kingdoms. Their corporate charters were granted by the popes, who claimed the universities as parts of the ecclesiastical realm to carry out the Church's duty to educate. University scholars were given clerical rank in the ecclesiastical order, which exempted them from the jurisdiction of all lay authorities. All scholars used the universal language of ecclesiastical Latin and all degrees were granted under the authority of the Pope. The license to teach granted by the universities gave the licensee the right to teach anywhere within papal Europe.

In keeping with the medieval culture's emphasis on corporate communities (political, religious, and economic), universities were essentially guilds of teachers and scholars. Organizationally, medieval universities were very similar to other guilds. As the apprentices, students were required to follow a definite course of study for a definite period of time, and to pass a definite examination in order to become full member of the guild. Upon receiving a Master of Arts or Doctor of Laws degree and fulfilling an obligation to teach for two years, they received all the privileges of the guild. The teachers of the universities were organized into faculties, with deans as their heads. Over the whole corporation was an elected rector. Like other guilds, the universities had a share in the collective governance of the towns. Universities that were heavily favored by popes and kings were granted special rights and privileges that not only exempted them from the authority of municipal rule, but also gave the heads of the universities considerable civil authority over the local community.

As incorporated bodies of scholars, the medieval universities had no libraries, laboratories, or buildings. Rather, they were institutions 'built of men' (Haskins 1923, pp. 3–5). But essential features of modern university organization can be traced back to the medieval schools: the university tradition of being an association of masters and scholars leading a common life of learning; a curriculum of study definitely specified with regard to time and subjects, tested by an examination, and leading to several types of degrees; organized bodies of faculties with their deans and higher officers such as chancellors and rectors; and the residential college (Haskins 1923, pp. 34–35).

Two Models of Medieval Universities: Bologna and Paris

The name 'university' emerged from Latin terms used during the Middle Ages to denote gatherings of scholarly learners. Almost any academic gathering was commonly referred to as a *studium* (place of study) or a *discipulorum* (an association of persons devoted to scholarly pursuits). With the early Renaissance in the late Middle Ages, learning became more specialized. Where teachers of specialized subjects, such as law or theology, gained sufficient reputations to draw large numbers of students from beyond the local areas, the term *studium generale* indicated an international place of study. Originally referring to any corporate association of the kind common in medieval life, *universitas* became used specifically to indicate a teaching–learning community. *Universitate* was sometimes also used to designate an association or guild of teaching masters or students. At some point, the scholastic guilds and *studia* became essentially identical, and *universitas* gave rise to the modern term 'university' (Lucas 1994, pp. 41–42).

While historians have incomplete information about medieval universities in their formative period, there is agreement that two universities provided institutional models that were emulated by the other medieval universities. Those were Bologna in Southern Europe and Paris in Northern Europe.

Bologna emerged as an academic center in the first half of the 12th century, when teachers of civil and Roman law developed a reputation that attracted many students from throughout Europe. The beginning of the university as an organized guild of learning came when the international students, being far from home and undefended, united for mutual protection and assistance. As a corporate body, the students received from Frederick Barbarossa a formal decree or charter granting a special ecclesiastical jurisdiction. In 1189, a papal document granted by Pope Clement III confirmed those rights and privileges. The students were now organized in a guild (or in several sub-guilds called 'nations' organized on basis of the geographical homes of the students). There was a strong economic motive for the students seeking guild status. Because the grant of rights and privileges did not specifically mention any place or any university by name, and as the university had no buildings, the students could threaten to move in mass to another location within the Lombard Kingdom. That collective bargaining power was first used against the townspeople who had taken advantage of the rising demand for rooms and necessaries by raising rents and prices. Through their guild representatives, the Bologna students were able to fix the prices of lodgings, foods, and books (Haskins 1923, pp. 12–14).

The guild of students then turned their monopsony power against the professors, whose dependence on student fees for their livelihood rendered them even more subject to threats of collective boycotts by the students. Professors were put under bond to abide by detailed regulations intended to guarantee that students would receive the full value for money paid. The earliest statutes of Bologna prohibited professors from being absent without leave, even for a single day. A professor who wanted to leave town would be required to leave a deposit to ensure his return. Any professor who failed to draw an audience of five for a regular lecture was fined as if he was absent, under the rationale that anyone unable to draw five students must be a very poor lecturer. Professors were required to begin with the bell and quit within one minute after the next bell. They could not skip a chapter in their commentary, nor postpone difficult concepts or problems to the end of the lecture hour. They were obliged to systematically cover so much ground in each specific term of the year. No professor could spend the whole year on introduction and bibliography (Haskins 1923, p. 15).

Excluded from the 'universities' of students, the professors formed a guild or 'college.' Admission requirements in the form of certain qualifications ascertained by examination prevented any student from entering without the guild's consent. As the ability to teach was viewed to be a good test of knowing a subject, students came to seek the professor's license as a certificate of attainment, regardless of their future career. That certificate or license to teach became the earliest form of academic degree. The Master of Arts degree became the certification to teach the liberal arts and the Doctor of Laws the certification to teach law (Haskins 1923, pp. 16–17).

In Northern Europe, the origin of universities was in the cathedral school of Notre Dame in Paris. At some point in the 12th century, it ceased to be a cathedral school and became a university. In 1200, King Philip Augustus recognized the exemption of the students and their servants from lay jurisdiction, creating a special position of students before courts that was long lasting. In 1231, the Pope issued a bulletin that confirmed the existing exemptions for students who were attending at least two lectures per week. It also regulated the chancellor's discretion in conferring the teaching license, and recognized the right of the masters and students to make constitutions and ordinances that regulated not only academic manners but also prices of lodgings and coercion of members. (One of the more interesting provisions was that students were forbidden to carry arms!) But while the University of Bologna was a corporation of students, the University of Paris was a corporation of masters, with four faculties, each under a dean. The masters of arts (the most numerous faculty) were further grouped into four 'nations.' Those 'nations' chose the head of the university – the rector – who would serve for a short term. That organization encouraged a great amount of internal feuding that often led to physical blows. Apparently, the members of the 'nations' spent much of their time spending the fees that were collected from new members and new officers in taverns (Haskins 1923, pp. 22–25).

An institutional feature of modern universities going back to 12th century Paris is the college. Originally an endowed hospice or hall of residence established for the purpose of securing board and lodging for poor scholars who could not pay for it themselves, colleges became the normal centers of life and teaching, absorbing much of the activity of the university. The colleges had buildings and endowments, even if the university did not (Haskins 1923, pp. 26–27).

Paris was pre-eminent in the Middle Ages as a school of theology, which was the supreme subject of medieval study, and became the source and model for Northern European universities. In England, Oxford branched off from this parent stem late in the 12th century and Cambridge sometime later. In Southern Europe, Bologna became pre-eminent in law, with at least two universities for law, as well as one for medicine and arts, and one for theology. Salerno became noted for medicine.

There were interesting differences between the types of students attending the medieval universities. The Southern European universities drew mostly mature professional men as students. Those studying law were preparing to take remunerative positions in the municipal government of Italian cities ruled by Roman law. They paid their own fees and appointed their own rectors. In contrast, the northern universities drew very young boys, some of whom had not yet learned to read or write. Because books were scarce and very costly before the invention of the printing press in the 15th century, the learning process was listening to lectures by teachers who had their private libraries of books. Even where medieval universities had libraries, they had only a small number of books.

THE ENGLISH UNIVERSITIES

The English universities of Oxford and Cambridge were founded as medieval universities in the 12th century. In their long evolutionary development into federations of semi-autonomous colleges, they were frequently affected by social and political developments, and occasionally by strong personalities within the institutions. Throughout the centuries, external authorities – officials of the Catholic Church, the Crown, the Church of England (and for a short time also Cromwell's Puritans), and Parliament – intruded in various ways, sometimes to found colleges, grant privileges, and provide endowments, but often to disrupt and alter the direction of change. The Renaissance brought changes to medieval universities everywhere. The English universities were also heavily impacted by the War of Roses, the Reformation, the English Civil War, and the Restoration, as well as the quieter political and religious conflicts that occurred in the 17th and 18th centuries. During periods of religious and political conflict, members of the universities and colleges often were partisans, and consequently suffered or were rewarded depending on which religious/political faction held or lost power. The following is a brief account of Oxford University as it evolved from the 12th century to become the 18th century institution that Smith attended for six years and later criticized in *Wealth of Nations.*

The University of Oxford's Early Development

Scholars have suggested that a migration of English students from Paris to Oxford in 1157 indicated that Oxford had become known for its teachers. Those early Oxford students were desperately poor. Facing hostility and economic extortion from the local townspeople, they did not lodge in inns and houses as in Paris. Instead, they resided in their own 'halls' that were rented or bought by cooperative effort and ruled by a principal elected among its members. For instruction, students went to any teacher in town, who was free to offer his teaching services on whatever terms he wished, with his income depending entirely on fees paid by the students. The University suspended operations for a time after a violent conflict erupted between students and townspeople in 1209. A number of students fled Oxford and started the University of Cambridge. Some five years later, a papal legate reinstated the University, conferring many privileges on it and its scholars and imposing numerous penances upon the townspeople for their transgressions against members of the University (Hobhouse 1946, pp. 2–3; Mallet 1924, Vol. I, pp. 31–32). The chief official of the University was the Chancellor, and the discipline of students was placed under the Proctors. Until new statutes were enacted under the reign of Elizabeth I, the governance of the university was largely in the hands of the collective body of scholars (see Cobban 1999, pp. 64–76).

Violent conflicts between University members and townspeople continued, with a particularly ferocious battle occurring in 1354. On each occasion, the Church and the Crown supported the University, awarding it greater privileges and expanding its authority over the civil and economic life of the town of Oxford. As examples of the University's substantial powers over those living and working in Oxford, the Vice-Chancellor licensed brewers and bakers, set days for brewing and fixed the prices, checked the color and quality of bread, licensed book-sellers, and closely watched their transactions with students.

Oxford functioned like the other medieval universities under papal authority, with essentially the same requirements for degrees. Degrees were granted on passing examinations, with four years study for the Bachelor of Arts, and three more years for the Masters of Arts. Students could subsequently continue studying for a degree in theology, law, or medicine. The curriculum was much the same as at Paris. The faculties of liberal arts and theology were the most popular, and the emphasis was on philosophy and dialectic in the scholastic tradition. Oxford, however, gave somewhat more attention to grammar and substantially more to mathematics and science. In the earliest period, the University treated the students as mature scholars who were part of the corporate foundation, and thus gave little attention to discipline. The average age of entering students, however, was between 15 and 17 years. While there were serious students, many were non-serious ones who preferred lectures on canon law because they started later in the morning (see Cobban 1999, pp. 20–21).

In its earlier period, the University was quite poor. Its income was largely derived from fees, and for centuries much attention was given to the collection of numerous fees levied on students from matriculation to the conferring of degrees. Until 1249, the University's only other regular source of income was one shilling a week paid by the town of Oxford as a fine for past mistreatment of university scholars. The shilling went into the University chest from which loans were made to poor students. But in that year, the Archdeacon of Durham left the University an endowment for Masters of Arts, which was used to purchase property that would later become University College.

Concurrent with the establishment of the University, several monastic orders devoted to teaching came to Oxford. The schools that they established with their own lecturers practically became colleges of the University. Indeed, some historians argue that the teaching friars largely gave Oxford its reputation. During the 13th century, the friars were intellectuals who were almost universally popular with both the rich and the poor. Better educated than parish priests, they had been trained to speak with eloquence and wit, telling stories that had moral points. With their extensive network of contacts throughout Europe, they were the local sources of news of the world. Later, however, their influence would decline, due in part to their own behavior, which became increasingly self-indulgent and neglectful of their teaching and community service missions. Their decline came also because others resented the wealth and influence of the monasteries. While the monastic orders easily gained recruits among young boys who were encouraged by the Church to take the scholarly step toward becoming parish priests, they also gained enemies. The founding of the first colleges in the university was in part in an effort to neutralize the influence of the regular monastic orders.

The English Colleges

Two particularly distinguishing features of the English universities were their colleges and the tutorial system of teaching. The early colleges established by benefactors were little more than alms houses for poor students. Students lived in the colleges, but attended lectures in the University 'schools.' But over time, the colleges came to be the most characteristic feature of University life, arrogating to themselves practically all teaching as well as direction of social life, until the University became merely an examining and degree-conferring body (Haskins 1923, p. 28). Less famous were the numerous halls where students lived, some of which later became colleges (see Cobban 1999, pp. 145–159). Balliol College was founded when the Bishop of Durham made John de Balliol endow a hostel for 16 Oxford students as part of his punishment for being 'unduly odious to episcopal authorities' (Hobhouse 1946, p. 4). Subsequently, benefactors established other colleges, which received statutes of governance and various endowments. By the beginning of the 14th century, Oxford was described as a community of several thousand scholars and three colleges with libraries, halls, and 'sumptuous places of worship' (Hobhouse 1946, p. 5).

All of the founding benefactors were men holding high Church positions. Indeed, Oxford was built with revenues coming from various religious institutions and organizations, reflecting the great wealth claimed by the higher offices within the Church. The major source of that wealth was tithes and rents paid by the lower classes. The medieval Church facilitated such diversion of wealth to the University by requiring celibacy (no offspring to whom to bequeath wealth) and allowing pluralism (a higher cleric could hold numerous Church positions, claiming the incomes without doing the work).

Each college was a corporate foundation of fellows and scholars, with its own governing body consisting of a head and a body of fellows. The colleges held their own estates and other endowments, and had their private staffs of teachers or tutors, usually taken from the fellows. Loyalty of students was to their colleges rather than the University, and the wealthier ones gave benefactions and bequests to their own colleges. As the various colleges accumulated endowments, some became very wealthy. College heads gave senior fellows special positions of authority, in some cases practically vesting the government of the college in their hands. By the end of the 17th century, the senior fellows were frequently using that authority to appropriate for themselves the surplus income of the colleges (Mallet 1924, Vol. II, pp. 1–7).

As the colleges became the real substance of the University, the heads of the colleges became the real governors of the University. Under statutes enacted during the reign of Elizabeth I, the University became a federation of independent and autonomous colleges. A revised governance system was created which remained largely in place until the Parliamentary reforms of the 1850s. The Chancellor was the head, usually a non-resident person of importance whom the University wanted for political protection. The acting executive was the Vice-Chancellor, a position that rotated among the heads of the colleges. Proctors maintained discipline outside the colleges. A Hebdomadal Board, consisting of the heads of colleges, initiated all legislation, which would then be submitted to two bodies of faculty and masters, called congregation and Convocation. The University matriculated students (each of whom was required to be admitted to a college), conferred all degrees, and policed the students and townspeople outside the college walls. Within the college walls, neither the town civil authorities nor the University proctors had any authority (see Cobban 1988, pp. 64–110).

Teaching and Curriculum

During the Renaissance era (1450–1558), Oxford gained additional colleges and the curriculum slowly changed to admit the classical learning in the humanistic form. By 1500, men were lecturing at Oxford who had studied in Renaissance Italy. But the medieval Scholasticism did not give way without a struggle. Greek was viewed as the typical study of the new humanistic learning and its opponents (who called themselves the 'Trojans') tried to bully the 'Grecians' out of Oxford. The latter gained the support of King Henry VIII and Sir Thomas More, and the 'Trojans' were silenced. But the results, as judged by scholarly product, were disappointing. By mid-16th century, there were few great scholars and the attendance had fallen. More organizational structure was introduced in the educational sphere. Under the older system, a 'school' could be set up by anyone. There was a street of 'schools' with more than 30 teachers competing for students and the fees they would pay. But that changed with establishment of a central School for Arts and a School of Divinity, which provided both lecture rooms and libraries (Hobhouse 1946, p. 21).

One effect of Renaissance learning was increase University people's contempt toward the monks who lived in cloisters and continued to teach in the old way. The monastic houses in Oxford were diminishing in influence even before Henry VIII seized most of their properties and wealth in the 1630s. Henry VIII and Cardinal Woolsey suppressed the colleges associated with monastic orders. After the Civil War, Puritan Commissioners sent by Cromwell attempted to purge Oxford of all papist influence. They destroyed libraries, burning many valuable manuscripts and throwing papers and pages of books to the wind. When the Catholics returned to power, reciprocal violence was done to University people and colleges associated with the Puritans. By the end of the 17th century, the University was firmly under the influence of the Church of England. The Religious Tests for enrolling in or graduating from Oxford or Cambridge excluded both Catholics and Protestant dissenters. The University became a closed institution to anyone outside the established Church of England (Hobhouse 1946, pp. 20–25).

These developments had important impacts. The dissolution of the religious houses dried up a stream of scholars for the University, most of whom were poor young men preparing for ecclesiastical careers within the Catholic Church. In their place came a large increase in the sons of country gentlemen. In earlier days, the colleges had accepted some noblemen's sons, as well as sons of wealthy men who were known as 'gentlemen commoners' (Mallet 1924, Vol. II, p. 8). Those young men were not scholars who were members of the college, but were essentially paying guests of the colleges. According to their rank, they were exempt from many of the regulations and enjoyed special privileges. Those of noble rank had all the privileges of high table and the commons room as the senior fellows and heads of colleges. With the monasteries suppressed, grammar schools were founded which enabled poor boys to gain scholarships. But increasingly the average undergraduate was a rich 'gentleman commoner,' who required a servant. Poor boys were able to work their way through the University by acting as 'Servitors' to the rich students, often doing their academic work as well as performing personal servant duties (Mallet 1924, Vol. III, pp. 65–67).

With the religious tests effectively excluding non-Anglicans, dissenting academies appeared to offer theological training. A number also offered a more utilitarian curriculum than the Universities, adding sciences and mathematics to humanistic studies. In attracting those who seriously desired an education, the academies gained a major advantage in offering the advantages of a residential education at only a small fraction of the cost of studying in a university. A more direct impact of the Reformation on English universities was the elimination of canon law and degrees in canon law. Henceforth, clergymen would be trained to be parish ministers rather than ecclesiastical scholar-lawyers. University study became more a matter of confirming high social class or status rather than providing entry into professional careers within the Church. This brought a change in the students from clerics to the sons of nobility and gentlemen, and lessened the prospects for the poorer students.

By the 1500s, the old teaching system of Regents lecturing to students in the 'schools,' receiving only the income from fees collected from their students, was giving way to the new system of teachers supported from college endowments. Those holding University chairs or professorships were supposed to give public lectures, but the tutorial system became dominant. The beginnings of the tutorial system were early in Oxford history. The view that senior members of a college had some responsibility for the conduct and instruction of their younger colleagues was a natural development of the collegiate idea. The earliest tutors were not primarily teachers, but rather were intended to be personal guardians to superintend the 'gentleman commoners'' conduct and expenditure. Protecting the financial interest of the college was at least as important as instruction of the student. College lecturers were also increasing in the 17th century, but the educational functions of tutors developed quietly. In the Laudian Statutes implemented, the tutor's responsibility was a recognized part of the University system. All scholars had to have a tutor, and all tutors had to be approved by the heads of colleges, and if necessary by the Vice-Chancellor (Mallet 1924, Vol. III, pp. 56–64 and Vol. II, p. 321).

By the end of the 17th century, a tutor's responsibilities depended upon his own view of them and with the habits of his students. The tutor had a two-fold obligation – to his college and to the student's parents. He had to see that statutory requirements were met and that the college was saved from loss or discredit. But he expected to receive a special remuneration from the parents of the richer students. There were complaints that tutors only read to their students and paid insufficient attention to their conduct and discipline. Some students had tutors who were serious teachers, while other students were allowed to waste their time.

The Academic Decline of Oxford

During the 16th and 17th centuries, the behavior of University students, fellows, and officials – drinking, consorting with women, carousing, fighting, and playing football – became a matter of some notoriety. Some chancellors did more than express concern. Most notably, in the 1630s, Archbishop Laud used his autocratic powers to issue a new body of statutes (the Laudian Statutes) that regulated all aspects of student and faculty activities and life (Mallet 1924, Vol. II, pp. 303–348). His intent was to bind the University to the new established Church of England, but also to tightly and completely regulate the conduct of the members of the university in all aspects – academic and personal. His powers of regulation and enforcement extended also to townspeople, including allowing night searches of their houses by University proctors. When townspeople objected, the University informed Parliament that the town of Oxford was an out-of-the way place that was of no use to the public, existing only for the entertainment of scholars on whose patronage it depended for its existence.

While many of the minute regulations under the Laudian Statutes pertained to academic garb, ceremonial requirements, etc., there was a serious intent to curb the wasteful behavior of students, fellows, and professors, to restore the academic environment. Although the statutes remained the governing code until the 1850s, by the end of the 17th century, much of the Laudian Code was scarcely observed. The University had entered into a serious state of academic decline. Heads of colleges, fellows, and students alike were notoriously heavy imbibers, and the elected offices and fellowships often went to drinking companions. Incompetence and disregard of academic standards increased. As Oxford University moved into Adam Smith's 18th century, there were some individuals among the masters and among the students who would excel, but overall the University was at an academic low point.

In Adam Smith's time, the colleges were still governed by obsolete statutes of medieval times, which were disregarded by the fellows who shared the corporate revenues from endowments. A few fellows in each college added to their incomes by holding tutorships, but make little effort to actual teach. The obligation of being in resident was practically annulled, so that a great part of the fellowships became sinecure stipends held by men unconnected with the University. Some colleges accepted only gentlemen commoners who paid high fees and did what they pleased. All Souls' College took no students at all and became a mere club, which was limited to men of high family by a strange perversion of their statutes (see Mallet 1924, Vol. I, p. 383). Scholarships established for poor students were often given to sons of wealthy men.

A formidable group of critics, including Adam Smith (whose criticisms will be noted in Chapter Three), Jeremy Bentham, and Edward Gibbon, complained of indifferent teaching and lack of interest in academic standards (Mallet 1924, Vol. III, p. 130). A holder of the Chair of Botany for some 36 years (until 1784) gave only one lecture during that time (Mallet 1924, Vol. III, p. 126). But few voices within the University suggested any reconsideration of the teaching of the past. The days when Oxford gave a lead to science seemed in the 18th century unlikely to return (Mallet 1924, Vol. III, p. 126) Classics, logic, and philosophy continued to be the favorite studies, but showed little development (Mallet 1924, Vol. III, p. 127).

Both tutors and fellows were inclined to curry favor with the wealthier students, and some parents preferred a tutor who would 'make their sons into men of fashion to one who would make them work' (Mallet 1924, Vol. III, p. 64). That was still true at the end of the 18th century, when finally institutional reform was in sight. Young men with titles were often given very special treatment, e.g., a Vice-Chancellor gave a Doctor's degree to a young duke. Critics inside the University complained that the distinctions of rank were too prominent, that 'gentleman commoners' were far too numerous, with too much money to spend and enjoying too many privileges.

The processes of examinations for degrees were severely criticized by those calling for reforms. It was claimed that the 'greatest dunce' competing for a Bachelor's degree could get his testimony signed with as much credit as the 'finest genius' (Mallet 1924, Vol. III, p. 164). Candidates acquired little books of stock examination questions and the examiners (based on their own student experiences) knew what questions they were supposed to ask. Examiners were often drinking companions of those being examined. Examinations for the Master's degree were often no more serious that those for the Bachelor's degree. The majority of candidates were not residents, but 'term-trotters' who spent the minimal weeks in the University to qualify them according to the letter of the Statutes. In many respects, the exercises required for higher degrees merely repeated those for lower degrees. Thus, one reformer:

> ... boldly begged the Prime Minister to call in Parliament to revise the Statutes and customs of the University, to abolish useless and antiquated forms, to alter and diminish the oaths required, to insist on longer residence, more discipline, less luxury, to put down the privileges of the Gentlemen Commoners, to increase the duties and the pay of College Tutors, to make education offered at Oxford worthy of the name (Mallet 1924, Vol. III, p. 165).

In the 19th century, the University began slowly to reform the examinations. While the rigor of the ordinary Pass Examination was left at a low level, an Honors examination was added and the number of students taking that examination gradually increased. In 1850, a Parliamentary Commission was sent to inquire into the state of the University (Mallet 1924, Vol. III, pp. 300–353). Its members encountered resistance from a number of factions, especially from the heads of colleges who refused to provide information about college finances. The commission's report cited a number of problems and recommended reforms. There should be greater access for poor and middle-income students. The curriculum should include more preparation for professional life and more science. Professors (as opposed to tutors) should do more of the teaching and examining. While the number of professorships had increased, it had not resulted in more professorial teaching. The commission described tutors and professors as being complementary methods of teaching. Lecturing by knowledgeable researchers was as effective for teaching some subjects as tutorials over assigned readings. The salaries of many professorships were too low. More professorships and higher pay were called for, with the funds for the higher pay to from fees and contributions from the well-endowed colleges. With only 22 of the 542 fellowships at Oxford not controlled by patronage or locality, the commission recommended that fellowships should be opened to free competition on merit. New fellowships should be created in the newer fields of study, but some fellowships should be closed and the funds reallocated to University professorships. It was also recommended that fellows should not have to take religious orders (Mallet 1924, Vol. III, pp. 315–316).

The commission's report met with strong opposition from influential individuals and powerful groups in Oxford. One leading opponent demanded that the University be kept under control of the Church. Others opposed reintroducing the lecture method, falsely claiming that it had failed in the German universities. The college heads wanted to retain their powerful autonomy and college wealth. Despite the opposition, the University Act of 1854 implemented a number of the recommended reforms. The University was opened to non-collegians and religious dissenters, but the religious demands were not clear. Finally, in 1871, the Religious Tests were eliminated. Subsequent Parliamentary commissions and legislation brought additional reforms. The curriculum, the examination system, and the honors list were modernized, with all departments of academic work recognized and domiciled in the University. Science was returned to a prominent position, the University professoriate was restored, and the fellowships opened to merit (Mallet 1924, Vol. III, p. 327).

THE SCOTTISH UNIVERSITIES

The first three Scottish universities were chartered by papal action before the Reformation ended the ecclesiastical authority of the Catholic Church. The University of St. Andrews was established in 1411. Forty years later, the King of Scotland persuaded the Pope to grant a bull authorizing the Bishop of Glasgow to set up a university. Thus, Scotland, like England, now had two universities. Because the University of Glasgow was Adam Smith's university as a student (before going to Oxford) and later as a faculty member and administrator, its evolutionary development will be discussed in more detail below.

The history of the University of Aberdeen is actually of two fiercely competing institutions – King's College and Marischal College – that were finally were forced by The Scottish Universities Act to merge in 1860. In 1495, the Bishop of Aberdeen wanted an institution to educate Scottish lawyers and clerics. A papal bull authorized him to create a university, which opened as King's College in 1505 with 36 staff and students. The structure was based on the bishop's experiences at Paris, Orleans, and Glasgow. The curriculum was Latin and Greek, medicine, and law (both canon and civil). With the Reformation, a Protestant principal took over. A second university emerged essentially because of local rivalries between the two separate burghs of Aberdeen – Old Aberdeen and the New Town. The Earl Marischal wanted the New Town to have a seat of higher learning and sponsored the chartering of Marischal College in 1593. There was continual friction between the two colleges, and although the Bishop was chancellor of both until 1641, each operated with almost complete autonomy. In that year, the office of Bishop was abolished, and the revenues split between the two colleges, with King's receiving the majority of the funds. Attempts to merge the two colleges failed, and the two colleges engaged in continuing legal disputes over funds and to compete fiercely for students. That competition was harmful to both schools, as revealed in a Royal Commission's report in 1858 that both universities were inadequately funded, suffering declining enrollments, and in great need to renovate buildings. In 1860, The Scottish Universities Act forced a merger of the schools. Marischal was given the medical and law schools, while Kings continued to teach arts and divinity.

The fourth Scottish university, the University of Edinburgh, differed from the other three in two important ways. First, it was the first post-Reformation university in Scotland. Second, it was the first civil university in Britain. Granted a Royal Charter in 1582, the university was founded by the Town Council of Edinburgh in the following year, known as King James' College or the Town's College. While maintaining a close relationship with the city of Edinburgh, the University soon established itself internationally. By the 18th century, it had become a leading center of the European Enlightenment and one of the continent's principal universities.

Relative to the two English universities, the four Scottish universities were poorly funded, and none ever gained the wealth in endowments enjoyed by the colleges of Oxford and Cambridge. The Scottish universities also differed from the English universities in the general characteristics of the students. The Scottish students matriculated at a very young age – twelve years old was rather common, and completed their first degrees at roughly the age that English university students were matriculating at Oxford and Cambridge. Thus, the Scottish universities essentially served as both high schools and colleges. Despite their relative poverty and the young ages of their students, the Scottish universities gained reputations in the 18th century for teaching in a number of subjects, and their faculties included an unusually large number of scholars with international reputations. While under the influence of the established Presbyterian Church of Scotland after the Reformation, the Scottish universities were never subjected to the type of religious oppression that was imposed on Oxford by Parliament and the Church of England.

The University of Glasgow

The papal bull that authorized the establishment of the University recognized Glasgow as a place admirably suited by climate and 'supply of victuals' to have a university. The school was to promote the Catholic faith, educate the simple folks, and develop the minds and intellects of men (Mackie 1954, p. 7). It was expected that theology, canon and civil law, as well as the arts and any other lawful faculty might flourish. The officials, faculty, and students were granted all the privileges, honors, and immunities held by those in Bologna. Perhaps the most important of the privileges was the right to divert ecclesiastical revenues to maintenance of the University. The Bishop of Glasgow was the University's chancellor, with the authority to give degrees and licenses to teach to all whom passed the proper examinations. Those licenses and degrees were valid throughout the Latin Christian world of learning (Mackie 1954, pp. 8–12).

The University was supposed to be modeled after Bologna, with students electing a rector who had jurisdiction over professors. Instead, the Chancellor (the Bishop of Glasgow) was the supreme authority, who saw the preparation of clergy for his own great diocese of Glasgow as being the first business of the university. For such a small institution (before the Reformation in 1559–1560, the average number of students was 50–60), the system of governance was rather complex, involving officials, positions, duties, ceremonies, and activities of an archaic medieval nature (Mackie 1954, pp. 14–19). As with other medieval universities, the foundation was essentially that of a guild of learning. The students were apprentices, who upon receiving the Master of Arts degree were required to formally teach for two years before being granted full master status. The ordinary teachers of the Universities were the masters. The head of each faculty was a dean, corresponding to the head of a craft guild, who was called a deacon in Scotland. Over the whole corporation was the rector, elected by the masters and students organized in four nations based on geographical origins. But effective power lay in the hands of the masters, and in the early days laymen of standing were sometimes made masters without undergoing the proper examinations (Mackie 1954, p. 17).

The University depended heavily upon the Bishop of Glasgow for sources of finance, and also for immunity from taxes, duties, and the rule of secular authorities. The Bishop used his authority to encourage both the King and churchmen to provide funds and services to the University. He also granted the University privileges in the city of Glasgow that assured the faculty and students would receive good treatment in rents and prices of goods. Members of the University were free to buy and sell goods without paying customs, and were to pay the same prices for local goods as paid by local residents. A panel of representatives from the University and the local community set rent rates. The Rector of the University had jurisdiction in all civil matters, not only between members of the University but also between members of the University and local citizens. The Rector was also given precedence over all ecclesiastic men within the diocese except the Bishop himself (Mackie 1954, p 18).

The University granted the Bachelor degree, the license to teach, the Master's degree, and the Doctor's degree based on studies, examinations, and payment of numerous fees. After residency of at least 18 months, and provided he was 15 years of age (the faculty could reduce that to 14), the student could be examined for the Bachelor's degree. After a residency of nearly four years, the student could be examined for the teaching license. Those receiving the license were required to take a formal oath of obedience to the University and to take the Master's degree within four months. The student had to be 20 years of age to receive that degree, which involved considerable expense in fees and the requirement to teach for two years (Mackie 1954, pp. 30–31).

Directly or indirectly, the university was substantially financed with revenues from ecclesiastical sources. A major form of financial support provided by the Church was allowing teachers and students holding Church positions to retain their stipends while in the University. Many of the early teachers and students were among the clergy, and all the university officials held Church positions. Over the years, the university was given certain ecclesiastical revenues, but those remained rather small. The Church also provided the buildings that housed the University.

But the Bishop of Glasgow failed to provide an adequate endowment, and like the other Scottish universities, Glasgow remained poorly financed, heavily dependent on incomes from fees. The University assessed students a number of fees from entry to being awarded a Master's degree, and imposed various fines for violations of university rules. Some of those fees were apparently difficult to collect. After a student received a Bachelor's degree (after passing an examination and payment of fees), the next step was to be licensed to teach. A fine was imposed if he failed to take his Master's degree after four months. Since the formal degree was of no use outside the University, in the early days those receiving the license to teach seldom completed the Master's degree. There was continuing frustration over the University's inability to collect the fines from those who failed to meet that requirement (Mackie 1954, pp. 21–24).

The faculty of arts became the major faculty. The Church retained the teaching of clerics and canon law, and the University lacked the resources to develop faculties of medicine and civil law. The faculty developed a governance system that paralleled that of the University. The University teachers were called regents, with professorships established later. Newly made masters were expected to give formal teaching the 'ordinary books' to the younger students for two years, while the regular regents handled the more advanced 'books.' The initial curriculum was similar to that at St. Andrews, which had been copied from Paris. The method of instruction was typical of the period before printed books were available for students to read. Teachers read from chosen books in Latin at a speed that permitted dictation, and the notes taken by the students became their textbooks. Thus, the lecture method became firmly established (Mackie 1954, pp. 25–41).

In the absence of University endowments, the faculty had no secure financial foundation. Apparently, the position of Regent paid no salary. From their University work, the regents depended on fees paid by students attending their lectures. Those fees varied not only between early and advanced courses but also between courses themselves. In many cases, faculty members also held Church positions, receiving the stipends while someone else did the actual Church work (Mackie 1954, pp. 38–39).

The original charter suggests that the Bishop envisioned the students living in houses occupied by the various masters. But the statutes for Glasgow omitted the regulation that St. Andrews University had borrowed from Paris that prohibited students from moving from teacher to teacher and teachers from poaching students from each other. That omission seemed to suggest a gathering of all students into a college, which the faculty of arts subsequently founded. As the College emerged and gained modest endowments, the Faculty of Arts encroached more markedly on the University, with the College becoming the core of life of the University. In the earlier days, the students were treated as mature men and given their appointed place in the election of the Rector. But attitudes soon changed, and the students became regarded as boys who were to be subjected to the severe discipline of the University and the College. The Principal was the supervisor of the College. Election of Regents was in the hands of the Rector, Dean of Faculty, which became increasingly an important officer, and the Principal. Academic matters were under the control of the faculty (Mackie 1954, pp. 43–56).

Post–Reformation Developments

Having been an ecclesiastical foundation of the Catholic Church, the University was nearly ruined by the Reformation, with its income severely reduced. Under the Protestant leaders' *Book of Discipline*, a plan for a national education establishment called for primary, secondary, and university education to be provided under the auspices of the new established Church of Scotland (Mackie 1954, p. 57). Implementation of that grand plan, however, was weakened by a lack of Church funds because noblemen had largely appropriated the old Church revenues and lands. Although legal battles over the funds went on for more than a century, the Church reclaimed relatively little and the universities got even less. Throughout the post-Reformation period into the 19th century, the University was subjected to numerous inspections by commissions and individuals called 'visitors' appointed by the Church of Scotland, the King, or Parliament, depending upon the political situation at the time. Those inspections were usually followed with recommendations for changes. On several occasions, when political authority and/or church authority underwent change, the University was ordered to conform to the new authority, sometimes in very detailed manner.

In 1573, the Glasgow town council granted the College a new constitution that confirmed the College's old possessions and endowed it with all the privileges and immunities granted by the King or his ancestors to any Scottish university that were within the council's limited ability to protect. Under that constitution, the College was to consist of a Principal, who was also to act as the Professor of Theology, two Masters or Regents, and 12 poor students who would receive room and board free for three and one-half years. The Principal was to be elected by the University officers – the Chancellor, Rector, and Dean of Faculty – and several Ministers of the Kirk. He was appointed for life, but could be removed by the electing body. The Regents were removable every six years at the will of the Principal, Rector, and Dean of Faculty. Under the practice of each Regent taking the entire class through a three-year curriculum leading to the Masters degree, the six-year rule allowed each Regent to take two classes through before he was evaluated. The Regents would to receive a small salary and their keep, plus the student fees. Local officials, the Rector, and the Dean of Faculty (usually a local minister) were to be the College's 'visitors' to assure that it was operating appropriately (Mackie 1954, pp. 62–63).

The foundation was modeled upon the medieval college, with each member – master and student alike – required to publicly accept the Confession of Faith of the Church of Scotland and swear to obey the statutes of the College. The curriculum was approximately the medieval form. The College was the center of academic life, with the Chancellor, Rector, and Dean of Faculty essentially the shell of a University that could grant degrees. The conduct of the University, whose primary function was preparing young men for the ministry, was very much under the eye of the Church, with the town officials sharing in the supervision.

In 1577, Glasgow College was granted a new charter by the Crown, which set forth a new constitution that endured with a few changes until the mid-19th century. That constitution was generally similar to the one granted by the town council in 1573, which left the College essentially a pre-Reformation college. While the charter made references to the Chancellor, Rector, and Dean of Faculty, their duties were not defined, creating governance difficulties for years to come. The College that was chartered in 1577 was a very small establishment, consisting of a Principal, three Regents, a Steward, four Poor Students, and three servant/porters. All were required to live in college. The 'Poor Students' were given free room and board, but it was expected that other students would come who would pay their own way. The Senior Regent served as Deputy-Principal. Appointment of the Principal was in the hands of the Crown, but the subsequent examination, election, and admission were entrusted to the Archbishop of Glasgow, Chancellor of the University, Rector of the Academy, Dean of Faculty, and various ministers (who became the electing body). The Principal had full jurisdiction over every person in the College, but his chief duty was teaching theology and preaching. The Steward collected and disbursed all of the College revenues and provided for the common table. With the consent of the 'visitor,' he could use any surplus in such purposes as repairing buildings (Mackie 1954, pp. 66–68).

The election of the Regents was in the hands of the Rector, Dean of Faculty, and Principal. Three Regents were deemed sufficient for the teaching in Arts. Previously, each Regent had taken one class – normally the whole entry of a single year – right through the complete curriculum, and when the three-year course was completed, started over with a new class of students. Under the new system, that system was discontinued, and Regents began specializing by subject, which led to the establishment of 'Chairs.'

The four Poor Students were admitted by the Principal, and entered College for three and one-half years free of all expense. Other students paid their own way. Many were the sons of lords and lairds, and some were notoriously rowdy in their behavior and indifferent in their studies. But Glasgow would not go the way of Oxford. In 1578, aristocratic privileges were demonstrably curbed when the Principal took resolute action to force a public apology from a student who had been disciplined, standing firm in the face of several hundred of the student's noble kin who had threatened to destroy the College and harm the members. Historians view that action as a defining moment, signaling that the University was committed to providing a high quality of education (Mackie 1954, p. 71).

Despite the civil and political turbulence of 1600s in Scotland, the College gained ecclesiastical revenues, received various sources of revenues from the Crown, added bursaries (scholarships) to subsidize poor students, added Regents and other teachers, and constructed buildings. The Regents were apparently good teachers, but normally were young Masters who were waiting for parish minister positions. Throughout the 17th century into the 18th century, ministers of the Kirk outranked university professors in the General Assembly of the Kirk and ceremonial activities. Officers of the University were required to also be ministers.

The governance of the University was based on statutes enacted in 1582. The term 'Moderators' was given to the Chancellor, Rector, Dean, Regents, and other officers. The Chancellor, who was identified with the Archbishop of Glasgow, granted the degrees, but was prohibited from doing any academic business without consent of the Moderators and Masters. (The latter term sometimes referred to the faculty but was also the list of those who had received their Masters degrees from Glasgow.) The Dean of Faculty was elected annually by the Moderators and Masters, and was usually one of the Glasgow ministers. He was concerned with appointment and supervision of teachers and examiners, and supervising the examinations. The Quaestor was in charge of finances and the library. The man holding that position was elected annually by the Dean of Faculty and the Masters, but only a Regent could be elected. That effectively placed the financial administration of the College and University in the hands of the faculty (Mackie 1954, pp. 74–75).

For more than a century after the Reformation, it was uncertain whether the governance of the church in Scotland would be episcopacy or presbytery. The College was affected by the conflict between the Presbyterians, who opposed a system of church governance by bishops (episcopacy), and the Crown, which wanted the bishops to be the king's instruments of control as in the case of the Church of England. When the Crown increased its control over the Kirk, the Chancellor was the Archbishop of Glasgow, and the Rectors were agents of the Crown. When the episcopacy was deposed and the Presbyterians gain control, the College officials were brought into line with the Presbyterians. While the College sought some of the ecclesiastical revenues that had gone to the bishops, it gained only a little. The General Assembly sent several commissions to investigate the University and ordered changes to conform to the new Church and political authorities. When episcopacy was restored in 1661, the College went through another period of adjustment as the bishops came back into power. When William IV became king in 1691, the Presbyterians were back in authority and the episcopal authority of the Chancellor was ended. Henceforth, the Principal of the College rather than the Chancellor or Rector was the chief administrator of the University (Mackie 1954, pp. 78–90, and pp. 119–134).

Glasgow University in the 18th Century

During the period 1701–1727, the salaries of professors were enhanced and a number of new Chairs were established. The Regents gave way to professorships with Chairs, lecturing in their specialized fields. Among the Chairs added were ones in law and medicine. (Curiously, before it began teaching medicine, the University had granted the M.D. degree based on examination of individuals who had studied elsewhere. Until that point, the University had provided general instruction and prepared men for the ministry. Awarding the M.D. degree marked to a change to also equipping its alumni to follow professions in which instruction had previously been by professional associations outside the walls of the College (see Mackie 1954, p. 168).)

While this was a period of growth, it was also marked by disorderly conduct by students and factional conflict among the faculty. Appointments to Chairs were heavily influenced by patronage and partiality under a dictatorial Principal who pursued his own pecuniary interests and his own ambitions in his administration of the College. In 1727, a Commission's findings led to new statutes for the University, which restored the right of students to vote for the Rector, and laid down exact rules for the conduct of University business, including specifying faculty meetings, the classes that would be taught, and who would teach the classes (Mackie 1954, pp. 178–179).

The era 1727–1801, which included Adam Smith's time at Glasgow as a student for three years and later as a faculty member, has been called by 'The Rule of the Faculty' (Mackie 1954, p. 185–214). During that period, the University earned a brilliant reputation for teaching and scholarly work by some of its faculty. But internally, factional conflicts and disputes over constitutional authority continued to occur. In part, that was due to the academic staff of the College being recruited from the ranks of a small society of men closely connected with the Church of Scotland. This contributed to alliances with patrons who influenced appointments to Chairs and offices in the University, and brought clannish disputes from within the Church into the College.

The regulations of 1727 continued the problem of leaving unclear where the ultimate authority in academic matters rested. Under the 1577 charter, the institution was essentially two distinct corporations – the University and the College – with two distinct governing bodies. The Senate, comprised of the Rector, Dean of Faculty, the Principal, and the faculty, governed the University. The management of the University's revenues was under that body. The Principal and the faculty governed the College. A major contentious issue was the authority over the control of the College's revenues, which were much larger than the University's revenues. After a long series of conflicts, the civil court ruled that the revenues and properties of the College were vested in the Principal and Faculty, and they had the sole right of administration. At the same time, the Rector, Dean of Faculty, and Minister of Glasgow had to give their advice and consent before any surplus revenues (revenues remaining after salaries and other ordinary expenses) could be spent (Mackie 1954, pp. 204–205).

Patronage was important to the University and the College, so the influential Dukes of Montrose were given the largely honorary Chancellorship. The influence of the Church of Scotland remained strong, although weakening over time somewhat. The Dean of Faculty was usually chosen from among the Glasgow ministers. Appointments to professorships that were vested in the College were in the hands of the Principal and faculty, although influential patrons played a large role. The College meeting was to inform the Crown of the vacancies for the Principal and those professorships that were in the gift of Crown. If nominations were not forthcoming, the College meeting was to take steps to fill the vacancies. But patronage was important to the individuals seeking appointments to any of the Chairs or who were hoping to advance to a more desirable Chair. Many of the professors in the Scottish universities had served as tutors in the houses of their patrons. Mackie (1954, pp. 187–188) described the faculty as feeling so secure in their positions with the backing of their patrons, that they regarded themselves as having vested interest in the houses provided for them by the College as well as their Chairs and salaries. Apparently, the townspeople complained that the houses of the faculty members were much too fine. Moreover, faculty members usually took in students as boarders and sometimes also acted as private tutors for some of the wealthier ones.

Under the Settlement of 1727, the Chairs of the 'higher subjects' (the lower 'gown' classes were required for the M.A. degree) were compelled to teach their subjects for a term if five students presented themselves.

Otherwise, they were required only to give one public lecture per week at a time specified by the faculty. Mackie (1954, pp. 188–195) reported that a number of those holding chairs drew their salaries for years without doing any teaching. One faculty member who had ambitions toward becoming Principal contrived to get awarded the honorary degree of Doctor of Divinity.

In Adam Smith's time, Glasgow College had some 300 students in all. The numbers of students in the classes varied between subjects, with some being more popular, and between the 'public' or ordinary classes taken for graduation and the 'private' or upper level classes. A larger number attended the 'public' classes, paying fees that were 50 percent higher than the 'private' class fees. Some students, especially the divinity students attending the 'private' class, were exempt from paying any fees. The average faculty income was derived partly from a moderate salary from College endowments and somewhat more from lecture fees. Those who boarded and tutored students collected extra fees from those students. Throughout the 18th century, fee incomes for professors at all the Scottish universities were affected by economic conditions, sometimes varying considerably from one session to another (Rae 1965, p. 50).

In addition to teaching students, the University of Glasgow provided a workshop for James Watt in the College, and made him mathematical instrument maker to the University when the trade corporations of Glasgow refused to allow him to open a workshop in the city (Mackie 1954, pp. 218–219). A printing office was also opened to advance the art of printing. To help the University printer, the University heads established a type-foundry on its grounds and appointed the type-founder to the University. A new Chair of Astronomy was endowed, and the type-founder was made the first professor. That individual had been trained as a physician, and brought reputation to the College and himself by observing sunspots. An Academy of Design for the teaching of the arts of painting, sculpture, and engraving was the first school of design in Britain (Rae 1965, pp. 72–74). The intent was to anticipate some aspects of modern 'academic capitalism' in combining technical teaching and revenue-generating outputs through the sales of productions through outlets in such places as Edinburgh. Efforts were also made to provide extension education through night lectures to working-men, which was acknowledged to improve the technical knowledge of the higher grades of artisans. Curiously, while the Principal and faculty strongly agitated against the building of a public playhouse in the area, there were some support (albeit unsuccessful) for establishing an academy of dancing, fencing, and riding in the University (Rae 1965, p. 79).

THE NEW GERMAN UNIVERSITIES

German universities originated in the Middle Ages modeled after the University of Paris. But the modern university is often viewed as beginning with the founding of the University of Berlin in 1809. In turn, the emergence of the modern American universities with graduate programs leading to research-based doctoral degrees in the latter part of the 19th century has been linked to the institutional influence of the new German universities.

Humboldt and the University of Berlin

As head of the Prussian educational system in the Ministry of the Interior, Humboldt's efforts at educational reform in Prussia included establishing a new institution of higher education in Berlin. The existing provincial universities had a number of reputable scholars among their faculty members. But those schools were small institutions, and the professors were overloaded with lecturing to indifferent and ill-prepared students. Humboldt's new university in Berlin was designed to be uncompromisingly committed to *Wissenschaft* (fields of pure scholarly learning) and *Bildung* (personal culture). The core of the university would be the philosophical faculty rather than the traditional faculties of theology, law, and medicine. While the word 'university' had become associated with the failed traditional institutions of the 18th century, Humboldt chose to retain the name in order to attract non-Prussians (both German and foreigners) (Sweet 1980, pp. 55–56).

Initially, Humboldt made a special effort to bring the various academies and institutes in Berlin into an organic relationship with the university. The latter was to be the central institution but it would not absorb the Academy of Sciences, which had its own special function as the ultimate sanctuary of *Wissenschaft*. Humboldt's early view that the Academy's function was enlarging knowledge and the University's function was disseminating that knowledge was revised as he became critical of the performances of the academies. Since universities had done more to advance knowledge, they should be both centers of research and teaching. An important institutional difference between the two institutions in Humboldt's scheme was that academies should be free to choose their own members but the appointment of university teachers must remain exclusively reserved to the state. Where university faculties chose their own members, universities became either citadels of sectarian indoctrination or controlled by particular cliques or interest. Faculty members were too vulnerable to sectarian influence and guild politics. But within the limited autonomy left to the university, the state should leave it free (Sweet 1980, pp. 60–62).

Humboldt's fundamental assumption was that the university should be the place where *Wissenschaft* in the deepest and broadest sense would be cultivated. In contrast to the academy, which consisted of men of proven scholarly and scientific competence, the university was a community of professors and students. The gymnasium's function was to concentrate on teaching what is already known, while the university was to wrestle with problems whose answers are not known. The gymnasium must impose discipline, but the university must emphasize freedom. Students must learn how to learn in the gymnasium. But within the university, there should be emancipation from being actually taught. Structured lectures should be a very small part. Unstructured activity, with professors and students cooperating as they choose, without compulsion or fixed purpose, was university work. There should be a maximum of opportunity for individuals to go about the quest for *Wissenschaft* in their own individualistic fashion. University professors do not have the duty of serving the student. Rather, both the professor and the student serve the cause of advancing *Wissenschaft*. Creative activity is the essence of the university. The true value of university teaching is that some scholars are more creatively productive when they are also teaching (Sweet 1980, pp. 66–68).

The University of Berlin, however, did not develop exactly along the lines of Humboldt's vision. He was unsuccessful in his attempts to persude King Fredrick William III to grant the university a permanent endowment in landed property. *Wissenschaft* as the central concern of the university proved to be an ambiguous concept (Sweet 1980, p. 70). Rather than the wholeness of knowledge, the term became commonly synonymous with specialized knowledge. Accordingly, the university became viewed as an institution for advanced professional training rather than as the final stage in a general education. Nevertheless, the Humboldtian vision provided a conceptual standard that influenced universities and judgments of how universities function, not only in Germany but in other countries as well, particularly in America. Writing in 1930, Flexner declared that:

The German university for almost a century and a half fruitfully engaged in teaching and research. As long as those two tasks combine in fertile union, the German university, whatever its defects of detail, will retain its importance. It has stimulated university development in Great Britain; from it has sprung the graduate school of the new world; to it industry and health and every conceivable practical activity are infinitely indebted. Neither utility nor even practical professional training is of its essence. Indeed, from time to time, it has been more open to criticism on the ground of indifference than to criticism on the ground of worldliness (p. 315).

A central authority, the education ministry in each of the federated states, ultimately governed each German university. The university's business affairs were handled by a local administrator, who was presumably both the confidential representative of the government and the trusted representative of the university in its dealing with the administration. The faculties of philosophy (arts and sciences), medicine, jurisprudence, and theology were distinct, autonomous, and as a rule equally prominent and equally developed. Internal business was transacted by committees of the faculty, who through their deans negotiated with the appropriate division of the ministry on matters that required governmental approval. Despite the bureaucratic slowness of progress and occasional expressions of local dissatisfaction, it was generally conceded that no other country made as much progress in equipment, finance, and expansion in the 75 years preceding World War I (Flexner 1930, pp. 316–317).

Special Features of German University Life

Four special features of German university life merit special note (see Flexner 1930, p. 317–327). First, there was a great deal of freedom. Each teacher, regardless of rank, held an intellectual post in which he was free of any supervision from either the faculty or the ministry. As a proven scholar or scientist, his function was conserving and advancing knowledge through teaching and research. How he would accomplish that function was left for him to determine. The topics covered, the manner of presentation, and the format of his seminar were left to the professor's own choice. Flexner (1930, p. 318) disputed the common notion that the German professors cared only about research and took their teaching lightly. German university professors did not engage in 'spoon-feeding' students, who were not supposed to require it.

Theoretically, the students were similarly free in their own right. With his credentials being recognized at face value, the student was free to go where he pleased, selecting his own teachers, wandering from one university to another. But the student's task was to prepare for one or both of the two examinations that were given. The examination that was the gateway to a professional calling was given by the state. The other examination that led to the doctorate degree was given the university. Preparation for those examinations required a prescribed course of study, and the responsibility for that preparation rested entirely with the student. He was regarded as being competent to take care of himself and to accept the full consequences of his behavior. Neither faculty members nor deans had any responsibility to supervise his preparation. When the student thought he was prepared for the exam, he took it. He could not earn a degree or qualify for an examination by accumulating a number of credit hours.

The second feature was the manner in which the full professors were selected. The process started with a committee of faculty suggesting three names to the faculty, which was free to modify the list before it was submitted to the state education minister. That official was free to appoint one from the committee or an outsider. Usually, the three candidates on the list had gained prominence in some other university. As a check on the state ministry's power to veto the choice of professors, only the faculty could grant the license to teach.

Relative to that, the third feature was the 'wandering' university instructor. After obtaining his degree and license to teach, usually after studying at several universities, he would begin his professional career by serving as an unsalaried *Privatdozen* in one university. He would offer a lecture course or two for fees, and attempt in some way to become attached to a laboratory, clinic, or library to continue his productive work. If his career developed successfully, he would subsequently be called to a faculty position in one of the provincial universities, beginning as lecturer or associate professor. If his reputation as a teacher and researcher grew sufficiently, he could advance in academic rank and move to a more renowned university. Before World War I, this was a severe system, with the *Privatdozen* making up a large group that collectively supplied a host of low paid workers for universities, secondary schools, governmental service, and industry. Many would remain in that status for years while waiting to be called to a university.

The German students were also 'wanders,' moving easily from one university to another, forming no sense of institutional loyalty. Students with ability were free to go where their particular subjects were best taught. Presumably, that stimulated professors to do their best to attract the most competent students to enhance the reputation of their seminar and laboratory. Moreover, professors' incomes depended to some extent on the quality of their students.

Fourth, the German universities were entirely dependent upon the state for funds. Departments could not be developed unless the state provided the money; new Chairs could not be established without the sanction of the education ministry. The state regulated and participated in examinations; in large measure it managed the budget. The safeguards to the universities' autonomy were law, idea, and tradition going back to Humboldt. The pre-World War I German university full professors received substantial salaries, and their lectures had to be paid for by students (even if they did not attend) because the professors had to attest to students' readiness to sit for the examinations. Professors preferred lectures rather than breaking their classes into smaller ones because the lecture fees were more remunerative. The fee incomes ranged from every low to very high, reflecting both the reputation of the professor and the popularity of the field to students.

THE EMERGENCE OF MODERN AMERICAN UNIVERSITIES

The earliest institutions of higher learning in America essentially reproduced the 17th century type of English college. But in the emergence of the doctoral degree-granting universities in the later 19th century, America borrowed heavily from the 19th century German universities. Three of the universities with which Veblen was associated as either a student or faculty member – Johns Hopkins, Chicago, and Stanford – were new institutions established with endowments from wealthy individuals and their organizational structures were designed by strong individuals serving as presidents. In contrast, Yale University, where Veblen completed his studies for the doctoral degree in philosophy, grew out of one of the earliest American colleges.

The American Colleges

The nine American colleges established before the Revolutionary War had the dual missions of preparing men for the clergy through 'divine learning' and educating civic leaders, particularly in the learned professions, through 'humane learning.' The motives for their founding and the sources of their funding reflected a blending of sectarian religions and public interest. Harvard was established in 1636 when the government of Massachusetts's colony appropriated funds. It was to educate Puritan clergymen and also to prepare men for positions of responsibility and leadership in society. Yale was founded in 1701 as a public institution to train clergy for the Congregational Church, apparently out of a desire to establish a new institution that would promote the Puritanism that allegedly was in decline at Harvard. As an expression of gratitude for a donation from Elihu Yale, a wealthy officer of the East India Company, the college took his name. Princeton was established because Presbyterians wanted an institution of higher education of their own. Similarly, New England Congregationalists founded Dartmouth; Brown University by the Baptists founded Brown University, and Rutgers by the Dutch Reformed Church. The newly founded American colleges tended to stress that they also had the larger aim of serving society by advancing liberal education. In contrast to the English universities, few American colleges were long dominated by any particular sect or denomination. Religious tests for admission or graduation were never firmly implemented, and in most cases students of minority religious affiliations had freedom of religious belief (Lucas 1994, pp. 105–107).

The legal distinction between the 'public' and 'private' colleges was unclear until the Supreme Court's decision in the Dartmouth case in 1819. While colonial and state governments heavily supported the colleges financially, they never became state institutions in the modern sense. The social interest in higher education was relatively weak. Only one person in a thousand in the population attended college and fewer actually completed a degree. The American colleges had copied the curriculum of the English colleges, although by the end of the 18th century, practical subjects such as navigation, surveying, and mathematics were being included at some schools.

The American colleges emulated the British colleges as residential institutions, although they lacked the funds to construct quadrangles to enclose the college from the outside world. Student behavior seems to have been little different from that of the English students, although the special privileges of nobility were never strongly established in America. Initially, poor students were provided with opportunities to attend by 'charity' scholarships and allowing them to teach school on a part-time basis. But rising costs in the 18th century began to restrict attendance to the sons of wealthy men. Benjamin Franklin reported that in his youth Harvard had already become a rich man's school, a place where wealthy parents sent their sons to learn nothing more than the social skills of gentlemen (Lucas 1994, p. 109).

The legal issue in the Dartmouth case was whether the College was a public corporation whose charter could be changed at will by the state legislature or a private corporation whose charter was could not be altered by the state. Dartmouth College's charter, received from the English Crown, provided for a self-perpetuating board of trustees and a president who was authorized to appoint his own successor. When the college's second president challenged the right of absentee trustees to meddle in the school's internal affairs, the board voted to dismiss him. In support of the president, the state legislature amended the charter to provide for a reorganized university. New members were added to the board, all of whom pledged to support the president. The board members opposed the change and two institutions, Dartmouth College and Dartmouth University, became involved in a legal contest over the institution's records and original seal. The state's supreme court ruled that Dartmouth was a public corporation, but the United States Supreme Court declared that it was a private corporation. As such, Dartmouth's charter was an inviolate contract that could not be altered by the state (Lucas 1994, pp. 114–119).

After the Dartmouth case, the number of private colleges increased for several reasons. The majority of the new colleges were founded by religious denominations, often without sufficient funding or academic staffs. The general intellectual quality declined, in part because anti-intellectual evangelicals displaced academic educators. At the same time, there was an increase in popular support and interest in higher education. In part, rivalry among states was responsible for the founding of public colleges and universities, as each state attempted to keep the young people from going out-of-state to college. Geographical isolation sometimes accounted for establishing colleges. Even those founding a private college tended to stress that a local or regional public interest would be served. Where England with a population of some 23 million had only four institutions of higher education, Ohio with a population of about three million had 37 colleges before the American Civil War (Lucas 1994, p. 117). Under the influence of Jacksonian democracy, colleges experienced the stress of contradictory social philosophies about higher education. On the one hand, there was great respect for uneducated common men succeeding through hard work and common sense. Hence, opportunities for attending college were regarded as unimportant. On the other hand, there was a strong dislike of the monopoly over college training that was held by the privileged wealthy classes, and it was deemed important to provide greater opportunities for members of the working class to attend college.

Before the Civil War, American colleges remained small and mostly poor, with tuition as the primary source of revenues. Those affiliated with religious sects were partially supported by donations from the churches of those sects. Not all students paid tuition. Many were on stipends or scholarships reserved for the needy. Colleges sometimes had to accept payment in kind or promissory notes. Charitable donations, largely from churches of the religious sects that had founded private colleges, and occasional endowments, supplemented tuition revenues. While the colleges sought financial support from state governments, they insisted on retaining control over internal policy-making, allowing only limited public representation on the governing boards. Although state subsidies to colleges fell off substantially after the Dartmouth case, private colleges continued to receive public funds. Regarding colleges more as philanthropic institutions justified that rather than as arms of the state, which also led states to reduce their efforts to control colleges not established as state institutions. The emphasis on endowments for the leading schools began during this period. In 1800, Harvard received 55 percent of its funds from public sources. By 1840, endowments were providing 40 percent of the college's income (Lucas 1994, pp. 114–116).

American colleges employed two types of teachers – tutors and regular professors. Tutors were the more numerous, typically a young man recently graduated from the college, willing to accept a temporary position while waiting for a more permanent outside position, usually as a minister. A regular professor had more academic training, had been a tutor, and was usually appointed by his alma mater after having a non-academic career, again usually as a minister. Stringent rules of behavior, which the faculty was expected to enforce, tended to create adversarial relationships within the colleges that sometimes became intense. On most campuses, religious observances were mandatory (Lucas 1994, pp. 123–124).

Governance of the American colleges was essentially in the form of college presidents exercising authority, answerable only vaguely to non-resident boards. When presidents met with challenges from students or faculties, the boards invariably backed the presidents. Still, an enduring compromise emerged under which faculty were allowed to largely control decisions regarding student admissions, academic standards, and curricular specifics, while the president and the board to handle all other matters. There was a growing acceptance of the notion that college administrators and academics were two different breeds, with the academic men considered too impractical to handle the administrative functions. It became popular for boards to seek men who had been in business to serve as presidents, to whom they could delegate their power (Lucas 1994, pp. 124–125).

Colleges that were established in the pre-Civil War 19th century tended to be located in rural areas, with residential campuses in attempts to isolate students from bad influences. Efforts were made to create residential halls on the model of the English colleges. On many campuses, the practice of making lower classmen subservient to upper classmen became installed. Lectures and recitations were the usual methods of instruction. The isolation, enforced seclusion, and rigorous routine resulted in numerous student fights and occasional rebellions against authorities. One of the few diversions approved by college authorities were activities sponsored by religious societies. While religious revivals occasionally broke up the monotony, they also brought stricter morals, at least for a time. Literary societies and debating clubs were popular, with amateur theater and orchestras, dancing in some schools, hunting, foot races, bowling, skating, shooting marbles, and free-for-all versions of football or soccer. Gymnastics became popular. Greek-letter societies also appeared in the early 1800s, which early opposition from faculty members proved unable to suppress (Lucas 1994, pp. 126–131).

American Graduate/Research Universities

The prototype American university as a large multi-level institution with the multi-purpose of research, teaching, service, and other activities appeared in the second half of the 1800s. In some cases, new institutions were established with contributed private funds, e.g., Johns Hopkins,

Clark, Chicago, and Stanford. In other cases, graduate and professional programs were added to existing institutions, both private and public. Yale and Harvard are prime examples of private colleges that became universities, while Michigan, Wisconsin, and California were examples of state schools that became modern universities.

Several developments contributed to the emergence of American universities. One was a growing movement for changes in the curricula and the range of activities undertaken by colleges. Before the Civil War, attempts were being made to revise curricula to offer more training for professional and technical employment, to include more science, mathematics, and engineering, and to allow students to choose among a number of specialized subjects. Increasingly, colleges in the late 19th century responded to those demands. The federal government encouraged more utilitarian curricula by giving to states public land that was to be sold and the revenue used to provide for agricultural and mechanical programs. The states responded to the land-grant programs in different ways. Some states created new land-grant universities, which then competed with the existing state schools for state appropriations. Other states added agricultural and mechanical programs to existing schools. Initially, land-grant schools experienced difficulty in attracting students, and the funds provided were often insufficient to make the schools self-supporting (Lucas 1994, pp. 146–153). Cities also became involved, establishing new universities whose curricula and perceived missions were to train 'non-traditional' urban students for employment. Part-time students constituted a significant portion of those attending the municipal schools.

Along with the greater emphasis on utilitarian curricula, there was also a growing movement to allow students to choose electives (Lucas 1994, pp. 165–170). While this was viewed by many academicians and intellectuals as weakening the academic functions of universities, two developments were occurring that closely related to one another. First, fields of study were becoming more specialized, with academic departments emerging and becoming more narrowly delineated. As schools became larger, the organization became more complex, with departments and colleges. With the depth and breadth of knowledge rapidly increasing, especially in the scientific and technical fields, more and larger physical facilities, including libraries and laboratories, were constructed. Universities became associated in the public eye with campuses and buildings.

The notion that universities were to provide public service also became entrenched during the late 19th and early 20th century. The University of Wisconsin as a state institution perhaps best exemplified a commitment to social service, using the resources of the university to try to find solutions to society's problems. With the appointment of Richard T. Ely in 1892 as director of the newly established School of Economics, Political Science, and History, the university took the lead in preparing students for positions in state government civil service and for faculty members to become advisors to governmental leaders. Extension programs, short-courses for farmers and housewives in practical matters, training courses for all kinds of occupations and professions, applied research, field work in social work, health, hygiene, and so forth became a permanent feature of American universities (Lucas 1994, pp. 174–176).

The second development was post-graduate programs leading to the doctoral degree, which meant a heavy emphasis on research and teaching mature advanced students in the methods of research. This reflected the strong influence of the German universities on both the philosophy and structure of American higher education (Lucas 1994, pp. 170–174). In some instances, the German-style university structure was simply superimposed upon an existing English-type undergraduate college. In other cases, new institutions to emphasize post-graduate studies were established with funds provided by wealthy private donors. The notable examples were Johns Hopkins, Clark University, the University of Chicago, and Stanford University. But those universities were 'American' in being complex institutions that included not only graduate studies but also undergraduate colleges, professional and technical schools, and various types of public service activities. In addition, with the exception of Johns Hopkins, the other universities engaged in the types of activities such as athletic teams that became a unique feature of American universities.

The founding of Johns Hopkins University is a case example of several features of the new American universities. The funding came from a wealthy private donor, who formed two corporations in 1867, one to maintain a hospital and one to found a university. In his will, he left to the proposed university an endowment of 15,000 shares of common stock in a railroad company and an estate outside of Baltimore. The trustees of the university were advised not to sell the stock but keep it as a safe investment. He chose 14 trustees from Baltimore business and professional men, ten of whom also served on the board of the hospital. They were advised not the sell the stock but keep it as a safe investment, to maintain the University out of revenues from student fees and the annual revenue from the principal fund, and to establish free scholarships for scholars from Maryland, Virginia, and North Carolina (Hawkins 1960, pp. 3–20).

The type of university to be created was left up to the trustees, who selected Daniel Coit Gilman as president. His plan for the new university called for postponing the creation of departments of medicine and law (Cordasco 1960, pp. 65–68; see also pp. 81–83). While the intent may have been to emphasize post-graduate studies in the German model, concentrating on research first, and teaching second, an undergraduate college was also established, offering Bachelor degrees in both classical studies and scientific studies. Master of Art and Doctor of Philosophy degrees would be awarded at the graduate level. Publishing learned journals to disseminate the results of research became visible features of the new American research university. Twenty graduate fellowships were established in 1876, and the Ph.D. as it evolved at Hopkins became the standard for the American graduate school. The requirements for the doctoral degree included having an earned Bachelor's degree from an institution of recognized standing, completion of a prolonged and arduous study of one primary subject and one subsidiary subject, preparation of a thesis requiring the labor of the greater part of an academic year, defending the thesis to examiners in writing and in oral questioning, demonstrating the ability to read Latin, French, and German and a familiarity with the methods of modern scientific and scholarly research (Cordasco 1960, pp. 87–88). The fellowships provided a nucleus of advanced students, the undergraduate college supplied a potential source of graduate students, and the permanent faculty was selected for their research abilities. In addition, publication of research results was emphasized, and several journals and monograph series were established.

The University of Chicago was founded in its modern form through funds given by John D. Rockefeller, which led to success in raising funds from other donors. The educational plan was the work of its first president, William Rainey Harper, who demanded and received from Rockefeller enough funds to raise the new school from a college to a comprehensive university and to pay salaries high enough to recruit the faculty that he wanted. The university was organized into three general divisions – the university proper, the university extension, and the university publication work. The first category included colleges of liberal arts, science, literature, and practical arts. In addition to the graduate school there were the divinity school, the medical school, the engineering school, school of pedagogy (education), school of fine arts, and school of music. The extension division would offer evening courses for those who could do regular work on campus, regular courses of lectures in and about Chicago, correspondence courses for people all over the world, special courses in Bible studies, and library extension through lending books to students not in Chicago. The publishing work included the usual printing and publishing of official documents, books, special papers, journals, and reviews prepared by Chicago faculty. A fourth division was subsequently added, that of libraries, laboratories, and museums. Yet a fifth was added, University affiliations, to establish working relationships with other colleges and universities to assist them in raising their standards (Goodspeed 1916, pp. 134–137).

The president was the immediate head of the University proper, with directors appointed to head the other divisions. The first two years of undergraduate studies was under one college (the Junior) and the last two under another (the Senior). Other Schools or colleges were added, e.g., the College of Commerce and Administration in 1898, later renamed the School of Commerce and Administration, by 1902 ranked as a separate professional school to prepare students for practical business professions.

A faculty Senate was to have purview over matters of education, and a Council over matters of administration. The Senate included the President, the University Recorder as secretary, all Head Professors (heads of departments), and the University Librarian. The Council consisted of the President, the Examiner, the Recorder, the Registrar, all Deans of colleges, and all Directors. Harper also developed plans for the academic year, including a summer school, and classification of courses, including major and minor fields of study, and electives. Changes subsequently occurred in the university's ruling bodies, but the power of the President remained largely intact (Goodspeed 1916, p. 140).

The University of Chicago became the prototype American university in yet another way. From the beginning, Harper emphasized the importance of athletics. In his 1896 spring convocation address, he stated that the 'athletic work' of students is a real and essential part of their college education, and that the athletic field is one of the University's laboratories, and by no means the least important one. Harper insisted that athletics be strictly of an amateur nature. The director of the athletic board was not a professional coach who had to win games to keep his job, but a permanent member of the teaching staff with professorial rank. Members of athletic teams were to be held to high grades of scholarship. Intercollegiate contests would be restricted within reasonable limits, e.g., seven or eight football games, both to prevent exhaustion and to prevent undergraduates from becoming so absorbed in sports as to neglect their studies. Football soared in popularity, and the ceremony of football games – e.g., cheers, cheerleaders, pep rallies – quickly became a feature of American university life. Between 1892 and 1915, the revenues from football just about paid for the cost of the total athletic programs. Twice during that time, the baseball team traveled to Japan. Alonzo Stagg became a person of influence with both students and alumni (Goodspeed 1916, pp. 387–382).

Another characteristic the American universities emerged at Chicago at the beginning, the fraternity system. The first order of business at the first meeting of the faculty in 1892 dealt with the issue of 'Greek-letter societies.' A committee was appointed to consider the acceptance of those societies, with Alonzo Stagg as one of the five members named by the president. Students wanted the societies. Apparently, the faculty did not, but declined to make any formal recommendation to the Trustees. The trustees gave their approval, with some superficial restrictions (Goodspeed 1916, p. 253 and p. 451).

Chicago also developed a financial management system of accounting, budgeting, and investment that utilized the latest in business techniques adapted to the non-profit university. Most of the gifts to the university were in bonds, with some stock also given. The investment manager for the university balanced the portfolio by making real estate loans on manufacturing and business property, and some farm mortgage loans. The university also bought some well-located central business property in Chicago. Chicago became a model of university finance that was copied by many other universities (Goodspeed 1916, p. 386).

The Governance of American Universities

One feature of the American colleges generally retained by the new research/graduate universities was the powerful authority of the president. Officially, the universities were in the hands of boards of trustees. Increasingly, business and professional people replaced the ministers who had been on the boards of the colleges. The board appointed the presidents and delegated their powers to him, typically giving him almost total freedom in his administration of the institution. Faculty could be hired and fired at his will. Academic freedom became a major concern for faculty members. Professors could be and were fired for expressing unpopular views, usually on religious issues but increasing on social issues that involved criticism of powerful businessmen. A professor at Chicago was fired in 1895 for criticizing monopolies and the railroad industry. But others were fired for their approval of free trade and free silver. The wife of the founder of Stanford University, acting as the sole trustee, ordered the president of the institution to fire an economics professor, E. A. Ross, for his failure to oppose municipal ownership of public utilities (Lucas 1994, pp. 194–195). Some historians explain the changes that occurred in curricula and activities in part as a new generation of entrepreneurial presidents replacing those who had held strongly to the more traditional classical education functions of colleges. Thus, a great deal of credit for the new is given to those individuals, such as the presidents of Johns Hopkins and Chicago.

Internally, universities became increasingly bureaucratized with colleges and departments headed by deans and department heads appointed by the president. Faculty positions became hierarchically ranked, with temporary or short-term appointments in the ranks of instructors and assistant professors, and the more permanent faculty in the ranks of associate and full professors. Some universities had additional ranks, such as readers and lecturers among the temporary appointments and head professor above the full professor level. The departmentalization of academic studies into quasi-independent bureaucratic organizations created provincialism and considerable internal competition for students and funds.

The funding of the major universities became a major determinant in what the universities did. While major state universities received appropriations from state governments, they also depended heavily on student fees and on private donors. Student fees were never intended to cover all the costs. The private universities of the research institution class depended very heavily on endowments, which led to major efforts to gain the good will of potential donors and retain that of existing donors. The rapid growth of the popularity of football became a major tool in soliciting the good will of both private donors and state legislators, and the competition on the playing fields became the visible feature of competition among the institutions for funds and for students.

3. Adam Smith on Failures of English Universities

Adam Smith's criticism of the English universities in *Wealth of Nations* appears in Book V, 'Of the Revenue of the Sovereign or Commonwealth,' Chapter 1, 'Of the Expences of the Sovereign or Commonwealth,' Part III, 'Of the Expence of Publick Works and Publick Institutions,' Article II, 'Of the Expence of the Institutions for the Education of Youth.' In that quaint manner, Smith treated the education of young men attending universities as well as that of children in local parish schools and boys attending British public schools as a legitimate subject in public finance.

The primary thrust of Smith's inquiry was posed by three normative questions:

> Ought the publick . . . give no attention, it may be asked, to the education of the people? Or if it ought to give any, what are the different parts of education which it ought to attend to in the different orders of the people? and in what manner ought it to attend to them? (p. 781).

With respect to the first question, Smith observed that 'The institutions for the education of the youth may . . . furnish a revenue sufficient for defraying their own expence. The fee or honorary which the scholar pays to the master naturally constitutes a revenue of this kind' (1776 [1976, pp. 758–759]). But he also asserted that the 'expence of the institutions for education' was 'no doubt, beneficial to the whole society, and may, therefore, without injustice, be defrayed by the general contribution of the whole society' (1776 [1976, p. 815]).

On that basis, Smith's response to the second question was that the 'publick' ought to provide for those 'different parts of education' that generated public benefits. Those 'parts' that he discussed included not only the basic education of children – the teaching of reading, writing, and arithmetic – but also university-level education. Indeed, Smith began with universities and the entire discussion of education of the youth devoted more attention to university education for the sons of 'gentlemen and men of fortune' than to the basic education of the 'common people.'

The nature of the public benefits that Smith perceived to derive from basic education has been subject to debate. As West (1965) pointed out, Smith definitely argued that educated people make better citizens. The dulling routine of most work under specialization and division of labor makes people generally:

> . . . as stupid and ignorant as it is possible for a human creature to become. The torpor of his mind renders him, not only incapable of conceiving any generous, noble, or tender sentiment, and consequently of forming any just judgement concerning many of the ordinary duties of life. Of the great and extensive interests of his country, he is altogether incapable of judging; and unless very particular pains have been taken to render him otherwise, he is equally incapable of defending his country in war (Smith 1776 [1976, p. 782]).

West (1965) denied, however, that Smith claimed that society gained any economic benefits, e.g., economic growth, from education. The following passage in *Wealth of Nations* might seem to suggest otherwise.

> There is scarce a common trade which does not afford some opportunities for applying to it the principles of geometry and mechanicks, and which would not therefore gradually exercise and improve the common people in those principles, the necessary introduction to the most sublime as well as to the most useful sciences (Smith 1776 [1976, p. 786]).

The second part of that statement indicates that such work can provide reinforcement of classroom educational experiences, giving rise to opportunities for mental stimulation and the learning of the 'principles of geometry and mechanicks.' But the first part clearly suggests that productivity in those trades could be improved by applications of mathematical and mechanical knowledge, as does the phrase 'the most useful sciences.' It might be argued, of course, that the increase in productivity from applying mathematical and scientific knowledge would be in the form of purely private benefits to be realized as returns on investment in human capital by those who gain and use that knowledge.

But there is also Smith's statement that the 'publick' could impose upon 'almost the whole body of the people' the necessity of acquiring 'those most essential parts of education' by requiring examinations as a condition for entering any trade in a town or village (1976 [1776, p. 786]). The discussion following that statement related to how the Greeks and Romans managed to instill a 'martial spirit' in their citizens. But the idea of requiring evidence of education as a condition for entering a trade would definitely seem to indicate an expectation of economic benefits to society. Smith's general theory that maximizing the wealth of nations requires conditions of complete freedom of individuals to employ their capital and labor where ever their self-interests are served would preclude any interference with that freedom by requiring qualifying examinations unless education is conducive to greater productivity in those trades. The economic efficiency of competitive markets would not permit the exclusion of individuals who were capable of performing the work of any particular profession or trade and who were seeking to maximize their own interests by choosing to do so. That would be highly inconsistent with Smith's repeated assurances that free individuals will make rational choices in employing their capital and labor. Such interference as requiring examinations could only be detrimental to maximizing the wealth of the nation in Smith's general theory unless the education enhanced the ability of individuals to create that wealth.

Although Smith was even more vague about the specific nature of the public benefits of university education, he was more explicit in stating that there were public benefits. Curiously, his most revealing comment on the subject was a general statement that the benefits were sufficiently large to be on net positive even while universities were failing to function properly.

> The parts of education which are commonly taught in universities, it may, perhaps, be said are not very well taught. But had it not been or those institutions they would not have been commonly taught at all, and both the individual and the *publick* would have suffered a good deal from the want of those important parts of education (1976, p. 765, emphasis added).

The bulk of Smith's discussion of universities in *Wealth of Nations* had to do with the third question – the 'manner' in which the 'publick' should 'attend' the education of youth. His response essentially divided into two related inquiries. The first identified the type of education that students should receive. To the extent that Smith expressed his views on a good university education, it was largely in terms of the curricula that universities should offer and diligent competence in teaching by faculty as the prime input in the education production function. Scholarly and scientific research appeared to be important only in assuring that faculty members would be sufficiently knowledgeable to effectively teach their subjects. Publication of books and papers was not even mentioned.

The second inquiry provided an economic perspective on how 'good' education could be most effectively supplied. As Skinner (1996) observed, 'the analysis of principles which are of general application refers primarily to the universities' (1776 [1976, p. 196]). Smith's normative views conditioned his perception that English universities were failing to function properly. How his own experiences as a student, faculty member, and administrator may have influenced his normative views is discussed in Appendix A. But Smith's discussion of the causes of those failures and his suggestions for reforms were supported by a positive analysis that explained universities' behavior in terms of the motives, interests, and the set of incentives and constraints faced by those individuals whose decisions and activities determined the institutional functioning of universities.

Smith's positive analysis essentially extended his basic economic theory of human behavior to an explanation of the behavioral tendencies of universities and their faculties. Similarly, his suggestions for reform called for institutional arrangements and practices that would create incentives for faculty to approach their teaching with diligence and competence. This involved removing constraints on the freedom of student-consumers to choose and forcing faculty members and universities to compete for student-consumers on basis of the attractiveness of the curriculum offered and the reputations of the teachers. The principles involved were the powerful motivating force of self-interest on part of faculty members, channeled through the market-like approach of making faculty incomes dependent upon class fees paid by students, appropriately constrained and channeled to the proper ends by the intertwining principles of student-consumer sovereignty and supply-side competition. Where universities operated in accordance with these principles, good education would be assured. But where universities operated under a different system, only failures could be expected.

THE INSTITUTIONAL NATURE OF UNIVERSITIES

While Smith introduced university education under the heading of duties of the sovereign, and generally stated that such education provided sufficient public benefits to warrant financing it from general revenue, his analysis of universities' behavior had essentially nothing to do with governmental finance or with public benefits. Instead, his commentary dealt primarily with the private benefits received by university students, both in terms of why students were not receiving maximum benefits and how that problem could be rectified through institutional reforms that would make universities function more like competitive market suppliers of education to student-consumers. Indeed, it would be possible to interpret Smith's perception that English universities were failing as simply another case of monopolistic behavior were it not for the unique institutional nature of universities, some of which were noted in *Wealth of Nations*.

On an institutional basis, Smith dealt with the European and British universities as they existed in his time but with an analytical perspective on their evolutionary development. Overall, the educational system in Britain was still in a rather primitive state. With the exception of the small parish schools in Scotland, anything resembling a system of public schools for children of working class families scarcely existed in Britain. Smith himself noted in *Wealth of Nations* that the establishment of charity schools in England was not so universal as that of parish schools in Scotland (1976, p. 785). England did not catch up with Scotland in that regard until the 1830s (West 1965, p. 115). There were only a few universities, most notably the English universities of Oxford and Cambridge and the four Scottish universities of Glasgow, Edinburgh, St. Andrews, and Aberdeen. As John Stuart Mill noted in his 1867 inaugural address as Rector of St. Andrews, the Scottish universities were actually both high schools and universities. Smith himself entered Glasgow University at the age of 14, which was actually older than the average (West 1976, p. 41).

The rather sketchy discussion of the institutional nature of universities in *Wealth of Nations* tended to be mixed in with Smith's more extensive discussion of the curriculum. The existing universities and especially the curriculum were explained in terms of their historical evolution. Smith noted that most European universities were originally 'ecclesiastical corporations' established to educate churchmen. Founded by papal authority, universities had the advantage of being under the pope's protection. Students and faculty enjoyed 'benefit of the clergy,' which meant they were exempted from the civil authorities and subject only to ecclesiastical tribunals. While theology or subjects that were preparatory to theology was initially taught, Smith noted that universities gradually drew to themselves the education of almost all other people, particularly the sons of gentlemen and men of fortune (1776 [1976, p. 773]).

University Endowments

One institutional characteristic of universities noted by Smith was that early on they became endowed institutions. While universities were institutions that could properly fall under the 'duties of the sovereign,' Smith observed that universities in the greater part of Europe actually received little support from the general revenue. Instead, they were funded by 'publick endowments' that took several forms. Smith mentioned the following: some dedicated local or provincial revenue, rent of some landed estate, or interest on some sum of money that had been allotted and put under the management of trustees for that purpose, sometimes by the sovereign and sometimes by private donors (1976, p. 759).

Smith also noted that subsidies were provided for a number of students by charitable foundations of scholarships, exhibitions, bursaries, etc. (1776 [1976, p. 759]). Earlier, in Book I of *Wealth of Nations*, Smith had critically commented on these subsidies as a topic under the general heading of the effects on wages of 'the policy of Europe' (1776 [1976, p. 146]). There he observed that in all 'Christian countries' very few churchmen were educated at their own expense. With many of those so educated not going into 'holy orders,' many 'men of letters' were educated at 'publick expense,' by which he meant from endowments.

Governance of Universities

In *Wealth of Nations*, Smith briefly mentioned two general forms of university governance, neither of which met with his approval. In some universities, the authority rested in the 'body corporate – the college or university,' which meant that the faculty or fellows or masters governed. That was the case with the English universities of Oxford and Cambridge. As we will examine in detail later, much of his criticism of how the English universities were functioning centered on this form of institutional governance. But Smith noted that authority could reside in some extraneous authority, e.g., bishop, governor of the province, or some minister of state. The French universities were cited as case examples. As we will also note later in this chapter, Smith was highly critical of this form of governance as well.

Students

While Smith mentioned the internal organization of the English universities in colleges, there was no indication in *Wealth of Nations* of any difference between undergraduate and graduate students as in the case of modern universities. There was some comment about required attendance at universities as requisite for entry into the professions of law, medicine, and clergy, but otherwise his discussions seemed to pertain entirely to undergraduate students.

SMITH'S CRITICISM OF UNIVERSITIES

To explain Smith's claim that the English universities were failing to function properly, we need to establish more specifically what he thought should be taught and how the faculty should teach. Smith explicitly indicated that 'improvements' in the different branches of philosophy (1776 [1976, p. 772]) and science (1776 [1976, p. 764]) should be taught. A popular interpretation is that Smith was stating that universities should teach what is practical and useful. Ortmann (1997), e.g., argued that Smith's 'advice' for universities in 'post-industrial environments' was to provide curricula that teach 'marketable skills.' A 'vocational' education interpretation of Smith's position, however, hardly withstands close consideration. As we noted earlier, West (1965) argued that Smith did not view education as needed to promote economic growth (p. 118). We also noted that Smith's comment that scarcely any common trade did not afford some opportunity of applying the principles of geometry and 'mechanicks' (1776 [1976, pp. 785–786]) would seem to dispute that argument at the lower education level. But in his comments that related directly to university curriculum, Smith seemed to be focusing more on fashionable social conversation among 'gentlemen and men of fortune' rather than on economic effects with respect to university education.

It may seem that the 'vocational skills' interpretation is suggested in Smith's statement that there was no better method of spending the 'long interval between infancy and that period of life at which men begin to apply in good earnest to the real business of the world' ('the business which is to employ them during the remainder of their days') than attending 'the publick schools and universities' (1776 [1976, p. 773]). But it is not at all clear that he was suggesting that universities should be teaching the 'vocational skills' of business. Rather, a strong element of social fashion is evident in his discussion. He noted without any sense of disapproval that most of the young men attending universities were the sons of gentlemen and men of fortune (1776 [1976, pp. 772–773]). What universities should teach to prepare these young men for 'the real business of the world' was what 'the circumstances of the times' rendered 'either necessary, or convenient, or at least fashionable to learn' (1776 [1976, p. 780]). Similarly, in asserting the superiority of private instruction, Smith declared that if there were:

> ...no *publick* institutions for education, a gentleman, after going through, with application and abilities, the most complete course of education, which the circumstances of the times were supposed to afford, could not come into the world completely ignorant of every thing which is the common subject of conversation among gentlemen and men of the world (1776 [1976, p. 781], emphasis added).

While what was best taught by private teachers included 'the three most essential parts of literary education, to read, write, and account' (1776 [1976, p. 764]), his other examples of teaching the social skills of dancing and fencing reinforce the sense that universities should teach what is fashionably useful for gentlemen (1776 [1976, p. 764]).

Indeed, the strongest basis for the vocational interpretation of Smith's views on the appropriate university curriculum seems to be his approving discussion of the education of women for domestic purposes in contrast to the education received by the sons of gentlemen and men of fortune.

> There are no publick institutions for the education of women, and there is accordingly nothing useless, absurd, or fantastical in the common course of their education. They are taught what their parents or guardians judge it necessary or useful for them to learn; and they are taught nothing else. Every

part of their education tends evidently to some useful purpose; either to improve the natural attractions of their person, or to form their mind to reserve, to modesty, to chastity, and to economy: to render them both likely to become the mistresses of a family, and to behave properly when they have become such. In every part of her life a woman feels some conveniency or advantage from every part of her education. It seldom happens that a man, in any part of his life, derives any conveniency or advantage from some of the most laborious and troublesome parts of his education (1776 [1976, p. 781]).

It is unlikely that modern scholars who argue that Smith thought universities should teach what is vocationally useful would want to base their argument on that particular passage.

The method of teaching that was endorsed by Smith was simply well prepared lectures delivered by knowledgeable instructors. Good lecturing went far beyond reading from books, including interpreting books written in foreign languages, and making occasional comments. Smith referred to these practices as 'sham lectures,' which any faculty member with the 'slightest degree of knowledge and application' could easily do (1776 [1976, p. 763]).

Smith gave further insight into effective teaching in his discussion of the cases of universities pulling men of letters away from churches when Chairs provided better pay than church positions. He remarked that:

To impose upon any man the necessity of teaching, year after year, any particular branch of science, seems, in reality, to be the most effectual method of rendering him completely master of it himself. By being obliged to go every year over the same ground, if he is good for anything, he necessarily becomes, in a few years, well acquainted with every part of it: and if upon any particular point he should form too hasty an opinion one year, when he comes in the course of his lectures to re-consider the same subject the year thereafter, he is very likely to correct it. As to be a teacher of science is certainly the natural employment of a mere man of letters; so is it likewise, perhaps, the education which is most likely to render him a man of solid learning and knowledge (1776 [1976, p. 812]).

How and Why English Universities Were Failing

Smith repeatedly asserted that British universities were failing to teach what would seem to be 'the most proper preparation' for the 'real business of the world' (1776 [1976, p. 773]). Still being taught were what Smith termed 'an exploded and antiquated system of science' and 'a science universally believed to be a mere useless and pedantick heap of sophistry and nonsense' (1776 [1976, pp. 780–781]). Smith also expressed strong disapproval of the current fashion of the sons of gentlemen and men of fortune being sent to travel in foreign countries rather than attending universities. He declared that: 'Nothing but the discredit into which universities were allowing themselves to fall, could ever have brought into repute so very absurd a practice as that of traveling at this early period of life' (1776 [1976, p. 774]). But the alternative, he said, was for the fathers to see their sons 'unemployed, neglected, and going to ruin' at one of the English universities (1776 [1976, p. 774]).

Even if the universities should be offering the appropriate curriculum, Smith argued that members of the faculties were failing to instruct their students in a proper manner. He declared that 'In the University of Oxford, the greater part of the publick professors have, for these many years, given up altogether even the pretence of teaching' (1776 [1976. p. 761]). On a wider basis, he claimed that 'In the universities the youth are neither taught, nor always can find any proper means of being taught, the sciences, which it is the business of these incorporated bodies to teach' (1776 [1976, p. 764]).

Characteristically, Smith explained the outdated curriculum and teaching failures of universities in terms of individuals pursuing their own self-interest in an institutional environment that failed to provide appropriate incentives for those who had the power to determine the curriculum and who did the teaching. Here is a case in which Smith's views exemplify his perception of two conflicting behavioral tendencies of human nature noted by Rosenberg (1960). One is the pursuit of wealth, while the other is the tendency to become more indolent as wealth is achieved. When wealth or income can be acquired with varying degrees of effort, people tend to choose the easiest way. From that perspective on human behavior, Smith specifically criticized the following aspects of universities: (1) faculty control of the curriculum; (2) institutional practices that mandated attendance of certain universities for admission into certain professions ('privileges of graduation'); (3) institutional rules that tied those receiving scholarships and other forms of subsidies to attendance of certain colleges, with no freedom of choice of instructors within those colleges; (4) institutional rules which made it very difficult for even students of independent means to change colleges within a university; and (5) faculty members enjoying incomes from endowments rather than from fees paid by students. While these interrelate, we reserve discussion of the disincentive effects of income from endowments to last because it essentially constituted the major cause of the problem.

Faculty Control of the Curriculum

Smith argued that control of the curriculum by the faculty (masters or fellows) resulted in adopting and maintaining curriculum and teaching styles that would be easiest for the faculty (1776 [1976, p. 761]). Here the self-interest of the individual faculty member takes a curious turn.

> If the authority to which he is subject resides in the body corporate, the college, or university, of which he himself is a member, and in which the greater part of the other members are like himself, persons who either are, or ought to be teachers; they are likely to make a common cause, to be all very indulgent to one another, and every man to consent that his neighbor may neglect his duty, provided he is allowed to neglect his own (1776 [1976, p. 761]).

Since modernizing curricula would require effort, the indolent faculty will be content to simply keep the old curriculum intact. It should be noted that the administrative officials, e.g., heads of colleges, seemed to be in perfect agreement with the faculty members.

But Smith also indicated that transferring control over the curriculum from the faculty to external authorities was not the solution. An external authority could only require that faculty give a certain number of lectures 'What those lectures shall be, must still depend upon the diligence of the teacher; and that diligence is likely to be proportioned to the motives which he has for exerting it' (1776 [1976, p. 761]). Moreover, Smith argued that an external authority, as exemplified by the French universities, was even worse than corporate authority by the faculty. Not only were the external authorities unable to know what should be taught or to judge the effectiveness of teaching, they tend to be insolent and arbitrarily oppressive in their treatment of faculty.

> From the insolence of office too they are frequently indifferent how they exercise it, and are very apt to censure or deprive him of his office wantonly, and without any just cause. The person subject to such jurisdiction is necessarily degraded by it, and instead of being one of the most respectable, is rendered one of the meanest and most contemptible persons in the society. It is by powerful protection only that he can effectually guard himself against the bad usage to which he is at all times exposed; and this protection he is most likely to gain, not by ability or diligence in his profession, but by obsequiousness to the will of his superiors, and by being ready, at all times, to sacrifice to that will the rights, the interest, and the honour of the body corporate of which he is a member (1776 [1976, pp. 761–762]).

Rules and Practices

Smith strongly criticized the institutional practice of restricting the 'privileges of graduation in arts, in law, physick and divinity' to required attendance at universities. He argued that private instruction would more effectively prepare people for the examinations for admission into the professions (1776 [1976, p. 762, and p. 764]). He sarcastically described such requirements as 'a sort of statutes of apprenticeship, which have contributed to the improvement of education, just as the other statutes of apprenticeship have to that of arts and manufactures' (1776 [1976, p. 762]). Smith had, of course, argued earlier in Book I of *Wealth of Nations* that the statutes of apprenticeship negatively affected the arts and manufactures.

Smith's recognition of the difference between holding university degrees and gaining an education was also indicated in his discussion of the great teachers in ancient Greece.

> There was nothing equivalent to the privileges of graduation, and to have attended any of those schools was not necessary, in order to be permitted to practice any particular trade or profession. If the opinion of their own utility could not draw scholars to them, the law either forced any body to go to them, nor rewarded any body for having gone to them. The teachers had no jurisdiction over their pupils, nor any other authority besides that natural authority, which superior virtue and abilities never fail to procure from young people, towards those who are entrusted with any part of their education (1776 [1976, p. 778]).

In a letter written in 1774, Smith was more blunt on the consequences of 'the privileges of graduation' being tied to attendance of universities.

> A degree which can be conferred only upon students of a certain standing, is a statute of apprenticeship which is likely to contribute to the advancement of science, just as other statutes of apprenticeship have contributed to that of arts and manufactures. These statutes . . . have banished arts and manufactures from the greater part of towns-corporate. Such degree, assisted by regulations of similar tendency, have banished almost all useful and solid education from the greater part of Universities (1776 [1976, p. 762, fn.]).

The result to be expected was 'quackery, imposture, and exorbitant fees' (1776 [1976, p. 762, fn.]).

Smith also argued that the practice of tying scholarships and other financial subsidies to certain colleges, and allowing the head of the college to appoint students to particular teachers contributed to a lack of interest for their students on part of those teachers. This was true even if the students were paying fees.

> Were the students upon such charitable foundations left free to chuse what college they like best, such liberty might perhaps contribute to excite some emulation among different colleges. A regulation, on the contrary, which prohibited even the independent members of every particular college from leaving it, and going to any other, without leave first asked and obtained of that

which they meant to abandon, would tend very much to extinguish that emulation. If in each college the tutor or teacher, who was to instruct each student in all arts and sciences should not be voluntarily chosen by the student, but appointed by the head of the college; and if, in case of neglect, inability, or bad usage, the student should not be allowed to change him for another, without leave first asked and obtained; such a regulation would not only tend very much to extinguish all emulation among the different tutors of the same college, but to diminish very much in all of them the necessity of diligence and of attention to their respective pupils. Such teachers, though very well paid by the students, might be as much disposed to neglect them, as those who are not paid by them at all, or who have no other recompence but their salary (1776 [1976, pp. 762–763]).

Faculty Incomes from Endowments

Smith's criticism of faculty incomes from endowments rather than from student fees is particularly well known. Here he stated an economic principle of the greatest general application.

In every profession, the exertion of the greater part of those who exercise it, is always in proportion to the necessity they are under of making that exertion. This necessity is greatest with those to whom the emoluments of their profession are the only source from which they expect their fortune, or even their ordinary revenue and subsistence (1776 [1976, p. 759]).

Endowments which provided set incomes for faculty combined with university prohibitions against faculty receiving fees from students resulted in an indifference to diligence in teaching.

His interest is, in this case, set as directly in opposition to this duty as it is possible to set it. It is in the interest of every man to live as much at his ease as he can; and if his emoluments are to be precisely the same, whether he does, or does not perform some very laborious duty, it is certainly his interest, at least as interest is vulgarly understood, either to neglect it altogether, or, if he is subject to some authority which will not suffer him to do this, to perform it in as careless and slovenly a manner as that authority will permit. If he is naturally active and a lover of labour, it is his interest to employ that activity in any way from which he can derive some advantage, rather than in the performance of his duty, from which he can derive none (1776 [1976, p. 760]).

In reviewing education among the Greeks and Romans, Smith claimed that the practice of paying fees to the 'antient philosophers' resulted in them being superior teachers. Here is found what is perhaps his strongest statement for a market approach to university-level teaching.

Masters . . . had been found, it seems, for instructing the better sort of people among those nations in every art and science in which the circumstances of their society rendered it necessary or convenient for them to be instructed. The demand such instruction produced, what it always produces, the talent for giving it; and the emulation which an unrestrained competition never fails to excite, appears to have brought that talent to a very high degree of perfection (1776 [1976, p. 780]).

It is to be noted that the demand for such instruction came from 'the better sort of people.'

Smith was very critical of both the direct and indirect effects of university faculty receiving fixed stipends. The direct effects were repeatedly noted. For example, he declared that 'In modern time, the diligence of publick teachers is more or less corrupted by the circumstances, which render them more or less independent of their success and reputation' (1776 [1976, p. 780]). Smith was quite explicit on the negative impacts of endowment incomes on curriculum innovation. As a general rule, there was an inverse relationship between the wealth of universities and the speed at which they adopted improvements in the several branches of philosophy. The tutors in the richest and best endowed universities 'content themselves with teaching a few unconnected shreds and parcels of this corrupted course; and even these they commonly teach very negligently and superficially' (1776 [1976, p. 772]).

Smith asserted that since teachers in the poorer universities were dependent upon their reputations for the larger part of their incomes, they had to 'pay more attention to the current opinions of the world' (1776 [1976, pp. 772–773]). Thus, improvements in science and philosophy were thus more easily introduced into the curricula. In 'some universities' in which the faculty members were largely dependent upon class fee income, the necessity of application remained. Professional reputations were important, with each faculty member depending 'upon the affection, gratitude, and favourable sentiments he is likely to gain in no way so well as deserving them, that is, by the abilities and diligence with which he discharges every part of his duty' (1776 [1976, p. 760]).

It seems clear that the 'some/poorer' universities to which Smith referred were the Scottish universities, and Smith's own Glasgow University in particular, and perhaps the Protestant academies in England. According to Skinner (1996), the analysis in *Wealth of Nations* may reflect the content of a letter that Smith wrote in 1774 in response to a proposal that the medical college in Edinburgh require doctors to have attended a university for at least two years. In that letter Smith stated that he regarded the Scottish universities 'as, in spite of all their faults, without exception the best seminaries of learning that are to be found anywhere in Europe' (Skinner 1996, p. 196). Smith concluded that the reason for the superiority of the Scottish universities was because '. . . the salaries of the Professors are insignificant. There are few or no bursaries and exhibitions, and their monopoly of degrees is broken in upon by all other Universities, foreign or domestic' (Skinner 1996, p. 199).

In declaring that 'The endowments of schools and colleges have necessarily diminished more or less the necessity of application in teachers,' (1776 [1976, p. 760]), Smith appeared to have no real concept of university faculty who were not pecuniarily motivated so far as teaching was concerned. While he observed that 'rivalship and emulation' also encourage the greatest exertions (1776 [1976, pp. 759–760]), the subsequent discussion suggests that the effects would be very weak in the case of university teachers. A faculty member whose income was independent of student fees was expected to pursue activities 'from which he can derive some advantage, rather than in the performance of his duty, from which he can derive none' (1776 [1976, p. 760]). At best, Smith argued that it might be unpleasant for a teacher who is a 'man to sense' to realize that he was delivering a poorly prepared lecture and was not respected by his students. But in such cases, Smith thought the teacher would take the easy way out, offering 'sham lectures' such as reading from a book and making an occasional comment on it (1776 [1976, p. 763]).

The indirect negative effects of endowment incomes for university faculty were on the private teachers who had to compete with them. Smith stated that:

> Their salaries . . . put the private teacher, who would pretend to come into competition with them, in the same state with a merchant who attempts to trade without a bounty, in competition with those who traded with a considerable one. If he sells his goods at nearly the same price, he cannot have the same profit, and poverty and beggary at least, if not bankruptcy and ruin, will infallibly be his lot. If he attempts to sell them much dearer, he is likely to have so few customers that his circumstances will not be much mended (1776 [1976, p. 780]).

But the plight of the private teacher was not totally due to the endowed incomes of the 'publick teachers.' It was due in part to the 'privileges of graduation' that restricted entry into certain professions to those who attended the universities and colleges, where they had to attend the 'lectures of publick teachers' (1776 [1976, p. 780]). Private teachers were more able to teach what students needed to know and would demand if they had a free choice. But they had been reduced by endowments of schools and colleges and the artificial demand created for 'publick teachers' by 'privileges of graduation' to the most humiliating and unprofitable employment. Those endowments had not only 'corrupted the diligence of publick teachers' but had rendered it almost impossible to have a good private teacher (1776 [1976, p. 780]).

The indirect negative effects of endowments were not limited to the behavior of university faculty. Earlier in Book I of *Wealth of Nations*, Smith had argued that the institutional practice of those endowments that subsidized the cost of students attending universities had resulted in a larger number of 'men of letters' than the market could absorb at natural wage levels. The result was that many of these men became teachers at income levels comparable to ordinary workers (1776 [1976, pp. 146–150]), indicating an excessive supply of teachers in the market at the natural wage level.

PROPOSALS FOR REFORM

Smith's proposed solutions were essentially to create more of a free market-like environment by increasing the opportunity for student-consumers' freedom of choice of institutions and teachers based on earned reputations and competition among the providers of university courses of study. He argued strongly for private teachers and against any requirements of university attendance in order to take examinations to enter professions. This would appear to indicate that universities had no particular social functions other than to supply lectures on subjects that buyers demand at any particular time, with those buyers being sons of gentlemen and men of fortune. Smith proposed that university teachers should be dependent upon student fees and that students be free to choose their instructors.

Reputations and Competition

Thus, teachers would compete for students, and universities would compete not only with other universities but also with private teachers. Smith touted competition or 'emulation' for students based on reputation of teachers and the ability to provide the type of instruction demanded by students. He remarked that 'where competition is free, the rivalship of competitors, who are all endeavouring to justle one another out of employment, obliges every man to endeavour to execute his work with a certain degree of exactness' (1776 [1976, p. 759]). If students were left 'free to chuze' which college or university to attend, Smith stated that 'such liberty might perhaps contribute to excite some emulation among different colleges' (1776 [1976, p. 763]). If teachers' incomes were dependent upon student fees and students were free to choose teachers, 'emulation' would be stimulated among the teachers (1776 [1976, p. 763]). Smith remarked that:

The improvements which, in modern times, have been made in several different branches of philosophy, have not, the greater part of them, been made in universities, though some no doubt have. The greater part of universities have not even been very forward to adopt those improvements, after they were made; and several of those learned societies have chosen to remain, for a long time, the sanctuaries in which exploded systems and obsolete prejudices found shelter and protection, after they had been hunted out of every other corner of the world. In general, the richest and best-endowed universities have been the slowest in adopting those improvements, and the most averse to permit any considerable change in the established plan of education. Those improvements were more easily introduced into some of the poorer universities, in which the teachers depending upon their reputation for the greater part of their subsistence were obliged to pay more attention to the current opinions of the world (1776 [1976, pp. 772–773]).

INCOMPLETENESS, WEAKNESSES, AND CONTRADICTIONS

Smith's analysis and criticism of the behavior of English universities were curiously incomplete, being limited to selected subjects, primarily reward structures and their influence on the performances of faculty members as teachers. There was no mention of research efforts by faculty members that resulted in publications. While Smith criticized stipends for faculty from endowments and lauded private teachers who lived on fee income, he made no mention of the importance of libraries in *Wealth of Nations*. Yet, his biographers note that he benefited enormously as a student from having access to the Balliol College library, one of the best at Oxford. The idea of an education as the product of several inputs, including the students' own efforts and library resources as well as instruction from faculty, was inadequately developed in *Wealth of Nations*.

Even though universities of the period were much smaller and certainly less bureaucratically structured than those of the 20th century, there were important aspects of university operations in that era that Smith did not mention at all. Internal disputes among faculty and in particular between faculty and administrators over the locus of authority, how those disputes were settled, and the effects of those settlements on university academic operations, including curriculum, were not discussed. Indeed, there was no mention of the organizational structure of universities other than the occasional mention of the 'head of the college' (1776 [1976, p. 763]). And while Smith's discussion focused primarily on the teaching function and particularly on the diligence of those who were charged with the lecturing, there was no discussion of any evaluation of student performances by colleges or faculty members. Instead, the context was primarily suggestive of student-consumers receiving (or failing to receive) knowledge that they desired from the university lecturers as suppliers. The only examinations mentioned were those required to enter a profession.

Even Smith's discussion of the selected topics was somewhat incomplete. Perhaps the most curious omission in light of the emphasis on the determination of natural and market prices and wages in Book I of *Wealth of Nations* was of any substantive discussion of the types and levels of fees charged for universities' services. Smith emphasized that making teachers dependent on class fees paid by students created incentives to diligence and competence on part of lecturers, and remarked in the opening paragraph that such fees constituted natural revenue, which indicates that a natural price of sorts was possible under competitive conditions. But the actual determination of the level of fees that universities imposed on students was not explained. On the one hand, the quasi-monopolistic position of universities would seem to lead to an expectation of higher prices. But the peculiar institutional nature of universities as endowed institutions led to under-pricing in Smith's era as it does in the modern era. There is one definite indication in *Wealth of Nations* that this was the case, and another somewhat ambiguous indication.

The latter appears in Book I, where Smith observed that the various types of subsidies for students from both private and public sources allowed more students to attend universities than would have been the case if they had had to pay the full fees. This may or may not be interpreted as under-pricing since the fees could be set high and a portion paid for the students by the subsidies. The former is found in the discussion of the education of youth. Smith stated emphatically that private teachers could not compete with university ('publick') teachers because the latter effectively enjoyed subsidies. But clearly those subsidies had reduced fees that students paid to universities to levels at which private teachers could not compete.

Curiously, while Smith described British universities as having rules that prohibited faculty from accepting fees, and the faculties of those universities as becoming indolent from incomes from endowments, he never suggested that self-interest might encourage faculty members to enhance their incomes from endowments by also collecting fees from students. While rules at Oxford disallowed that practice, if the faculty really governed they could change rules that constrained such pursuit of their economic self-interest. In addition, there was no recognition that faculty members would have an economic interest in striving to increase endowments and how that might affect their regard for students. If wealthy parents were pleased with the education of their sons, such parents would represent potential contributors to the endowments of the particular colleges.

On the issue of competition, Smith emphasized reputations of teachers (and by association also the reputations of colleges and universities). But little was said about price competition. He did indicate that the greater the reputation the greater would be the fee income of the teachers in his discourse on the high incomes enjoyed by famous teachers in ancient Greece and Rome. Here again, Rosenberg's observation that Smith perceived two conflicting behavioral tendencies of human nature – pursuit of wealth and the tendency to become indolent when wealth is achieved – has particular relevance. The corollary that if a certain amount of wealth can be achieved with varying degrees of effort, people tend to choose the easiest way was clearly the case for teachers enjoying incomes independent of student fees. But will teachers who enjoy higher incomes from student fees be subject to this behavioral tendency? Smith gave no indication that such would be the case. On the contrary, he remarked in Book I of *Wealth of Nations* on the high incomes received by the 'most eminent' teachers in Athens and their 'splendid even ostentatious' way of living without any suggestion that slothfulness was setting in (1776 [1976, pp. 149–150]).

There is also the question of the incentive effects of piece-rate pay. In Book I of *Wealth of Nations*, Smith warned that workers who were paid 'liberally by the piece' would tend to overwork themselves (1776 [1976, p. 100]). Why would university professors not be subject to some variant of the same behavior? Perhaps a possible answer might be that Smith simply did not have very 'liberal' rates of class fees in mind. In commenting on Smith's curious silence on how class fees at universities would be established, Rosen (1987) noted that fees would presumably be set by university policy based on competitive environments but would be the same for all faculty members (p. 563). In such a case, increasing income would be possible only by increasing the number of students. Smith explicitly mentioned small fees paid by pupils in the small parish schools (1776 [1976, p. 785]), with the rest of the teachers' incomes to be paid from non-fee sources. If the same applied for university professors, the disincentive effects of 'liberal' payments would not come into play. Smith explicitly introduced non-economic incentive effects, stating that 'great objects,' i.e., high incomes, from success may sometimes motivate 'the exertion of a few men of extraordinary spirit and ambition' but are not necessary to encourage 'the greatest exertions' because 'rivalship and emultation render excellency, even in mean professions, an object of ambition, and frequently occasion the very greatest exertions' (1776 [1976, pp. 759–760]).

But that might well be offset by another factor that Smith did not address. Additional students may impose relatively low additional costs for the professor supplying the lectures. That would encourage university faculty to attempt to gain students since the marginal increase in fee income would exceed the marginal cost. A market failure may occur because the marginal cost for students may become quite substantial as room space becomes excessively crowded or large lecture halls make it more difficult for students to hear the lecturer. Smith gave no indication of such developments.

In addition to the curious incompleteness of Smith's analysis and critique of universities, there were also several contradictions in his commentary. One appeared in his statements pertaining to the social usefulness of universities. On the one hand, he stated that 'Were there no publick institutions for education, no system, no science would be taught for which there was not some demand; or which the circumstances of the times did not render it, either necessary, or convenient, or at least fashionable to learn' (1776 [1976, p. 780]). Yet, he also stated that:

> The parts of education which are commonly taught in universities . . . are not very well taught. But had it not been for those institutions they would not have been commonly taught at all, and both the individual and the publick would have suffered a good deal from the want of those important parts of education (1776 [1976, p. 765]).

Smith's comments on endowments for students were also somewhat contradictory. On the one hand, he argued that the various endowments which subsidized students had resulted in an excessive supply of teachers, causing their incomes to be very low, which he said 'may somewhat degrade the profession of the publick teacher.' But he went on to declare that 'the cheapness of literary education is surely an advantage which greatly over-balances this trifling inconveniency' (1776 [1976, p. 151]). Still, we must note that Smith added that 'The publick too might derive still greater benefit from it, if the constitution of those schools and colleges, in which education is carried on, was more reasonable than it is at present through the greater part of Europe' (1776 [1976, p. 151]).

Perhaps the greatest weakness in Smith's analysis was in his high confidence in the viability of student-consumer sovereignty. Quite clearly, his thesis rested on highly idealistic presumptions about the rationality and mature seriousness of university students.

> The discipline of colleges and universities is in general contrived, not for the benefit of the students, but for the interest, or more properly speaking, for the ease of the masters. Its object is, in all cases, to maintain the authority of the master, and whether he neglects or performs his duty, to oblige the students in all cases to behave to him as if he performed it with the greatest diligence and ability. It seems to presume perfect wisdom and virtue in the one order, and the

greatest weakness and folly in the other. Where the masters, however, really perform their duty, there are no examples, I believe, that the greater part of students ever neglect theirs. No discipline is ever requisite to force attendance upon lectures which are really worth the attending, as is well known whenever such lectures are given. Force and restraint may, no doubt, be in some degree requisite in order to oblige children, or very young boys, to attend those parts of education which it is thought necessary for them to acquire during that early period of life; but after twelve or thirteen years of age, provided the master does his duty, force or restraint can scarce ever be necessary to carry on any part of education. Such is the generosity of the greater part of young men, that, so far as being disposed to neglect or despise the instructions of their master, provided he shows some serious intention of being of use to them, they are generally inclined to pardon a great deal of incorrectness in the performance of his duty, and sometimes even to conceal from the public a good deal of gross negligence (1776 [1976, p. 764]).

Note that the last sentence in above quoted passage appears to contradict the argument that effective teaching will be assured by rational consumer behavior on part of students. If they like the teacher, they will tolerate 'a good deal of gross negligence' and 'a great deal of incorrectness in the performance of his duty.'

If parents of the potential student-consumers were expected to act as agents for their sons, Smith gave little indication that they would make rational choices, both by what he said and by what he did not say. He strongly criticized decisions by gentlemen and men of fortune to send their sons on tours of the continent. He blamed the failures of the English universities on the alternative that he mentioned, namely, a dissipated life-style of young men. But if such behavior occurred simply because faculty gave poor lectures and show little interest in students, what does that say about the failure of parents to instill moral character in their sons? More directly, Smith indicated that there were other (and poorer) universities in which faculty members depended largely on fee incomes. Not only were the teachers more diligent, the curricula of those universities were more modern. Thus, the question becomes 'Why did not more English gentlemen and men of fortune not send their sons to those universities?'

4. John Stuart Mill on Universities

John Stuart Mill's perspectives on universities were revealed in his published writings and personal correspondences that related to his views on education in general, which were deeply rooted in his utilitarian philosophy and his own ideal of human improvement. Much of his commentary on education dealt with the legitimate role of the state with respect to a national system of elementary education. But in several essays, he specifically discussed the special social functions of universities, and declared that British universities were failing, although by the 1850s he was acknowledging some improvements. Like Smith, 'public' university teachers referred not to state-supported institutions but to universities with endowments.

There were major similarities in Smith and Mill's perspectives on the behavior of the English universities. But there were also several notable differences in both their normative and positive economic analyses. Mill's views on the special functions of universities, which he suggested was the generally accepted opinion, are examined in the following section. Those views merit attention for two reasons. First, the nature of the perceived failures of the English universities can only be explained in terms of what they were supposed to be doing. Second, Mill's conception of the true functions of universities was more similar to Veblen's than to Smith's, thus positioning him as a transitional figure between the two.

An examination of Mill's analysis of the nature and causes of the failures of the English universities then follows. One major difference between Smith and Mill is easily observed. Mill placed a much greater blame on a non-economic external factor, specifically the sectarian dominance of the universities by the Church of England. That difference was perhaps merely one of omission on Smith's part. From his commentaries on education of the youth and on religious instruction in *Wealth of Nations*, it could easily be inferred that he would agree with Mill's call for universities to be free of sectarian influence and exclusivity. Here again there is some similarity with Veblen's analysis of the failures of the early 20th century American universities, although the external influences and the ways by which they intruded into the internal functioning of universities were very different in the two cases.

External factors aside, Mill's assessment of the behavior of the English universities involved an economic analysis that strongly endorsed Smith's assessment of the disincentive effects of faculty receiving fixed incomes from endowments and the positive effects of making those incomes depend in large part on fees paid by students. But Mill qualified Smith's analysis by adding the principle of payment by results, based on how well students performed on meaningful examinations. At the same time, Mill expressed a fundamental disagreement with Smith on the applicability of market principles in education. He essentially rejected a key assumption in Smith's recommendations for reform in universities, namely, that student-consumers and their parents could be expected to be sufficiently rational to assure that a system in which the curriculum and teaching would function optimally under student-consumer sovereignty.

THE SPECIAL SOCIAL FUNCTIONS OF UNIVERSITIES

In Chapter Three, we noted that Adam Smith's discussion of the social benefits from education did not explicitly mention any economic benefits. In contrast, Mill argued that popular education contributes to national wealth by increasing industrial skills at the middle management and supervisory levels. Education directly improves the quality of labor by elevating it from mere habitual memorized routine to an intelligent activity incorporating some element of imagination and initiative. Education also has indirect positive effects on productivity by enhancing the practical and moral qualities of character (good sense, sound judgement, prudence, and self-restraint), which contribute to higher standards of work and productivity as well as improved labor relations.

But Mill did not relate the social function of universities to any economic benefits of education. Certainly, the society needs medical schools, as well as schools of law, engineering, and the industrial arts, but professional and technical education was not the function of universities. In his 1835 review of *Prof. Sedgwick's Discourse on the Studies of the University of Cambridge*, Mill stated that universities' special purpose was to keep philosophy alive by forming 'great minds.' Educating the 'common mind' for 'the common business of life' could safely be left to the stimulus of individual interest to seek and competition to appropriate supply because the public is capable of knowing best what that education should be. (Elsewhere he seemed to doubt that competence.) But the public can not be competent judges of university education aimed at forming 'great minds' (1882, pp. 218–231).

Similarly, in his 1836 essay *Civilization*, Mill declared that universities have the special duty to 'counteract the debilitating influence of the circumstances of the age upon individual character, and to send forth into society a succession of minds, not the creatures of their age, but capable of being its improvers and regenerators' (1963, Vol. 18, p. 128). In reference to the socio-cultural conditions of 19th century England, university education regenerates the character of the higher classes (1963, Vol. 18, p. 146) so they might better exercise the 'elements of importance and influence' that come from the 'powers and acquirements of mind' (1963, Vol. 18, p. 121). Rejecting Smith's contention that the universities should provide studies that (in Mill's own words) stood in 'a closer connexion with what it is the fashion to term "the business of the world"' (1963, Vol. 18, p. 139), Mill declared:

> We would have classics and logic taught far more really and deeply than at present, and we would add to them other studies more alien than any which yet exist to the 'business of world,' but more germane to the great business of every rational being – the strengthening and enlarging of his own intellect and character. The empirical knowledge which the world demands, which is the stock in trade of money-getting-life, we would leave the world to provide for itself; content with infusing into the youth of our country a spirit, and training them to habits, which would ensure their acquiring such knowledge easily, and using it well (1963, Vol. 18, p. 139).

University education rests on the cornerstone principle that the objective is 'to call forth the greatest possible quantity of intellectual *power*, and to inspire the intensest *love of truth*.' The essence of university life is the philosophical and academic freedom of great minds to inquire and critique, to formulate and express informed opinion. In educating university students, there must be absolutely no concern about what they may choose to think, even if they are led to opinions that diametrically oppose those of their teachers (1963, Vol. 18, p. 144). University teachers must be allowed to teach 'in the spirit of free inquiry, not of dogmatical imposition,' and must never be held to any particular creed (1963, Vol. 18, p. 144). The professors should be the most eminent intellectuals and scholars. Their eminence must arise not on any particular doctrines that they profess but because they are 'most likely to send forth pupils qualified in point of disposition and attainments to choose their own doctrines (1963, Vol. 18, p. 146).

In his inaugural address as honorary president of St. Andrews University in 1867, Mill stated that:

> The proper function of an University in national education is tolerably well understood. At least there is tolerably general agreement about what an University is not. It is not a place of professional education. Universities are not intended to teach the knowledge required to fit men for some special mode of gaining their livelihood. Their object is not to make skilful lawyers, or

physicians, or engineers, but capable and cultivated people . . . . What professional men should carry away with them from an University, is not professional knowledge, but that which should direct the use of the professional knowledge, and bring the light of general culture to illuminate the technicalities of a special pursuit (1963, Vol. 21, p. 218).

Mill described the 'higher limit' of the university in the following manner 'its province ends where education, ceasing to be general, branches off into departments adapted to the individual's destination in life' (1963, Vol. 21, p. 219). But he noted that the 'lower limit' is more difficult to define. The university is not concerned with elementary education, which is to be acquired before coming to the university. In the imperfect world of schools in the 19th century, the question of where elementary education ends and higher studies begins had not been answered at all well. While many argued that the university should teach not knowledge but the 'philosophy of knowledge,' schools adequate for teaching knowledge had never been developed. Consequently, universities had had to perform largely the functions that should have been taken care of at an earlier stage. Mill observed that the Scottish universities were both universities and high schools, and stated that if the English universities had not followed suit, it was only because the need to do so had been ignored. Sounding much like Smith, he declared that 'Youths come to the Scottish universities ignorant, and are there taught. The majority of those who come to the English universities come still more ignorant, and ignorant they go away' (1963, Vol. 21, p. 220).

Subsequently, Mill engaged in a lengthy discussion of the continuing controversy with respect to the curriculum in higher education – whether general education should be classical (literary), or scientific (1963, Vol. 21, p. 220). In *Autobiography*, Mill wrote that in his inaugural address he had strongly vindicated 'the high educational value of the old classic and the new scientific studies,' and that it had been the 'stupid inefficiency of teaching' which had regarded them as competitors rather than allies (1963, Vol. 1, p. 287).

Interestingly, a professor at a Scottish university charged that Mill's inaugural speech indicated 'no conception of the limits of a University curriculum.' According to that critic, no one that had ever resided in a university would express such a view of the functions of a university. He added that on other occasions Mill had 'dogmatized on Universities in total ignorance of their working' (1963, Vol. 21, p. liii, fn.).

WHY THE ENGLISH UNIVERSITIES WERE FAILING

Mill's criticism of the two English universities was scathing, although by 1859, he was acknowledging that legislative intervention had brought about some improvement. In the essay *Civilization*, he declared that the universities had basely neglected their special duty for so long that 'as is usual with neglected duties, the very consciousness of it as a duty has faded from their remembrance' (1963, Vol. 18, p. 128). A large part of the failures was attributed to the sectarian dominance of the Church of England over the universities. But more importantly, economic factors were involved in explaining universities' behavior.

Sectarian Control of the English Universities

In his review *Prof. Sedgwick's Discourse on the Studies of the University of Cambridge*, published in 1835, Mill briefly indicated in the opening paragraph that English universities were failing. But his strongest criticism of the English universities was in the lengthy essay *Civilization*, published in 1836. There he wrote that:

> The difficulty which continues to oppose either such reform of our old academical institutions, or the establishment of such new ones, as will give us an education capable of forming great minds, is, that in order to do so it is necessary to begin by eradicating the idea which nearly all the upholders and nearly all the impugners of the Universities rootedly entertain, as to the objects not merely of academical education, but of education itself (1963, Vol. 18, p. 140).

The 'deep-seated' erroneous idea held by the English universities was that their purpose was not to develop student's ability to judge what is true or what is right, but rather it was to indoctrinate him, so that he sees as being true and right that which 'we think right – that to teach, means to inculcate our own opinions, and that our business is not to make thinkers or inquirers, but disciples' (1963, Vol. 18, p. 140). Under the sectarian control of English universities by the Church of England, students were not being trained to be determined and qualified seekers of the truth in an unshackled manner, but rather to accept a certain set of opinions (1963, Vol. 18, p. 141). Mill lamented that English universities had turned out very few 'great minds' over the past several centuries, and those few had succeeded in spite 'nearly everything which could be done to stifle their growth' (1963, Vol. 18, p. 141). The universities had done all they could 'to prevail upon their pupils, by fair means or foul, to acquiesce in the opinions which are set down for them' (1963, Vol. 18, p. 141). As long as the universities could prevent heresy, they did not care that the price was stupidity (1963, Vol. 18, p. 142).

Look at them. While their sectarian character, while the exclusion of all who will not sign away their freedom of thought, is contended for as if life depended upon it, there is hardly a trace in the system of the Universities that any other object is seriously cared for. Nearly all the professorships have degenerated into sinecures. Few of the professors ever deliver a lecture (1963, Vol. 18, p. 142).

Mill stated flatly that:

As a means of educating the many, the Universities are absolutely null. The youth of England are not educated. The attainments of any kind required for taking all the degrees conferred by these bodies are, at Cambridge, utterly contemptible; at Oxford, we believe, of late years, somewhat higher, but still very low (1963, Vol. 18, p. 143).

In Mill's view, the English universities compared very poorly with the German universities, and even with the French and Italian universities. He declared that when a man was pronounced by English universities as having excelled in his studies, the universities gave him an income 'not for continuing to learn, but having learnt; for not doing anything, but for what he has already done: on condition solely of living like a monk, and putting on the livery of Church at the end of seven years. They bribe men by high rewards to get their arms ready, but do not require them to fight' (1963, Vol. 18, p. 143).

For Mill, the very first step toward reforming the English universities should be to:

. . . . unsectarianize them wholly – not by the paltry measure of allowing Dissenters to come and be taught orthodox sectarianism, but by putting an end to sectarian teaching altogether. The principle of dogmatic religion, dogmatic morality, dogmatic philosophy, is what had to be rooted out; not any particular manifestation of that principle' (1963, Vol. 18, p. 144).

Mill cited the general rule followed by German and French universities of selecting the 'most distinguished teacher' whatever his particular views, who would consequently teach 'in the spirit of free inquiry, not of dogmatic imposition' (1963, Vol. 18, p. 144). Such 'is the principle of all academical instruction which aims at forming great minds' (1963, Vol. 18, p. 144). In a footnote, he declared that if such academic freedom was practiced in the English universities, the results would 'greatly eclipse France and Germany' because there were many individual minds in

Britain that were superior 'in variety and sterling value' (1963, Vol. 18, p. 144).

In a footnote comment to the reprinted text of *Civilization* in 1859, Mill stated that:

> Much of what is here said of the Universities, has, in a great measure, ceased to be true. The legislature has at last asserted its right of interference . . . and even before it did so, those bodies had already entered into a course of as decided improvement as any other English universities (1963, Vol. 18, p. 143, fn.).

Similarly, in his 'Inaugural Address,' he commented that the old English universities were doing better work, not only in teaching the ordinary studies of the curriculum but also in pursuing free inquiry. In his later years, Mill apparently had no problem in recommending that young men be sent to either of the old universities, stating that they were much changed. Free inquiry and speculation on the deepest and highest questions were being pursued, and the competition for honors provided strong stimulus for study.

MILL'S ECONOMIC ANALYSIS OF UNIVERSITIES' FAILURES

The similarities in Mill's and Smith's economic analyses of universities' behavior are most evident in their perspectives on the disincentive effects of endowments. Both Mill and Smith addressed the use of endowments to subsidize the costs of students attending universities and to pay the incomes of university teachers. But while Mill largely agreed with Smith in each case, he pointed to additional factors as being involved.

Effects of Educational Subsidies on Teachers' Incomes

The effects of educational subsidies on incomes of teachers were discussed in *Principles of Political Economy* in the chapter on wages. After reviewing Smith's principles of differential wages, he noted 'a modifying circumstance' that interfered to some extent with the operation of those principles. As a general rule, earnings in the types of employment that required 'school education' were at monopoly rates because of the impossibility of the masses of people of obtaining the requisite education. But the 'policy of nations' and the 'bounty of individuals' (by which he meant endowments that made subsidies possible) had offered 'eleemosynary instruction to a much larger class of persons than could have obtained the same advantages by paying their price' (1961, p. 394).

Mill then cited Smith's argument that educational subsidies had so largely increased the supply of 'men of letters' relative to demand that incomes in academic occupations had been driven to poverty levels. Agreeing completely with Smith's historical analysis, Mill quoted the lengthy passage from *Wealth of Nations* (Smith 1776 [1976, pp. 394–396]) that ended with the economic plight of 'men of letters.' Mill agreed that the supply of 'men of letters' in that early time period, who could only become public or private teachers, or scribes, had been increased to the point that the universities appeared 'to have often granted licenses to their scholars to beg' (1961, p. 296). But Mill observed that since Smith's time, educational subsidies no longer influenced the incomes of those engaged in 'literary labour.' The demand for their services had greatly increased while the 'provisions for eleemosynary education have nowhere been much added to' (1961, p. 397).

There was, however, a new supply-side factor that was unrelated to university endowments. Prices of 'literary labour' were now being negatively affected by competition from 'amateurs,' who were motivated more by vanity than by hopes of pecuniary reward (1961, p. 397) and who derived their subsistence from other types of employment or from independent means. Mill cited Jeremy Bentham and David Ricardo, among others, as celebrated 'amateurs' (1961, p. 397). Highly remunerative 'literary labour' was found mostly in newspaper work, where there was competition from those who received subsidized education, but not from amateurs because the type of work is 'more troublesome and disagreeable' and confers no 'personal celebrity' (1961, p. 397). The competition from the 'poor scholars' was not sufficient in itself to lower prices. While Mill did not mention it, there were relatively fewer poor scholars because the corruptness within the English universities during the 18th century had reduced the number of 'poor scholars' as the scholarships were given to the wealthier students. That vanity and 'personal celebrity' may motivate scholars and scientists was in keeping with Smith's competitive emulation. It also was something of an antecedent for the pursuit of prestige that figured so prominently in Veblen's later analysis.

Effects of Paying Fixed Faculty Incomes from Endowments

Mill was in complete agreement with Smith's analysis of the disincentive effects of paying faculty fixed incomes from endowments, although he had rather different views on endowments in general. In *Corporation and Church Property*, published in 1833, Mill stated that 'A doctrine is indeed abroad, and has been sanctioned by many high authorities, among others by Adam Smith, that endowed establishments, for education or other pubic purposes, are a mere premium upon idleness and inefficiency' (1963, Vol. 4, pp. 55–56). Mill agreed that was the situation in the English universities, and declared that the interested parties protested every attempt to regulate the use the endowments, claiming their private property rights were being violated (1963, Vol. 4, p. 56).

But Mill did not regard endowments themselves as the real problem. Rather, it was the absence of appropriate government regulation of their use, which is discussed in more detail below under the heading of 'Reforms.' Despite the general defects of government, Mill declared that endowed universities in France and Germany that were under government control were giving the best education that could be supplied. In his review of *Prof. Sedgwick's Discourse on the Studies of the University of Cambridge*, Mill briefly related the failures of the English universities to the absence of pay in proportion to exertion, made worse by the absence of any role of government to secure that exertion from those receiving incomes from endowments. Again, he declared that the universities, or more specifically, the faculties of the universities, would only respond to attempts to take away their endowments and encroach on their monopoly (1882, p. 124).

That Mill's defense of government regulation of the use of endowments did not contradict Smith's principal argument for fee-based incomes for university professors was made clear in an 1866 report to the Secretary of the Schools Inquiry Commission (1963, Vol. 21) and in his 1869 essay on endowments (1963, Vol. 5). Mill emphatically expressed his strong opposition to paying teachers fixed salaries out of endowments, describing that practice as 'almost fatal to the general usefulness of educational endowments, and quite sufficient in itself to account for the admitted fact of their extensive failure' (1963, Vol. 21, p. 209). The danger was that which Smith had cited, namely, that 'the teacher's duty will be idly and inefficiently performed if his remuneration is certain, and not dependent on pupils and their payments' (1963, Vol. 21, p. 624). Even if the fees paid by students went to a collective body (an arrangement similar to Smith's payment of fees to judges), no 'law of nature' required that all teachers should be equally paid from that fund (1963, Vol. 21, p. 624).

Despite his comments on 'amateurs' in 'literary work' being motivated by the pursuit of vanity and personal celebrity rather than pecuniary gain, Mill agreed with Smith that the motivating force of personal commitments to teaching could not be counted on to overcome the disincentive effects of fixed incomes for teachers. Essentially paraphrasing Smith, he declared that 'Every motive that acts upon a teacher thus situated, tends to render his work valueless, except conscience of a disinterested love for his duty; *and the insufficiency, in average cases, of these motives, is the principal cause which renders laws and institutions necessary*' (1963, Vol. 21, p.

210, emphasis added). But Mill went beyond Smith to assert that teachers' incomes should be based in part on the numbers of students but also on their effectiveness as judged by the *proficiency* of their students. Teachers should be awarded an extra payment for each student who passes a creditable examination upon leaving the institution in his department.

The Applicability of Market Principles in Education

Although Mill strongly agreed with Smith on the need for incomes of professors to be linked to fees paid by their students, he just as strongly disagreed with Smith on the applicability of market principles in education. In *Principles of Political Economy*, Mill appeared to question the viability of any market-related approach to paying teachers. In this discussion of the competition from amateurs keeping down the incomes of teachers and others in 'literary work,' he indicated doubt as to 'whether any social arrangement under which the teachers of mankind consists of persons giving out doctrines for bread, is suited to be, or can possibly be, a permanent thing – would be a subject well worth the attention of thinkers' (1961, p. 398). But there was a much more fundamental reason why Mill thought market principles did not apply. Education is one of those things for which demand in the market is not a test of its social worth (1961, p. 953). What will be supplied, quantitatively and qualitatively, in response to market demand 'will be anything but what is really required' (1961, p. 953).

In *Principles of Political Economy*, Mill briefly explained the market failure was because the public was not competent judges of education. He developed his argument more fully in several essays in which he criticized private schools and schoolmasters. In his 1833 essay on *Corporation and Church Property*, Mill asked whether the endowed seminaries of Great Britain were worse or even as bad as all of the other places of education in the country. Was the desire to gain as much money with as little labor as is consistent with saving appearances a tendency peculiar to the endowed teachers, or did it apply to private teachers as well (1963, Vol. 4, pp. 214–215)? His response was that 'nineteen-twentieths' of the unendowed schools, i.e., private schools that charged full fees, were an 'organized system of charlatenerie for imposing upon the ignorance of parents' (1963, Vol. 4, p. 215). Mill directly questioned 'whether parents do prove themselves as solicitous, and as well qualified, to judge rightly the merits of places of education, as the theory of Adam Smith supposes' (1963, Vol. 4, p. 215). He suggested that most parents gave very little thought about the merits of schools for their children, and those who do are unable to judge competently, becoming instead 'the ready dupes of the very shallowest artifices' (1963, Vol. 4, p. 215). Schoolmasters are more concerned with keeping parents in good humor, readily sacrificing the real ends of instruction not solely for the ease of the teacher as Adam Smith thought, but also to the 'additional positive vices of clap-trap and lip-proficiency' (1963, Vol. 4, p. 215). Those few schoolmasters who really endeavor to educate students are sure to be engaging in a 'losing speculation' (1963, Vol. 4, p. 215). Invariably, the 'merely trading schoolmaster' will 'teach down to the level of the parents' (1963, Vol. 4, p. 215). In his 1834 essay *Reform in Education*, Mill quoted this passage from his 1833 essay on endowments and church property (1963, Vol. 21, pp. 65–66).

In his 1835 essay *Prof. Sedgwick's Discourse on the Studies of the University of Cambridge*, Mill stated that 'All things in which the public are adequate judges of excellence are best supplied where the stimulus of individual interest is the most active; and that is where pay is in proportion to exertion' (1882, p. 121). But the public cannot pretend to be competent judges of university education. To accomplish its purpose of rearing up 'minds with aspiration and faculties above the herd' requires universities to be free of any dependence on the 'immediate pleasure' of the multitude (1882, pp. 121–122).

A somewhat more complex economic analysis appeared in the 1869 article on endowments. Mill (1963, Vol. 5, p. 622) posed the question of whether education is a marketable commodity, for which the self-interests of rival dealers is sufficient to assure provision of the required quantity and quality. Or is it a public want that is sufficiently met by the ordinary incentives of the principle of trade? Mill specified three conditions as being requisite for free trade to work. Consumers must have the ability to pay; they must care sufficiently for it; and they must be sufficient judges of the value. In the case of 'national education,' all three conditions were wanting (1963, Vol. 5, p. 622). The wishes of parents in regard to instruction of their children are determined by what will bring a pecuniary profit, and in that they consider themselves to be good judges, although Mill regarded most of them as being very incompetent (1963, Vol. 5, p. 623). (This statement seemingly contradicted his comment that self-interest would adequately provide for professional and technical education.) On those kinds of education that do not bring a pecuniary profit, the parents are totally ignorant and simply follow the rule of following the customs of their social class at all levels of education. In his review of *Prof. Sedgwick's Discourse on the Studies of the University of Cambridge*, Mill criticized the educated classes of England for not seeking real university education for their sons. Rather than turning away from Oxford and Cambridge teachers in contempt, they continued to send their sons to the universities. That enabled the universities to flourish quantity-wise while offering nothing quality-wise (1882, p. 125).

GOVERNMENT SCHOOLS VS. PRIVATE SCHOOLS

The inapplicability of market principles (or principles of trade) to education favored government provision of education but not exclusively. Smith stated that it was legitimate for the 'sovereign' to fund education of the youth based on social benefits, but lauded private teachers as superior to public teachers. In contrast, Mill argued that schools financed by government would be inherently superior to private schools. The 'real principle of efficiency in teaching,' payment by results, can be easily applied to public teaching. But it is totally inapplicable to private school speculations ('even when they subject to a general system of public examinations; unless by special agreement between schoolmasters and parents, which also is a thing we have no chance of seeing until the fashion can be set') (1961, p. 624).

In *Principles of Political Economy*, Mill distinguished between the 'authoritative interference' of government and the role of government providing something that people are free to either produce for themselves or acquire from private producers' (1961, p. 942). Government intervention is justifiable in education 'because the case is not one in which the interest and judgement of the consumer are a sufficient security for the goodness of the commodity' (1961, p. 956). Education is one of those things for which demand in the market is not a test of its social worth 'the supply called forth by the demand of the market will be anything but what is really required' (1961, p. 953).

In that context, the government should require elementary education and assure that it be available 'either gratuitously or at a trifling price' (1961, p. 954). Mill's basic rule was that government must claim no monopoly on education in either in the lower or the higher level (1961, p. 956). In contrast to Smith's view of the superiority of private teachers, Mill stated that 'the government teachers will probably be superior to the private teachers' (1961, p. 956). Even so, government teachers 'will not embody all the knowledge and sagacity to be found in all instructors taken together, and it is desirable to leave open as many roads as possible for the desired end' (1961, p. 956). One of his direct comments on colleges and universities in *Principles of Political Economy* is found in that discussion

Though a government, therefore, may, and in many cases ought to, establish schools and colleges, it must neither compel nor bribe any person to come to them; nor ought to the power of individuals to set up rival establishments to depend in any degree upon its authorization. It would be justified in requiring from all people that they shall possess instruction in certain things, but not in prescribing to them how or from whom they shall obtain it (1961, p. 956).

The word 'bribe' injects some confusion, as any cost difference between attending a school supported by the government and a private school could be interpreted as a 'bribe.' Mill's rejection of that interpretation elsewhere is noted below in the discussion of his views on the importance of government regulation of endowments.

Reforms

Mill insisted that good education must be provided from motives other than that of pecuniary gain (1963, Vol. 4, p. 215). In the world as it existed, enlightened government is 'probably a better judge of good education than an average man – even an average founder' (1963, Vol. 4, p. 215). As people grow more enlightened, they will become more able to appreciate and willing to pay for good instruction. Then the competition of the market will become more and more adequate to provide good education, and endowed establishments will be less and less necessary (*Collected Works* 1963, Vol. 4, p. 216). But he gave little indication that such a social development could be expected in the near future.

But Mill also criticized private schoolmasters whose self interest is providing only what ignorant parents are willing to accept. These are 'the natural fruits, of the trading principle in education' (1963, Vol. 5, p. 624). It is difficult to see in the operation of the trading principle any tendency to make these things better. When the customer's ignorance is great, the trading motive acts much more powerfully in the direction of vying with one another in the arts of quackery and self-advertisement than in merit' (1963, Vol. 5, p. 625). Of all of the modes of human improvement, parents' notion of what education is and its value is about the slowest (1963, Vol. 5, p. 625).

> Schools on the trading principle will not be improved unless the parents insist on their improvement, nor even then if, all other schools that are accessible being equally bad, the dissatisfaction can have no practical effect. To make those parents dissatisfied who care but little for good schooling, or are bad judges, and at the same time to make it a necessity for schoolmasters to pay regard to their dissatisfaction, there is but one way; and this is, to give to those who cannot judge of the thing itself, an external criterion to judge by; such as would be afforded by the existence of a certain number of places of education with the *prestige* of public sanction, giving, on a large and comprehensive scale, the best teaching which it is found possible to provide (1963, Vol. 5, p. 626).

If society wants its youth to have an education that is based on considerations other than the narrow exigencies of business life, the custom must be changed to make it the fashion to receive a really good education. Bringing about that change could best be done by offering models of good education in schools and colleges within easy reach of all parts of the country. But to accomplish that, the institutions must be able to forego any consideration of pecuniary profit and consider only the quality of education. The English universities were in a position to do just that because they were certain of sufficient customers (1963, Vol. 5, p. 623). The funds required for the means of being able to wait for years until people realized that the education they received had prepared them for all uses of life could only be derived from taxation or endowments? Which means of funding is preferable?

Reform of Endowments

Much of Mill's commentary about universities came in essays that dealt primarily with the topic of endowments. Despite his agreement with Smith on the disincentive effects of paying professors fixed incomes from endowments, Mill defended endowed universities, as opposed to private schools charging full-cost fees. But he recommended reforms in their use. In view of the great efforts by universities to increase their endowments that was noted by Veblen in the early 20th century and has continued unabated into the 21st century, an examination of Mill's thoughts on the legitimacy of universities' endowments is merited.

While endowments could easily be misused and wasted (see above), that was only if the law took no notice. The variety of endowed institutions, with the influence of the state exerted within its proper limits, would ensure adequate provision in the course of education what needs to be included in it. A major issue addressed by Mill in the essays on endowments was whether government should regulate the use of endowments, or more fundamentally, whether endowments should even be allowed for public purposes such as education. In the 1869 paper, Mill defended endowments from coming too far under public authority. The reference was to private schools without endowments and 'public' schools with endowments. The exception was that the endowment mission should have a limited life, so that when new circumstances make that mission irrelevant, the government could change the use of the endowment. Mill cited the private colleges in America as an example of the social worthiness of private endowments. They were 'covering America with the very institutions which her state of society most needs, and was least likely in any other manner to get – institutions for the careful cultivation of the higher studies' (1963, Vol. 5, pp. 616–617).

An important question was the extent to which those who give the endowments should be allowed to specify the use. Mill argued that subject to some restrictions, that control should be unlimited at least through the founder's life and as long after as his foresight can be assumed to reach (1963, Vol. 4, pp. 198–205). After that, the legislature can legitimately consider more appropriate uses. The next question is the rights of the actual holders of an existing endowment, such as universities. Mill rejected the arguments by the trustees and those supported by the endowments that these were their property rights. They are entitled only to payment for services provided in carrying out the educational function for which the endowments were intended. There is a clear intimation that trustees are prone to attempt to appropriate the benefits of the endowments for their own pleasures and to lay legal claim to having property rights to those endowments. It is incumbent upon the state, whose first duty is to assure that the endowments are employed as usefully as possible, to assure that they fulfill the requirements of their contracts, which was not happening in the English universities where professors neglected to teach.

Mill stated that 'Whether endowments for educational purposes are good or evil is a fair question for argument' (1963, Vol. 5, p. 617), but argued that the idea that public authorities should specify the nature of the organization and operations under fixed principles in anything that aims at producing a public benefit was wrong. But educational endowments were a 'peculiar case' (1963, Vol. 5, p. 621). Education would be provided, so the question was one of quality. Private endowments for schools were essential for providing variety and choices, preventing a public (government) monopoly over education which is subject to administrations' spasmodic interference with education in response to prevalent opinion in the country. Mill rejected the argument that endowments gave public schools a competitive edge over private schools through subsidizing the costs – bribing parents and underselling their competitors. As long as private schools are wanted in addition to the public ones, the market price will cover the cost of private schools (1963, Vol. 5, p. 626) because 'a political economist need scarcely be reminded that the price of a commodity is determined by that portion of the quantity required which is produced and brought to the market under the least favourable circumstances' (1963, Vol. 5, p. 626). While that seems to suggest that endowed universities will charge market prices equal to those charged by the private schools, the ability to pay was taken into consideration. Students being supported from the endowments should be those academically qualified who cannot pay the full cost themselves.

One limitation had to do the form of the endowment. It should be in the form of an annuity, so the trustees will have only the duty of expending the funds, not of realizing income from the endowment. He only mentioned land as a precluded form, stating that trustees may desire landed property as a source of power as an additional reason for precluding it. The extent to which modern universities are engaging in commercial development of their real properties, as well as other properties, makes his limitation particularly noteworthy.

Mill strongly endorsed endowments that make possible higher education for those who have the intellectual ability, the preparation, and who are worth receiving a higher education but cannot afford to pay for it. He also favored use of university endowments for 'the maintenance of professors,' and for encouraging students to enter esoteric studies in which it is in the interest of mankind to have a few knowledgeable people. That included the highest branches of almost all sciences, since speculative researches in science are not those by which money can be made in the general market (1963, Vol. 5, p. 628). As we will see in the next two chapters, Veblen would essentially apply a similar view to the entire university as the institution of higher learning. But given that Mill had agreed with Smith that university professors should not receive certain incomes from endowments, if Mill meant by 'the maintenance of professors' not only research support but also income support. As we will see in the next chapter, that suggests something of a precursor to Veblen's view that university scientists and scholars must receive certain fixed incomes.

5. Veblen on Failures of American Universities

Nearly a century and half after Adam Smith criticized the English universities in *Wealth of Nations*, Thorstein Veblen argued that American schools called 'universities' were failing to function as true universities. Relative to Smith's critique of English universities, which essentially consisted of only part of one chapter, Veblen's critique of early 20th century American universities was developed at greater length and in greater depth. In the last chapter of *The Theory of the Leisure Class*, published in 1899, Veblen had criticized the 'higher learning' in general as 'an expression of the pecuniary culture' (1945, pp. 363–400). But in *The Higher Learning in America*, published in 1918 with the provocative subtitle *A Memorandum on the Conduct of Universities by Businessmen*, he developed a different and more analytical perspective on the behavior of American universities. Unfortunately, a heavy overlay of sarcasm, while entertaining, distracts readers' attention from the serious analytical work that was presented. In this and the following chapter, we closely examine Veblen's normative and positive analyses of institutional behavior of universities.

In a number of respects, the universities observed by Smith and Veblen were different types of institutions in very different historical-cultural settings. The 18th century English universities as federations of self-governing colleges were few in number (essentially Oxford and Cambridge), small in size, and reflecting a deeply ingrained feudalistic social class system, extremely elitist. The students were largely undergraduates. In matters of curricula, the dominance of classical and theological doctrine was being only weakly challenged by pre-industrial revolution developments in scientific and technological knowledge. In contrast, American universities in the early 20th century reflected the wealth and affluence of a large industrialized economy and much more democratic attitudes toward education. Universities and colleges stood at the top of a fairly comprehensive system of education that included both public and private schools at all levels, with universities providing both undergraduate and research-oriented graduate programs. Broader and deeper curricula reflected increased specialization in academic subjects and enormous advances in scientific and technological knowledge, as well as the methods of modern business enterprise. Universities in Veblen's America were more numerous, enrolled many more students, both undergraduates and graduates, and engaged in a much wider range of academic and non-academic activities. Their governance structures were more centralized, and organizational structures were much more bureaucratic, with external authorities in the form of boards of trustees and powerful individuals as presidents playing dominating roles.

But while institutional differences account for some differences between Veblen's and Smith's critiques of universities' behavior, fundamental institutional similarities between the 18th century English universities and early 20th century American universities figured prominently in their analyses. Both Veblen and Smith recognized the special features of universities as non-profit educational corporations that had evolved from medieval institutions to currently exist in a market economy. Implicitly or explicitly, their *normative* critiques dealt with the question of how far removed universities *should be* from proprietary business firms. Implicitly or explicitly, their *positive* analyses dealt with the question of how far removed universities *actually were* in operational practices from business enterprises and the ruling forces of the market economy.

A major part of the differences in Veblen's and Smith's assessments of institutional failures reflected fundamental differences in their normative views on the social functions of universities. There were, to be sure, several notable similarities, e.g., both expressed a highly negative view of governance of universities by external authorities. But to a large extent, Smith's proposed 'reform' measures for the English universities – a more market-oriented approach that included student-consumer sovereignty and competition for students and vocational curricula – were essentially what Veblen saw as either contributing to or providing evidence of the failures of American universities.

In this chapter, we examine Veblen's argument that American universities were failing to function as true universities, primarily due to the intrusive influence of business values, principles, and practices. That argument was largely normative in nature. While his view of the functions of the true university was similar to Mill's, Veblen rested the analytical structure heavily on his own evolutionary theory of human nature and social institutions. Essentially, his normative critique of American 'university corporations' involved a social theory of institutional contamination under the principle of the efficiency of specialized institutions. The 'contamination' came partly from combining non-university schools with the true university. But the primary source was the intrusive influence of business values, principles, and practices.

While Smith's and Veblen's normative critiques were almost polar opposites, both rested on positive analyses that developed economic perspectives on universities' behavior in a generally similar fashion. Like Smith, Veblen explained institutional behavioral tendencies of universities in terms of self-interested behavior on part of individuals in positions to influence institutional decisions. Indeed, his analysis of universities' internal decision-making processes had sufficient breadth and depth to develop the conceptual framework of a behavioral 'model' of universities that largely anticipated modern economic models of universities as non-profit institutions. In Veblen's 'model,' which we examine in Chapter Six, *strategic* choices of institutional goals and *operational* decisions on academic policies and internal resource allocations were explained as outcomes that satisfied the personal 'motives' of the 'discretionary officials' within the institutions. That explains how business values, principles, and practices were able to influence of the behavior of American universities.

While primary attention in Chapter Six will be given to the features of Veblen's economic 'model' of the internal processes of universities' decision-making and the institutional behavioral tendencies that result, we will also note his limited 'suggestions' for 'reforming' American universities. In Appendix B, we consider the possible relationship between Veblen's own personal experiences at the University of Chicago and Stanford University and the critique that he presented in *The Higher Learning in America*. There we also note differences between the views on the 'higher learning' in *The Theory of the Leisure Class* and *The Higher Learning in America*.

THE SOCIAL IMPORTANCE OF KNOWLEDGE

Veblen's social norm for evaluating the performances of American universities was a concept of the university as an institutional ideal. It stemmed from the great social importance of knowledge, which he explained in terms of his social psychology of instincts. In every stage of civilization, a body of 'esoteric knowledge' exists which society regards as having 'great intrinsic value, in some way a matter of more substantial consequence than any or all of the material achievements or possessions of the community' (1918 [1993], p. 1). That knowledge constitutes 'the substantial core of the civilization in which it is found,' giving that particular civilization its 'character and distinction' (1918 [1993, p. 1]). All such bodies of 'esoteric' knowledge are rooted in the instinct of idle curiosity that impels people to instinctively seek knowledge and to value it for its own sake. Each society regards its own 'esoteric' knowledge as embodying 'a systematization of fundamental and eternal truth' (1918

[1993, p. 1]).

But in every case, the particular knowledge is actually shaped by, and is a part of, the institutional structure of that particular social environment. While the instinct of idle curiosity provides the impulse to acquire and value knowledge for its own sake, the content and scope of that knowledge, and the methods by which it is sought and maintained, are functions of the instinct of workmanship. That impulse to action leads to normative standards for judging the social worth of all human activities. Those standards reflect the dominant factors shaping social behavior in a particular time and place. In that manner, the knowledge that is so highly esteemed by a society always reflects the institutionalized norms, the criteria of what is accepted as truth, stemming from the predominant habits of life in the social environment. Hence, the nature, character, and content of knowledge are subject to the forces of institutional evolutionary change over time.

In earlier periods, the 'esoteric' knowledge or 'higher learning' had pragmatic importance, e.g., theological doctrines were valued because they guided people into the next world. In modern civilization, which Veblen described as being 'particularly intellectual,' the 'esoteric' knowledge or 'higher learning' is that of science and scholarship. It is conditioned primarily by the matter-of-fact nature of modern industrial technology, and secondarily by the current institutional system in which the dominant factor is business enterprise, with its own matter-of-fact pecuniary logic of business accountancy (1918 [1993, pp. 3–5]). Veblen repeatedly asserted that the modern 'esoteric knowledge of matter-of-fact' is viewed by society as being supremely worthwhile in its own right (1918 [1993, p. 7]). Even as a 'sterilized, germ-proof system of knowledge, kept in a cool, dry place,' it is held in the same high esteem as was once accorded to the much more personalized theological 'knowledge' of the feudalistic era (1918 [1993, p. 5]). This was a fairly recent development in the evolutionary development of modern civilization:

> . . . [i]n past times such a disinterested pursuit of unprofitable knowledge has, by and large, not been freely avowed as a legitimate end of endeavour; or such has at any rate been the state of the case through that later segment of history which students commonly take account of. A quest of knowledge has overtly been rated as meritorious, or even blameless, only in so far as it has appeared to serve the ends of one or another of the practical interests that have from time to time occupied men's attention. But latterly, during the past few generations, this learning has so far become an avowed 'end in itself' that the 'increase and diffusion of knowledge among men' is now freely rated as the most humane and meritorious work to be taken care of by any enlightened community or any public-spirited friend of civilization (1918 [1993, p. 7]).

Veblen repeatedly sought to impress upon his readers that he was not expressing a personal opinion. Rather, this had 'come to be the long-term common-sense judgement of enlightened public opinion' (1918 [1993, p. 7]). The 'modern learning' had become 'the most valued spiritual asset of civilized mankind' (1918 [1993, p. 8]) and society would not tolerate its miscarriage.

THE SOCIAL FUNCTIONS OF UNIVERSITIES

Veblen claimed total objectivity in critiquing American universities by postulating a social norm that defined the proper functions of universities, and insisting that only institutions that engaged in those functions and no others qualified as universities in the true sense. Indeed, he went to considerable lengths to assure readers that he was only evaluating the performance of institutions calling themselves 'universities' against what society had dictated that true universities are to do, and was not expressing his own personal opinion.

UNIVERSITIES AND THE PRINCIPLE OF INSTITUTIONAL SPECIALIZATION

In every society, the body of 'esoteric knowledge' is placed in the keeping of a particular group of specialists, e.g., medicine men, priests, scientists and scholars, depending on the particular stage of socio-cultural development. In the modern era, universities are the specialized institutions that have been entrusted with the keeping, diffusion, and expansion of the scientific and scholarly knowledge. By tradition, the modern university is more closely identified with the quest for knowledge than any other institution. It stands as 'the only accepted institution of the modern culture on which the quest of knowledge unquestionably devolves; and the visible drift of circumstances as well as of public sentiment runs also to making this the only unquestioned duty incumbent on the university' (1918 [1993, p. 11]).

As a political economist, Veblen applied the principle of efficiency advantages of institutional specialization to distinguish between the social functions of the true university and other types of schools (1918 [1993, pp. 14–15 and pp. 22–23]). As the 'seminary of the higher learning' (1918 [1993, p. 12]), the university exists in the form of 'a body of mature scholars and scientists, the "faculty"' (1918 [1993, p. 13]). While modern university work requires large plant and equipment and supporting personnel, those are only the appliances used by scientists and scholars in their work, not the university (1918 [1993, p. 13]). In fulfilling the function of conserving and advancing the 'higher learning,' the university engages in two distinct but closely bound lines of work. The 'primary and indispensable' line is scientific and scholarly research, the 'work of intellectual enterprise' (1918 [1993, p. 12]). The very nature of scientific and scholarly research requires that scientists and scholars be free to pursue whatever line of investigation that intrigues them. Mill had expressed essentially the same sentiment earlier.

Teaching in a highly specialized and differentiated form constitutes the second line of university work. Instruction of students belongs in the university only 'in so far as it incites and facilitates the university man's work of inquiry' (1918 [1993, p. 12]). University teaching has 'a particular and special purpose – the pursuit of knowledge,' and therefore has 'a particular and special character' that differentiates it from other teaching (1918 [1993, p. 13]). University teaching as 'a concomitant of investigation, is distinctly advantageous to the investigator; particularly so in so far as his work is of the nature of theoretical inquiry' (1918 [1993, p. 13]). The 'university man' is 'properly, a student, not a schoolmaster' (1918 [1993, p. 13]). His work is the pursuit of knowledge, 'together with whatever supervisory surveillance and guidance he may consistently afford such students as are entering on a career of learning at a point where his outlook and methods of work may be of effect for them' (1918 [1993, p. 13]). University-level teaching is only that which 'can readily be combined with the work of inquiry, at the same time that it goes directly to further the higher learning in that it trains the incoming generation of scholars and scientists for the further pursuit of knowledge' (1918 [1993, p. 12]). It aims 'to equip the student for the work of inquiry, not to give him facility in that conduct of affairs that turns such knowledge to "practical account"' (1918 [1993, p. 12]). Veblen emphasized the importance of teaching to university work with the comment that 'good, consistent, sane and alert' scientific work can only be carried on under the 'stimulus and safeguarding that comes of the give and take between teacher and student' (1918 [1993, p. 200]).

Since the work of scientists and scholars follows paths of inquiry dictated by their own interests and discoveries, the true university offers no set curriculum (1918 [1993, p. 18]). The relation of the university student 'to his teacher necessarily becomes that of an apprentice to his master, rather than of a pupil to his schoolmaster' (1918 [1993, p. 13]). Students come to the university for the pursuit of knowledge, and are expected to know what they want and to want it without compulsion. The university teacher is not responsible for any lack of knowledge on the student's part or for any failure of students to exhibit the requisite interest and initiative.

The university student has 'a legitimate claim' only to:

> . . . an opportunity for such personal conduct and guidance as will give him familiarity with the ways and means of the higher learning, – any information imparted to him being incidental to this main work of habituation. He gets a chance to make himself a scholar, and what he will do with his opportunities in this way lies in his own discretion (1918 [1993, p. 14]).

As an institution 'specialized to fit men for a life of science and scholarship,' the university is only concerned with such discipline over students that is necessary to 'give efficiency in the pursuit of knowledge and fits its students for the increase and diffusion of learning' (1918 [1993, p. 15]).

Clearly, Veblen's concept of the university as an institutional ideal was much more compatible with Mill's than Smith's. But Veblen would not agree with Mill's view that the social function of universities was to turn the upper classes into more effective social leaders.

EVOLUTIONARY DEVELOPMENT OF MODERN 'UNIVERSITY CORPORATIONS'

Veblen's use of the term 'modern university' was somewhat inconsistent. Sometimes it was in reference to the true university; at other times he was referring to the large American schools that had combined under the same corporate organization the true university and the 'lower schools' to form 'university corporations.' The 'lower schools' included undergraduate colleges, professional schools, e.g., law and medicine, and technical schools, e.g., engineering. In addition, 'university corporations' engaged in activities that were non-academic in nature as well as those that were quasi-academic.

Veblen emphasized that the true university did not exist as a separate and distinct institution in America. In the real world, 'many other lines of work, and of endeavour that may not fairly be called work, are undertaken by schools of *university grade*; and also, many other schools that call themselves 'universities' will have substantially nothing to do with the higher learning' (1918 [1993, p. 11], emphasis added). To the extent that the true university did exist, it was in the graduate divisions of the larger 'university corporations' which qualified as 'university-grade' schools. But as 'university corporations,' those schools engaged in a variety of 'enterprises' that had nothing to do with the higher learning. These included: professional training, undergraduate instruction by faculty members who were 'schoolmasters' rather than university-grade scientists and scholars, supervision and guidance of the secondary school system, 'edification of the unlearned by "university extension" and similar excursions into the field of public amusement,' training of secondary teachers, and 'encouragement of amateurs by "correspondence"' (1918 [1993, pp. 11–12]).

The critical institutional differences between the 'true university' and the other schools included under the modern American 'university corporations' were explained in terms of evolutionary institutional development. The base line feature in all of Veblen's analytical works was an emphasis on evolutionary processes of institutional development and change and technological progress. His normative interpretations of institutional evolution emphasized the negative social consequences of institutional lags. His positive comments on the true university, surprisingly, represent perhaps the only case in which a 'good' institution had evolved.

Veblen's evolutionary analysis of the emergence of modern universities and the nature of the failures of American universities essentially divided into two parts. The first, which is examined in this section, was a brief historical review of the evolutionary development of the universities to end of the 19th century. In this part of Veblen's evolutionary analysis of the development of universities there is a discernible suggestion of an irresistible movement toward the ideal institutional form in both Europe and America.

That suggestion was contradicted, however, in the second part of his evolutionary analysis, which dealt with conflicting forces at work within the modern American 'university corporations.' Those forces played a prominent role in influencing both the current behavior of American universities and the direction of change in institutional goals, academic policies, and internal resource allocations. This second part constituted the major thrust of Veblen's analysis of university behavior. It accomplished his stated purpose of the 'historical argument' that was to provide '*an intelligent appreciation of what things are coming to*' (1918 [1993, pp. 23–24], emphasis added). The characteristic behavioral tendencies that those forces were producing are examined later in this chapter. The micro-structure of these forces, i.e., Veblen's economic model of university behavior, is examined in depth in Chapter Six.

The Historical Development of European Universities

Veblen's review of the evolutionary institutional development covered both universities in general and the specific cases of European and American universities in their most recent stages of development. Modern universities had 'grown out of professional training schools' and 'modern science and scholarship have grown out of the technology of handicraft and the theological philosophy of the schoolmen' (1918 [1993, p. 24]). In discussing the 'genesis of the university at large' as 'an institution of civilized life,' Veblen declared that:

> In a general way, the place of the university in the culture of Christendom is still substantially the same as it has been from the beginning. Ideally, and in the popular apprehension, it is, as it has always been, a corporation for the cultivation and care of the community's highest aspirations and ideals (1918 [1993, p. 24]).

But as those ideals and aspirations changed as western civilization evolved, universities as institutions changed in character, aims, and ideals so as to remain 'the corporate organ of the community's dominant intellectual interest' (1918 [1993, p. 24]).

The European universities evolved from schools founded originally to meet the needs of professional training, particularly theological (and philosophical) training in earlier times (1918 [1993, p. 16]). Later in Chapter 1 of *The Higher Learning in America*, Veblen presented a more interpretative account in terms of his theory of institutions, in which 'An institution is . . . a prevalent habit of thought, and as such it is subject to the conditions and limitations that surround any change in the habitual frame of mind prevalent in the community' (1918 [1993, p. 25]). In that regard, he argued that 'The university of medieval and early times, that is to say the barbarian university, was necessarily given over to the pragmatic, utilitarian disciplines, since that is the nature of barbarism; and the barbarian university is but another, somewhat sublimated, expression of the same barbarian frame of mind' (1918 [1993, p. 25]). This was because 'The barbarian culture is pragmatic, utilitarian, worldly wise, and its learning partakes of the same complexion' (1918 [1993, p. 25]). The pragmatic utilitarian animus in that period was 'a boundless solicitude' of men for salvation, and 'Under the rule of such a cultural ideal the corporation of learning could not well take any avowed stand except as an establishment for utilitarian instruction' (1918 [1993, p. 26]).

The universities of early modern times which began as federations of professional schools or faculties of 'divinity engineering,' law, politics, medicine, and other professions that served utilitarian interests set an institutional mold. Universities that were established later were organized along similar lines. As it is the nature of all institutions to be resistant to change, further changes of academic policy and practice that were demanded by later growth of cultural interests and ideals were made reluctantly and with suspicious reserve (1918 [1993, p. 26]). But in a 'surreptitious' fashion, change did occur because the:

... human propensity for inquiry into things, irrespective of use or expediency, insinuated itself . . . and from the first this quest of idle learning has sought shelter in the university as the only establishment in which it could find a domicile, even on sufferance, and so could achieve that footing of consecutive intellectual enterprise running through successive generations of scholars which is above all else indispensable to the advancement of knowledge (1918 [1993, p. 27]).

Scholars masked their disinterested inquiries 'under some colourable masquerade of practicality' (1918 [1993, p. 27]).

Under the rule of such a cultural ideal the corporation of learning could not well take any avowed stand except as an establishment for utilitarian instruction, the practical expediency of whose work was the sole overt test of its competency. And such it still should continue to be according to the avowed aspirations of the staler commonplace elements in the community today. By subreption, and by a sophisticated subsumption under some ostensibly practical line of interest and inquiry, it is true, the university men of the earlier time spent much of their best endeavour on matters of disinterested scholarship that had no bearing on any human want more to the point than an idle curiosity; and by a similar turn of subreption and sophistication the later spokesmen of the barbarian ideal take much complacent credit for the 'triumphs of modern science' that have nothing but an ostensible bearing on any matter of practical expediency, and they look to the universities to continue this work of the idle curiosity under some plausible pretext of practicality (1918 [1993, p. 26]).

The 'spirit of idle curiosity' was so persistent and:

...so consonant with the long-term demands of the laity, that the dissimulation and smuggling-in of disinterested learning has gone on ever more openly and at an ever increasing rate of gain; until in the end the attention given to scholarship and the non-utilitarian sciences in these establishments has come far to exceed that given to the practical disciplines for which the several faculties were originally installed (1918 [1993, p. 27]).

Thus, 'what had once been incidental, or even an object of surreptitious tolerance in the university, remains today as the only unequivocal duty of the corporation of learning, and stands out as the one characteristic trait without which no establishment can claim rank as a university' (1918 [1993, p. 27]).
In that manner, European universities reached 'their mature development, in the 19th century, as establishments occupied with disinterested learning, given over to the pursuit of intellectual enterprise, rather than as seminaries for training of a vocational kind' (1918 [1993, p. 16]). That is, European universities of the mid-1800s were functioning as 'true universities,' and Veblen appeared to think that the European

universities (with the exception of war-time Germany) were still functioning as true universities. He commented that:

> ... it is interesting to note, by way of parenthesis, that even now a large proportion of the names that appear among the staff of these [American] institutions of research are not American, and that even the American-born among them are frequently not American-bred in respect of their scientific training' (1918 [1993, p. 201]).

But he also asserted that the forces responsible for the failures of American universities were 'already making the way of the academic scientist or scholar difficult and distasteful in the greater schools of the Old World' (1918 [1993, p. 201]).

American Colleges, Universities, and 'University Corporations'

Veblen remarked that 'In point of historical pedigree the American universities are of another derivation than their European counterpart;' but he added that 'the difference in this respect is not so sharp a matter of contrast as might be assumed at first sight' (1918 [1993, p. 15]). American universities emerged out of American colleges, which originally existed largely for professional training, chiefly for clergy and secondly for the training of schoolmasters (1918 [1993, p. 16]). But by the mid-19th century, American colleges, like the European universities, had reached their 'mature development' in becoming 'establishments occupied with disinterested learning, given over to the pursuit of intellectual enterprise, rather than as seminaries for training of a vocational kind' (1918 [1993, p. 16]):

> . . . the American college was, or was at least presumed to be, given over to disinterested instruction, not specialized with an occupational, or even a denominational bias. It was coming to take its place as the superior or crowning member, a sort of capstone, of the system of public education (1918 [1993, p. 16]).

Veblen seemed to view this arrangement with considerable approval. He remarked, for example, that colleges of that era rested on 'that ancient footing of small-scale parcelment and personal communion between teacher and student that once made the American college, with all its handicap of poverty, chauvinism, and denominational bias, one of the most effective agencies of scholarship in Christendom' (1918 [1993, p. 208]). In this mode, the American colleges provided an ideal institutional model that was emulated by state universities.

The life-history of any one of the state universities whose early period of growth runs across this era will readily show the effectual guidance of such an ideal of a college, as a superior and definitive member in a school system designed to afford an extended course of instruction looking to an unbiased increase and diffusion of knowledge. Other interests, of a professional or vocational kind, were also entrusted to the keeping of these new-found schools; but with a conclusive generality the rule holds that in these academic creations a college establishment of a disinterested, non-vocational character is counted in as the indispensable nucleus, – that much was at that time a matter of course (1918 [1993, p. 16]).

But that situation became altered by developments after the American Civil War. During that period, corresponding to the rise of large corporate business enterprise, the American university (Veblen was speaking of the true university) came into being and the college became 'an intermediate rather than terminal link in the conventional scheme of education. American universities emerged from the colleges by 'historical accident' (1918 [1993, p. 17]). The institutional result was that the two became linked as 'subdivisions of a complex whole' within the 'university corporation' through coupling the 'graduate' and 'undergraduate' programs. The 'holding together of the two disparate schools is at the best a freak of aimless survival' (1918 [1993, p. 17]).

Undergraduate departments did not rate as institutions of the higher learning, that is, as true universities. In the modern setting, the college 'takes its place in the education scheme as senior member of the secondary school system, and it bears no peculiarly close relation to the university as a seat of learning' (1918 [1993, p. 17]). At best, undergraduate colleges had become 'fitting schools' for universities, schools for 'preliminary training, preparatory to entering on the career of learning' (1918 [1993, p. 17]). More commonly, undergraduate colleges were closely related to vocational and professional schools, preparing people for further training required for the professions. But chiefly, the undergraduate college was 'an establishment designed to give the concluding touches to the education of young men who have no designs on learning, beyond the close of the college curriculum. 'It aims to afford a rounded discipline to those who goal is the life of fashion or affairs' (1918 [1993, p. 18]). Except for the strong sense of disapproval, this sounded very much like Smith's view of the function of English universities.

INSTITUTIONAL FAILURES OF AMERICAN UNIVERSITIES

An assessment of institutional failures requires an operational criterion against which the actual performances of universities could be evaluated. Under the principle of institutional specialization, Veblen repeatedly stressed that his criterion was *institutional efficiency* in pursuing the goals which society decreed for each set of institutions. Only institutional purity would permit achievement of society's desire to maximize the 'efficiency of its specialists' (1918 [1993, p. 23]). In the 'ideal scheme' of things, the 'lower schools, (which included the professional schools)' are 'designed to fit the incoming generation for civil life,' while the university is 'specialized to fit men for the life of science and scholarship' (1918 [1993, p. 15]). To achieve maximum 'efficiency in pursuit of knowledge' (1918 [1993, p. 15]), the scientists and scholars who constitute the faculty of the university must be completely unimpeded in their work aimed at the expansion and diffusion of knowledge.

The failures of American universities to function as true universities were the consequences of processes of institutional contamination from which created institutional environments that incompatible with and hostile to the disinterested pursuit of science and scholarship. One source of contamination was from the attitudes and practices of the undergraduate, professional, and technical schools. Fundamentally more important was the institutional contamination from the pecuniary animus of the culture of the business enterprise with its attendant business values, principles, and practices had intruded in the academic policies of universities.

Institutional Contamination from the 'Lower Schools'

Veblen denied that he was suggesting that the responsibility of universities for 'scholarship' was more important than the responsibility of fitting of young men for 'citizenship.' Rather, he was merely recognizing that university work was different and could not function efficiently unless the university (the graduate programs) was completely separated from the undergraduate college He insisted that the intent of his work was not to imply any 'undervaluing of the work of those men who aim to prepare the youth for citizenship and a practical career. It is only a question of distinguishing between things that belong apart' (1918 [1993, p. 14]). Unconvincingly, Veblen conceded willingly that the schoolmaster 'may be equally, or more, valuable to the community at large . . . but in so far as his chief interest is of the pedagogical sort his place is not in the university' (1918 [1993, p. 14]). The university exists only if the faculty is a 'bona fide university faculty, and not a body of secondary-school teachers masquerading under the assumed name of a university' (1918 [1993, p. 17]). Only if universities and lower schools are separated absolutely can any of the institutions 'do its work in a workmanlike manner' (1918 [1993, p. 23]).

Schools could not claim to be universities unless they had some core of disinterested pursuit of knowledge by mature scientists and scholars. But the outcome of combining undergraduate colleges with university work:

> ... in nearly all cases where the control of both departments vests in one corporate body, as it usually does, is the gradual insinuation of undergraduate methods and standards in graduate school; until what is nominally university work settles down, in effect, into nothing more than an extension of the undergraduate curriculum. This effect is had partly by reducing such of the graduate courses as are found amenable to the formalities of the undergraduate routine, and partly by dispensing with such graduate work as will not lend itself, even ostensibly, to the schoolmaster's methods (1918 [1993, p. 19]).

While the hybrid nature of the older universities was due to the university emerging from the colleges, it set the 'conventional pattern' of the inclusion of an undergraduate department (the college) with the graduate program (the university), along with professional and technical schools. That arrangement was emulated by the newer universities from a 'headlong eagerness on part of the corporate authorities to show a complete establishment of the conventionally accepted pattern, and to enroll as many students as possible' (1918 [1993, p. 18]). Veblen cited two reasons for the 'continued and tenacious connection' between these schools and the universities. One was 'ancient tradition, fortified by the solicitous ambition of the university directorate to make a brave show of magnitude', while the other was the desire of these schools 'to secure some degree of scholarly authentication through such a formal connection with a seat of learning' (1918 [1993, p. 30]).

The organizational nature of American universities that combined graduate colleges, undergraduate colleges, and professional and technical schools into one large complex institution:

> ... does not set aside the substantial discrepancy between their purpose, work and animus and those of the university proper. It can only serve to trouble the singlemindedness of both. It leaves the pursuit of learning and the work of preparation for the professions somewhat at loose ends, confused with the bootless illusion that they are, in some recondite way, parallel variants of a single line of work (1918 [1993, p. 19]).

While Veblen focused primarily on the private universities of the Chicago class, he occasionally mentioned state universities. He asserted that 'the greater number' American state universities were not, or were not yet, true universities except in name. They were founded with 'a profound utilitarian purpose . . . with professional training as their chief avowed aim' (1918 [1993, p. 31]). They were to 'train young men for proficiency in some gainful occupation', with some 'half-articulated professions of solicitude for cultural interests to be taken care of by the same means' (1918 [1993, p. 31]). American state universities were:

> . . . installed by politicians looking for popular acclaim, rather than by men of scholarly or scientific insight, and their management has not infrequently been entrusted to political masters of intrigue, with scant academic qualifications; their foundations has been the work of practical politicians with a view to conciliate the good will of a lay constituency clamouring for things tangibly 'useful' – that is to say, pecuniarily gainful. So these experts in short-term political prestige have made provision for schools of a 'practical' character; but they have named these establishments 'universities' because the name carries an air of scholarly repute, of a higher, more substantial kind than any naked avowal of material practicality would give (1918 [1993, p. 31]).

This stands in contrast to his earlier statement that state universities founded in the mid-19th century readily showed 'the effectual guidance of such an ideal of a college, as a superior and definitive member in a school system designed to afford an extended course of instruction looking to an unbiased increase and diffusion of knowledge' (1918 [1993, p. 16]).

Critics who have charged that Veblen regarded all teaching as waste are obviously wrong. On the contrary, he argued that good teaching is essential but that teaching undergraduates and teaching graduate students were very different (1918 [1993, pp. 12–13]). As did Smith, Veblen related teaching to both *perceived* actual behavior of students and *expected* behavior of students. With respect to the latter, Veblen's 'bona fide' students (1918 [1993, p. 75]) were very similar to Smith's idealistic depiction of undergraduates not requiring any institutional discipline. Veblen remarked that 'bona fide students will require but little surveillance in their work, and little in the way of an apparatus of control' (1918 [1993, p. 75]). But Smith placed responsibility for good student behavior on the faculty since young men would be serious students only if their teachers showed interest in their welfare and endeavored to teach them effectively. In contrast, Veblen's graduate students were mature self-motivated individuals who had serious aspirations for becoming scientists and scholars. They knew fully well why they were at the university. Faculty members had only one responsibility, which was to allow their students the opportunity to work with them, to learn experientially by serving as apprentices to master scientists and scholars (1918 [1993, pp. 12–15]).

With respect to perceived behavior of students, Veblen described the undergraduates in American universities as behaving much like the poorly taught undergraduates in Smith's English universities. But there was a difference in the alleged causes of that behavior. Smith blamed faculty members' indifference toward their students and laziness in carrying out their teaching duties. Veblen placed the blamed more broadly on the conspicuous consumption culture and the business enterprise system, and more specifically, on the manner in which the 'discretionary officials' were administering the universities.

For Veblen, effective teaching was not the well prepared and effectively delivered lectures endorsed by Smith, which was the conventional method of the relationship between the 'schoolmasters' and their undergraduate pupils. Rather, effective teaching required close personal contact between teacher and student (1918 [1993, p. 165]), e.g., 'intimately personal contact and guidance' is what 'makes up the substance of efficient teaching' (1918 [1993, p. 207]). That applied to undergraduate teaching as well, at least when the undergraduates were 'bona fide' students. There were such students, largely in the small colleges from which came the majority of graduate students. This was clearly indicated in Veblen's tribute to the American colleges of the mid-1800s. Veblen stated that the 'ancient footing of small-scale parcelment and personal communion between teacher and student . . . once made the American college, with all its handicap of poverty, chauvinism and denominational bias, one of the most effective agencies in scholarship in Christendom' (1918 [1993, p. 208]).

In several respects, Veblen's views on teaching were similar to Smith's. Just as Smith had argued that teaching is the best way for a man of science to learn, Veblen viewed teaching as an essential part of the learning experience for university scientists and scholars (1918 [1993, pp. 12–13]). Like Smith, he saw the importance of the relationship between teaching and research, remarking that 'good, consistent, sane, and alert' scientific work can only be carried on under the 'stimulus and safeguarding that comes of the give and take between teacher and student' (1918 [1993, p. 200]). Veblen also stated that:

...even in undergraduate work it remains true, as it does in all education in a degree, that the instruction can be carried on with best effect only on the ground of an absorbing interest on part of the instructor, and he can do the work of a teacher as it should be done only so long as he continues to take an investigator's interest in the subject in which he is called on to teach (1918 [1993, p. 80]).

Veblen was harsh in his condemnation of the lack of good teaching in the undergraduate programs in American 'university corporations.' Undergraduate departments were teaching through 'Exposition, instruction and drill' with the 'consistent aim . . . to instruct, to inculcate a knowledge of results, and to give the pupil a working facility in applying it' (1918 [1993, p. 14]). The 'lower schools necessarily take over the surveillance of their pupils' everyday life, and exercise a large measure of authority and responsible interference . . . in the moral, religious, pecuniary, domestic, or hygienic respect' (1918 [1993, p. 15]). Undergraduate work is 'task work,' and the schoolmasters:

> ...reduce it to standard units of time and volume, and so control and enforce it by a system of accountancy and surveillance; the methods of control, accountancy and coercion that so come to be worked out have all that convincing appearance of tangible efficiency that belongs to any mechanically defined and statistically accountable routine, such as will always commend itself to the spirit of the schoolmaster; the temptation to apply such methods of standardized routine wherever it is at all feasible is always present, and it is cogently spoken for by all those to whom drill is a more intelligible conception than scholarship (1918 [1993, pp. 18–19]).

Veblen asserted that in the common-sense view of society, the university is the seminary of the higher learning, a view earlier expressed by Mill. But he also stated that in the practical view of the public at large, the university is primarily an undergraduate school, with graduate and professional departments added to it (1918 [1993, p. 73]). In part, this was due to the large numbers of undergraduate students. The undergraduate or collegiate schools had undergone 'certain notable changes' in the latter part of the 19th century, with the numbers of undergraduates had rapidly increased (1918 [1993, p. 87]). ('Concomitant with their growth in numbers they have taken over an increasing volume of other function than such as bear directly on matters of learning' (1918 [1993, p. 74]).) One consequence of the growth in the numbers of undergraduates was that their 'usual and average age . . . has been slowly falling back into the period of adolescence' (1918 [1993, p. 75]), with little interest in pursuing knowledge. Rather 'By force of conventional propriety a "college course" – the due term of residence at some reputable university – has become a requisite of gentility' (1918 [1993, p. 74]). A large part of the universities' activities are now in providing for the life-style demanded by these students – football, club life, and discipline (1918 [1993, p. 75]). With 'such increased enrolment as comes of this competitive salesmanship among the universities is made up almost wholly of wasters, accessions from the genteel and sporting classes, who seek the university as a means of respectability and dissipation, and who serve the advancement of the higher learning only as fire, flood, and pestilence serve the needs of the husbandman' (1918 [1993, pp. 171–172]).

Thus, it becomes necessary to organize undergraduate instruction on a coercive plan, and hence to itemize the scholastic tasks of the inmates with a nicety of subdivision and with a meticulous regard to an exact equivalence as between the courses and items of instruction to which they are to be subjected' (1918 [1993, p. 75]). Instruction must be reduced to standard units of time, grade, and volume. Failure to do so result in 'injustice and irritation' on part of both pupils and schoolmasters (1918 [1993, p. 75]).

The larger American schools are primarily undergraduate establishments, – with negligible exceptions; and under these current American conditions, of excessive numbers, such a centralized and bureaucratic administration appears to be indispensable for the adequate control of immature and reluctant students; at the same time, such an organization conduces to an excessive size. The immediate and visible effect of such a large and centralized administrative machinery is, on the whole, detrimental to scholarship, even in the undergraduate work; though it need not be so in all respects and unequivocally, so far as regards that routine training that is embodied in the undergraduate curriculum. But it is at least a necessary evil in any school that is of so considerable a size as to preclude substantially all close or cordial personal relations between the teacher and each of these immature pupils under their charge, as, again, is commonly the case with these American undergraduate establishments. Such a system of authoritative control, standardization, graduation, accountancy, classification, credits and penalties, will necessarily be drawn on stricter lines the more the school takes on the character of a house of correction or a penal settlement; in which the irresponsible inmates are to be held to a round of distasteful tasks and restrained from (conventionally) excessive irregularities of conduct. At the same time this recourse to such coercive control and standardization of tasks has unavoidably given the schools something of the character of *a penal settlement* (1918 [1993, pp. 162–163]; emphasis added).

Like undergraduate colleges, the aims, methods, and achievements of technical and professional schools are 'foreign to the higher learning' (1918 [1993, p. 19]). Their 'aim and animus' are 'practical, in the most thoroughgoing manner' (1918 [1993, p. 19]), 'animated wholly by considerations of material expediency, and the range of its interest and efforts is strictly limited by consideration of the useful effect to which the proficiency that it gives is to be turned' (1918 [1993, p. 20]). While the 'animus' of the true university is 'idle curiosity,' the 'animus' of these schools is 'worldly wisdom' (1918 [1993, p. 20]). While technical schools have some bonds with the proper work of the true university, i.e., occupied in great measure with the same general range of materials and employ somewhat the same logical methods in handling these materials, this relationship is 'almost wholly external and mechanical' (1918 [1993, p. 20]). There is no reason for technical schools and true universities to be combined in a single institution (1918 [1993, p. 20]). (Interestingly, a later University of Chicago professor with a very different normative orientation argued along similar lines. Stigler (1963, p. 40) argued that even in the social sciences there were no historical evidence of sufficient complementarity of disciplines that they should be housed together.)

Because of the large importance of undergraduates, large universities operate with 'an administrative system of bureaux or departments, a hierarchical gradation of the members of the staff, and a rigorous parcelment and standardization of the instruction offered' (1918 [1993, p. 72]). Veblen remarked that:

> The need for a well-devised bureaucratic system is the greater the more centralized and coercive the control to which the academic work is to be subject; and the degree of control to be exercised will be greater the more urgent the felt need of a strict and large accountancy may be (1918 [1993, p. 72]).

The system of 'scholastic accountancy' which breaks up the continuity and consistency of the work of instruction and diverts the attention of students from the work in hand to the making of a passable record in terms of the academic 'miners inch' brings with it 'painstaking distribution of the personnel and the courses of instruction into a series of bureaux or departments to facilitate the oversight and control of the work' (1918 [1993, pp. 76–77]).

Veblen took special note of the entertainment activities provided by American universities catering to undergraduates. 'Well to the front of these undergraduate appurtenances of gentlemanship are the factional clubs known as Greek-letter fraternities' (1918 [1993, p. 89]). The necessity of keeping the behavior of the members of 'strict surveillance' 'affects the necessarily discipline of the school at large, entailing a more elaborate and rigorous surveillance and more meddling with personal habits than would otherwise be required, and entailing also some slight corporate expense' (1918 [1993, p. 90]). But for 'dissipating energy and attention' of undergraduates, 'college athletics is perhaps still the most effective,' and also the one pushed most by university authorities. It is also 'the most widely out of touch with all learning, whether it be the pursuit of knowledge or the perfunctory taskwork of the collegiate division' (1918 [1993, p. 90]). Veblen cited the pecuniary inducements offered by universities to students with high prospects as college athletes and the 'significant practice of retaining trainers and helpers at the university's expense and with academic countenance. There is the corps of workmen and assistants to take care of the grounds, buildings, and apparatus, and there is the corps of trainers and coaches, masseurs and surgeons, masquerading under the caption of 'physical culture,' whose chief duty is to put the teams in form for the various contests' (1918 [1993, p. 91]). Coaches were retained officially as faculty members, with highest academic rank and pay (1918 [1993, p. 92]). Mill would no doubt view this as another example of how private schools cater to the wants of the non-intellectual members of society who are unable to know the true meaning of higher learning.

The consequences of the institutional contamination from the 'lower schools' are grave for the work of university men. The undergraduate methods of the schoolmaster are heavily imposed upon the operations of the graduate programs.

> Perfunctory work and mechanical accountancy may be sufficiently detrimental in the undergraduate curriculum, but it seems altogether and increasingly a matter of course in that section; but it is in the graduate division that it has it gravest consequences. Yet even in undergraduate work it remains true, as it does in all education in a degree, that the instruction can be carried on with best effect only on the ground of an absorbing interest on the part of the instructor; and he can do the work of a teacher as it should be done only so long as he continues to take an investigator's interest in the subject in which he is called on to teach. He must be actively engaged in an endeavour to extend the bounds of knowledge at the point where his work as a teacher falls. He must be a specialist offering instruction in the specialty with which he is occupied; and the instruction offered can reach its best efficiency only in so far as it is incidental to an aggressive campaign of inquiry on the teacher's part (1918 [1993, pp. 80–81]).

Professional and technical men will have a larger impact on academic policies because they are 'to some extent trained to the conduct of affairs, and so come in for something of that deference which is currently paid to men of affairs' (1918 [1993, p. 22]). Their practical training gives them an advantage over their purely academic colleagues, 'in the great assurance and adroitness which they are able to present to the contentions' (1918 [1993, p. 22]). They will have little regard for purely scientific or scholarly work that has no practical use, and their presence on the academic staff will divert 'the university's forces away from disinterested science and scholarship to such palpably utilitarian ends' (1918 [1993, pp. 22]).

There is also a false image of academic importance that becomes attached to the work of the lower schoolmen:

> . . . the formal incorporation of these technological and professional men in the academic body, with its professedly singleminded interest in learning, has its effect on their frame of mind. They are, without intending it, placed in a false

position, which unavoidably leads them to court a specious appearance of scholarship, and so to invest their technological discipline with a degree of pedantry and sophistication; whereby it is hoped to give these schools and their work some scientific and scholarly prestige, and so lift it to that dignity that is presumed to attach to a non-utilitarian pursuit of learning (1918 [1993, p. 23]).

Veblen remarked that:

...this pursuit of scholarly prestige is commonly successful, to the extent that it produces the desired conviction of awe in the vulgar, who do not know the difference; but all this make-believe scholarship, however successfully staged, is not what these schools are designed for; or at least it is not what is expected of them, nor is it what they can do best and most efficiently (1918 [1993, pp. 23]).

Since the combining of undergraduate colleges, technical schools, and professional schools with universities, i.e., graduate programs, was a historical accident in institutional development, the institutional contamination from the 'lower schools' had shallow roots. At times, Veblen indicated that the drift toward the ideal university was virtually irresistible, as exemplified in the following comments on state universities:

Yet, in those instances where the passage of time has allowed the readjustment to take place, the quasi-'universities,' installed by men of affairs, of a crass 'practicality,' and in response to the utilitarian demands of an unlearned political constituency, have in the long run taken on more and more of an academic, non-utilitarian character, and have been gradually falling into line as universities claiming a place among the seminaries of the higher learning. The long-term drift of modern cultural ideals leaves these schools no final resting place short of the university type, however far short of such a consummation the greater number of them may still be found (1918 [1993, p. 32]).

Thus, if no other source of contamination was present, that from the 'lower schools' would be subject to erosion over time.

Institutional Contamination from Business Values and Practices

But the main thrust of Veblen's critique of American universities focused on the institutional contamination from the intrusion of business values and practices into university affairs. That contamination reinforced and rendered more permanent the contamination from the 'lower schools,' and added even more serious negative impacts on the functioning of 'university corporations' as seminaries of higher learning. Veblen explained how that intrusion was occurring with rather complex, inter-twining analyses. For clarity of understanding, we attempt to separate those analyses, and to examine each in some degree of isolation.

The first analysis, which is discussed here, applied Veblen's social theory of institutional behavior shaped by the interplay between instincts and acquired habits. The second, which is discussed in Chapter Six, was a more narrowly focused micro-analysis of the internal governance process. It developed the essential features of an economic model of organizational behavior driven by the personal motives of the key decision-makers within the institution. But the two analyses are closely linked as the personal motives of the decision makers, as well as the determination of just who becomes one of the decision makers, are shaped by the institutional environments that have evolved over time.

Conflicting Institutional Forces

In Veblen's social analysis, conflicting institutional forces were influencing American universities. What he termed the prevailing social sentiment in modern civilization, which was rooted in the instinctive impulses of idle curiosity and workmanship, endorsed the university as a seminary of the higher learning. But social attitudes toward universities were also affected by acquired habits, which interact with instinctive behavior in determining social behavior. Particularly important are habits of thought that are shaped by influence of the 'workday interests' of earning a living. Those conduce utilitarian pragmatic views that lead men to 'overrate ways and means as contrasted with the ends which these ways and means are in some sense designed to serve' (1918 [1993, p. 34]). Under their influence, inevitably:

> One class or another, biased by the habitual preoccupation of the class, will aim to divert the academic equipment to some particular use which habit has led them to rate high; or to include in the academic discipline various lines of inquiry and training which are extraneous to the higher learning but which the class in question may specially have at heart; but taking them one with another, there is no general or abiding consensus among the various classes of the community in favour of diverting the academic establishment to any other specific uses, or of including in the peculiar work of the university anything beyond the pursuit of knowledge for its own sake (1918 [1993, p. 34]).

At work is an ebb and flow process that involves one institutional drift toward the ideal of the university as a seminary of higher learning and another institutional drift toward the university as an academic version of a business enterprise. What actually happens depends upon the relative strengths of those two forces. Because the interests shaped by the workday life tend to be urgent and immediate, the drift toward the university as an academic enterprise will tend to be strong. But when the force of those interests is at low ebb, people are left free to take stock of the ulterior ends and values of life and the instinctive 'intellectual predection – the idle curiosity' – abides and asserts itself (1918 [1993, p. 33]). Even so, Veblen's primary argument was that the institutional forces countering that drift toward the ideal university, i.e., the urgency and strengths of the 'practical and expedient interests' from the work-day life, showed few signs of ebbing. On the contrary, those forces were growing stronger as the overall cultural influence of the pecuniary value system and institutional behavioral patterns gained ground in modern civilization.

Negative Influence of Business Habits on Universities' Behavior

While people's preoccupation with the material ways and means of life give rise to interests that are urgent and immediate, those interests are transient and change with time. So it is the 'practical and expedient interests' that influence universities in the direction of giving a utilitarian bent to the pursuit of knowledge. In the past, the two most notable interests in that regard were the ecclesiastical and the political. In the modern period, the pecuniary values and interests of business enterprise have replaced the church and state in social esteem (1918 [1993, p. 35]). Within modern universities, the new conflict is between the values and methods of science and scholarship on the one hand, and the pecuniary values and methods of seeking pecuniary gain on the other (1918 [1993, p. 35]). In general, the intrusion of business principles in the universities' academic policy weakens and retards the pursuit of learning by subjecting it to a pecuniary valuation standard, thus defeating the ends for which the university as a specialized social institution is maintained (1918 [1993, p. 165]).

The negative effects are both directly and indirectly observable. Business values and practices reinforced the contamination from the methods and practices of teaching undergraduates and the utilitarian curricula of the 'lower schools.' On a more fundamental level, the whole strategic concept of university work and behavior was affected. The pecuniary value system of business enterprise leads to putting a low value on the pursuit of knowledge for its own sake. In emulation of large business enterprises, especially retail department stores, universities put great strategic emphasis on competition for institutional prestige. In operational practice, that involves competition for larger numbers of students and for funds from donors. There are also negative effects on teaching and research arising from the influence of business values and practices on how faculty members are paid and their work assignments.

Reinforcement of Contamination from the 'Lower Schools'

While the institutional structures of the 'lower schools' had been the result of a historical accident, they simulated in academia the organizational features and practices of larger modern business coalitions which brought under one general business management a large number and variety of industrial plants (1918 [1993, pp. 140–141]). That was because the methods and practices of undergraduate colleges were highly compatible with business values, principles, and practices of large corporate enterprises. Thus, 'business principles take effect in academic affairs most simply, obviously and avowedly in the way of a businesslike administration of the scholastic routine; where they lead immediately to a bureaucratic organization and a system of scholastic accountancy' (1918 [1993, p. 162]). In commenting on the centralized bureaucratic organization of undergraduate colleges, Veblen stated that:

> . . . the ideal of efficiency by force of which a large-scale centralized organization commends itself in these premises is that pattern of shrewd management whereby a large business concern makes money. The underlying business-like presumption accordingly appears to be that learning is a merchantable commodity, to be produced on a piece-rate plan, rated, bought and sold by standard units, measured, countered and reduced to staple equivalence by impersonal, mechanical tests. In all its bearings the work is hereby reduced to a mechanistic, statistical consistency, with numerical stands and units; which conduces to perfunctory and mediocre work throughout, and knowledge, as contrasted with the pursuit of academic credits. So far as this mechanistic system goes freely into effect it leads to a substitution of salesmanlike proficiency – a balancing of bargains in staple credits – in the place of scientific capacity and addition to study (1918 [1993, p. 163]).

Utilitarian and Elective Curricula

The effects of the intrusive influence of business mentality were particularly visible in the recent trends toward elective curricula and vocational training. Here the contrast between Veblen and Smith who had advocated a form of student-consumer sovereignty is particularly stark. Veblen took a very dim view of electives, declaring that the introduction of electives which led to highly flexible curricula was responsible for carrying the American college off its footing as a school of probation and introduction to the scholarly life, and leaving it as a job lot of shortcuts into the trades and professions. The elective curricula reinforced the trend toward vocational training. Veblen noted that:

To meet the resulting range and diversity of demands, an increasing variety of courses has been offered, at the same time that a narrower specialization has also taken effect in much of the instruction offered. Among the other leadings of interest among students, and affecting their choice of electives, has also been the laudable practical interest that these young men take in their own prospective material success (1918 [1993, p. 143]).

Here the influence of workday-formed habits of thought on social attitudes was particularly evident. Parents support the vocational training/elective curricula approach because they want their sons to become equipped for material success. Businessmen laud this approach because they feel a need for a free supply of trained subordinates at reasonable wages. Veblen observed that 'this needed supply of trained employees comes to the business concerns in question at rates of wages lower than what they would have to pay in the absence of such gratuitous instruction' by the universities (1918 [1993, p. 144]). Doubtlessly, Smith would agree with Veblen's economic analysis, but perhaps not with the same degree of disapproval. Mill, however, would see this as exemplifying the tendency for private schools providing what the non-intellectual public wants.

But the prime mover behind the trend toward vocational training was the influence of the business animus on habitual attitudes in general, the 'current unreflecting propensity to make much of all things that bear the signature of the "practical"' (1918 [1993, p. 141]). The influence of the business animus is revealed as 'practical' means 'useful for private gain,' and as implying nothing about 'serviceability to the common good' (1918 [1993, p. 141]). Those outside the universities expect universities to be utilitarian training institutions, providing 'practical' training in the business sense. Those within the university establishments for vocational training were taking 'an apologetically aggressive attitude in advocating its claims' (1918 [1993, p. 140]). The same spirit shows up in the continuous revision of the undergraduate curriculum that leads to a multiplication of courses designed to provide or lead up to vocational training. Veblen observed that 'this permeation of the university's everyday activity is less visible to outsiders . . . but it touches the work within the university proper even more radically and insistently (1918 [1993, p. 142]). The consequences are that 'business proficiency' replaces the higher learning (1918 [1993, p. 142]).

Veblen declared that the 'incursion of pecuniary ideals in academic policy is seen at its broadest and baldest in the Schools of Commerce,' where 'facility in competitive business is to take the place of scholarship as the goal of university training, because, it is alleged, the former is more useful' (1918 [1993, pp. 149–150]). These seminaries of business had become the 'appointed keeper of the higher business animus' (1918 [1993, pp. 149–150]). Like the divinity schools, business schools are equally extraneous to the 'intellectual enterprise' on behalf of which the university is ostensibly maintained (1918 [1993, pp. 149–150]). But while divinity schools belonged to the old order and were losing their preferential hold on universities, schools of commerce belong to the new order and are gaining ground (1918 [1993, pp. 149–150]).

Wasteful Competition

Adam Smith had argued for competition based on reputation for students who are free to choose and who pay in large part the incomes of their professors. In contrast, Veblen argued that universities should not compete because scientific and scholarly research requires cooperation rather than competition – at the university level 'learning is in no degree a competitive enterprise' (1918 [1993, p. 171]). But he emphasized that American universities *were* competing, with negative consequences on true university work. He acknowledged that some extent universities engaged in competition because of location. But its persistence, form, and consequences all reflected the influence of business mentality. The most visible result of that competition is conspicuous waste, with excessive spending on buildings designed to impress rather than for service to scientists and scholars, and duplication of courses, programs, and publications, even in the graduate programs. Such competition is alien to true universities since the work of scientists and scholars is cooperative rather than competitive. But it reflects the businessman's emphasis on tangible assets as objects of expenditure and the non-pecuniary value of scientific and scholarly work. Veblen argued that the modern American 'university corporation' resembled a multi-product enterprise, especially those engaged in retail trade.

> It is one of the unwritten, and commonly unspoken, commonplaces lying at the root of modern academic policy that the various universities are competitors for the traffic in merchantable instruction, in much the same fashion as rival establishments in the retail trade compete for custom. Indeed, the modern department store offers a felicitous analogy, that has already been found serviceable in illustration of the American university's position in this respect, by those who speak for the present regime as well as by its critics. The fact that the universities are assumed to be irreconcilable competitors, both in the popular apprehension and as evidence by the manoeuvers of their several directors, is too notorious to be denied by any but the interested parties (1918 [1993, p. 65]).

Since universities are not business enterprises producing marketable products, what they compete for and the form that competition takes are different from the price competition of the business sector. Veblen emphasized that universities' competitive strategies were aimed at enhancing institutional prestige. The type of prestige most actively sought by universities is 'credible notoriety,' pursued through methods of publicity and salesmanship borrowed from business practices. That type of notoriety and the activities its pursuits induce conflict with the functioning of universities as seminaries of the higher learning:

> . . . any line of inquiry into the business management of the universities continually leads back to the cares of publicity, with what might to an outsider seem undue insistence. The reason is that the businesslike management and arrangements in question are habitually – are primarily – required either to serve the ends of this competitive campaign of publicity or to conform to its schedule of expediency. The felt need of notoriety and prestige has a main share in shaping the work and bearing of the university at every point. Whatever will not serve this end of prestige has no secure footing in current university policy. The margin of tolerance on this head is quite narrow; and it is apparently growing incontinently narrower (1918 [1993, p. 168]).

The 'gains' to the universities from their competitive pursuit of notoriety and prestige were increases in endowment funds and in enrollments. 'Painstaking cultivation of a reputable notoriety' is believed to be essential to avoid 'the more alert and unabashed rivals' diverting 'the flow of loose funds to their own use' and thus 'outstrip their dilatory competitor in the race for size and popular acclaim' (1918 [1993, p. 169]). Unlike in the business sector, the consequences of universities' competition based on notoriety and prestige were net losses because the costs of publicity promotion exceeded the gains in revenues, and wastes of resources:

> The net loss . . . is always much more considerable than would be indicated by any statistical showing; for this academic enterprise involves an extensive and almost wholly wasteful duplication of equipment, personnel and output of instruction, as between the rival seats of learning, at the same time that it also involves an excessively parsimonious provision for actual scholastic work, as contrast with publicity; so also it involves the overloading of each rival corps of instructors with a heterogeneous schedule of courses, beyond what would conduce to their best efficiency as teachers. *This competitive parcelment, duplication and surreptitious thrift, due to a businesslike rivalry between the several schools, is perhaps the gravest drawback to the American university situation* (1918 [1993, p. 170], emphasis added).

While the strategic goal was to enhance institutional prestige, the competition among universities on an operational basis is for students and endowments. Large numbers of students are of great importance in enhancing institutional prestige, and true university work is seriously compromised in the pursuit of that operational goal. Students are little interested in studies, and 'they have other interests that must be taken care of by the school, on pain of losing their custom and their good will, to the detriment of the university's standing in genteel circles and to the serious decline in enrolment which their withdrawal would occasion' (1918 [1993, p. 74]).

As a result of the business-like competition for students, there was an increase in the number of undergraduates enrolled, and Veblen speculated a decrease in the number of graduate students. That was occurring in part because the undergraduates were not being encouraged to go in for 'the disinterested pursuit of knowledge' that would lead them into graduate studies. The push of the movement toward 'a perfunctory routine of mediocrity' that had taken over the public schools and had made great headway in undergraduate work was certain to continue to the graduate level (1918 [1993, pp. 165–166]). Yet, Veblen noted that competition for students extended to graduate students, where competitive use of fellowships played a role. Whereas fellowships were previously 'an honorable distinction' while providing sufficient financial support for serious and capable graduate students to devote full time to scholastic work, under the influence of business principles rival universities now use fellowships to bid for graduate students. The purpose is to increase the numbers rather than the quality of graduate students. Fellowships were also being offered to 'induce enrolment in the professional schools' as well (1918 [1993, pp. 95–96]). Veblen added that the students 'are quite callously exploiting the system in that sense' (1918 [1993, p. 95]). In a footnote, Veblen observed that students intending to go to law school were accepting fellowships to enter academic doctoral programs, then switching to law (1918 [1993, p. 96]). While that would suggest that competition for graduate students would tend to increase the size of stipends, the business principles' influence on university policy led to just the opposite. Just as businessmen go for short-term returns, universities will be inclined to make the fellowships small and numerous to gain more graduate and professional students (1918 [1993, p. 96]).

While Veblen emphasized the extent to which business values and principles were influencing the competitive behavior of universities, he said nothing about pricing strategies in that competition. Indeed, he said surprisingly little about fees paid by students. It might be expected that universities emulating business enterprise would seek to maximize fee revenues, but that was not the case. Veblen stated that increasing enrollments will not increase universities' net revenues and that universities do not seek net revenues (1918 [1993, p. 171]). Fees were explicitly mentioned only once in *The Higher Learning in America*, and that was in relation to excluding middle and lower income students.

Veblen observed that while students do not bear the full cost of instruction of professional and vocational schools because that instruction was presumed to be worth more than its costs to students, the costs of attending schools of commerce effectively shut out those without income or wealth (1918 [1993, pp. 155–156]).

In contrast to Smith who said nothing about efforts to increase endowments, Veblen emphasized the competitive pursuit of donors and its consequences. He dwelled at some length on the use of endowment revenues for ornamental buildings to impress potential donors rather than paying faculty salaries and providing the libraries and buildings that support scientific and scholarly research. Veblen described the competitive pursuit of donors as being worse than a zero sum game. Prestige for universities does not bestow the pecuniary gains that it does for competitive business enterprise. It serves a pecuniary end only in the way of impressing potential donors, which was described as a 'highly speculative line of enterprise, offering a suggestive parallel to the drawings of a lottery' (1918 [1993, p. 101]). But the influence of habituation leads even the very well endowed universities to engage in the competitive quest for prestige, and universities pursue publicity well past the point justified by any comparison of gains from donors and the costs of the publicity (1918 [1993, p. 176]).

Negative Effects on Teaching and Research

Smith argued that the faculty members of the English universities as being induced into indifferent teaching because of assured incomes from endowments. In contrast, Veblen argued that university faculty members must receive sufficient incomes to enable them to give full attention to their scientific and scholarly work, and that those incomes must come in the form of stipends that must not depend in any way on any utilitarian pragmatic, i.e., pecuniary, value of the work involved (1918 [1993, pp. 85–86]; see also p. 110 and p. 124) because university work is 'extra-economic' in nature (1918 [1993, p. 85]) and cannot be classed as a gainful pursuit. It was largely the influence of business values that was causing poor teaching in American 'university corporations.' The business-like management in universities led to work being let to the lowest bidders on a roughly piece-wage plan. That arrangement could only produce inefficiency, waste, and stultification (1918 [1993, pp. 85–86]) because 'like other workmen, under the pressure of competition the members of the academic staff will endeavour to keep up their necessary income by cheapening their product and increasing their marketable output' (1918 [1993, p. 121]).

In the business view of the university as an academic enterprise, faculty members are employees who should be hired at the lowest possible wage.

Under the heavy influence of business mentality, American university teachers, especially those at the lower ranks, were so poorly paid that they engaged in outside work to supplement that income, which took time away from their academic work. In addition, universities offered so many different courses as part of their competitive publicity strategies that faculty members were assigned heavy teaching loads, which included too many different preparations in subjects that were not their specialties.

TRANSITIONAL STATEMENT

Thus, while institutional contamination could be attributed in part to the accidental institutional development of universities from existing colleges, the behavioral characteristics of competition among universities and the quest for institutional prestige were largely reflective of the extent to which business values, attitudes, and practices had intruded into the management of universities. Why and how that intrusion occurred, and how it related to the failures due to institutional contamination, were explained in Veblen's analysis of the internal decision-making processes through which universities' goals, academic policies, and internal resource allocations were determined. That analysis, which essentially sketched the main features of an economic model of university behavior, is examined in Chapter Six.

6. Veblen's Economic 'Model' of University Behavior

> . . . [i]t has appeared that the introduction of business principles into university policy has had the immediate and ubiquitous effect of greatly heightening the directorate's solicitude for a due and credible publicity, a convincing visible success, a tactful and effectual showing of efficiency reflected in an uninterrupted growth in size and other tangible quantitative features (Veblen 1918 [1993, p. 98]).

Veblen's normative critique emphasized the incompatibility between business values, principles, and practices and the societal function of universities as seminaries of the higher learning, devoted to scientific and scholarly work with no utilitarian interest. How business mentality was able to influence universities' institutional goals, academic policies, and resource allocations was explained in his positive analysis of the micro-structure of the internal decision-making processes of the large American 'university corporations.' While that analysis was linked to Veblen's social theory of instincts and institutional habits, it applied the economic approach of explaining decisions in terms of self-interested behavior of individuals within the institution. In this case, Veblen, who is usually regarded as being outside the mainstream of economics, developed the essential features of an 'economic model' of non-profit corporations that anticipated to a surprising degree the models developed by modern mainstream economists.

In Veblen's 'model,' the internal decision-making processes permit the personal 'motives' of the 'discretionary officials' of the university to influence institutional decisions. With several groups of 'discretionary officials' involved, the actual outcomes depend upon the extent of influence that each group is able to exert over the institutional decisions. Where Veblen's 'model' fundamentally differs from the modern economic models is in linking the motives of different groups of 'discretionary officials' to different systems of values.

The primary purpose of this chapter is to review Veblen's economic 'model' of the university as a non-profit institution. This involves identifying the discretionary officials and their value systems that give rise to conflicting motives. Why American universities were failing to function as true universities is then explained in terms of institutional behavior that satisfies the motives of those discretionary officials who are in dominant positions in the institutional decision-making systems of non-profit (private) universities.

Veblen assiduously avoided offering any suggestions for (or expressing any hope of) reforms in his critical analyses of the modern business enterprise system and its attendant social environment. Rather, he insisted that his purpose was only to describe *what was* without any pretense of knowing what *should be*. But in *The Higher Learning in America*, Veblen did comment, albeit in limited and obviously unrealistic fashion, on what his analysis might imply about institutional reforms that would allow American universities to function as true universities. Those 'reforms' are critically examined in the last section of this chapter.

UNIVERSITIES AS NON-PROFIT CORPORATIONS

Veblen consistently criticized the welfare aspects of neo-classical economics throughout all of his writings. At the same time, he accepted the profit-maximizing assumption of neo-classical models. In his analyses of the business enterprise system, firms and businessmen seek to maximize profits from production of 'vendible' or 'merchantable' outputs, and financial institutions and financiers seek to maximize gains from transactions in the securities markets. But Veblen explicitly recognized that universities constitute a different type of institution, with neither a formal proprietary interest nor a marketable output. While he mentioned state universities and their nominal control by state governments (politicians), his analysis dealt primarily with the decision-making processes for private universities, which in modern terminology would be non-profit institutions. Indeed, in the 'Preface' to *The Higher Learning in America*, Veblen acknowledged that he had initially drawn heavily from observations of the University of Chicago. And just as large 'public' state universities today function essentially as non-profit institutions, the 'university-grade' state universities in *The Higher Learning in America* became very similar to non-profit (private) universities (see, e.g., 1918 [1993, p. 32]).

In that respect, Veblen's use of the term 'university corporation' was particularly significant. His economic model of university behavior explains the internal decision-making processes within the corporate organizations of private (non-profit) universities. While there is no proprietary motive of maximizing pecuniary profits, university decision makers ('discretionary officials') use their discretionary power to make institutional goals, policies, activities, and internal resource allocations serve their own motives. The relationship between the motives of groups of 'discretionary officials' and the values and practices of business enterprise is the primary conduit through which 'university corporations' increasingly become subject to the influence of the methods and practices of modern large corporate business (1918 [1993, pp. 48–49]).

Two features of non-profit institutions figure prominently in Veblen's economic 'model' of universities' behavior. Those are the importance of endowments as a source of funds, and the form of governance in the absence of proprietors.

ENDOWED INSTITUTIONS

Veblen described modern universities as corporations of large funds (1918 [1993, p. 62]), 'possessed of large property and disposing of large aggregate expenditures' (1918 [1993, pp. 46–47]). Like Smith, Veblen placed heavy emphasis on the importance of endowments in university finance. The university 'is an endowed institution of culture, whether the endowment take the form of assigned income, as in the case of the state universities, or of funded wealth, as with most other universities' (1918 [1993, p. 110]). The endowments of 'university corporations' came largely from 'that more select body of substantial citizens who have the disposal of accumulated wealth' (1918 [1993, p. 134]). It had become an 'honourable custom among men of large means' to give to institutions without 'many restrictions on the character of the enlightenment which it is to serve' (1918 [1993, p. 134]).

Veblen differed from Smith on the role of endowments in two respects. The first difference is in how universities used endowments and the consequences of that use. The second was that unlike Smith, Veblen heavily emphasized the strategic efforts of modern 'university corporations' to solicit funds from donors. With respect to revenues received by universities, Veblen spoke almost exclusively about incomes generated from endowments, both in terms of the magnitude of those incomes and the purposes for which they were expended. Curiously, while he emphasized the competition among 'university corporations,' and the cost of pursuing competitive strategies, he said very little about incomes from fees and nothing about price competition. Indeed, all of the competition that he described was non-price competition that was aimed directly or indirectly at increasing donors and increasing student enrollments.

Governance and Control

In the absence of any proprietary interests, the question of governance and control of the university corporations arises. The charters that established the American universities (or the colleges from which the universities evolved) placed the ultimate control of the properties, endowments, and incomes in the care of governing boards. But these boards have relatively limited direct involvement in corporate governance of modern universities. Rather, the individuals who serve on the governing boards are members of the group of 'discretionary officials' who collectively make decisions. Veblen's economic model of university behavior explains the selection of institutional goals, academic policies, and internal resource allocations in terms of the 'motives' of the 'discretionary officials' and the degree to which each group of such 'officials' is able to influence university decisions.

IDENTITIES AND MOTIVES OF DISCRETIONARY OFFICIALS

Like Smith, Veblen applied the rule of self-interested behavior in his analysis of universities' decision-making process. His analysis, however, was more complex than Smith's analysis, in part because the institutional environment was more complex and in part because it was linked to his evolutionary social theory of behavioral tendencies. Institutional goals, academic policies, and internal allocations of resources were explained in terms of the motives of individuals in positions to have some influence on those decisions and the incentives that were provided (or the constraints that were imposed) by the institutional environment. But those motives were shaped by fundamental values that were explained in terms of his evolutionary social theory. The 'executive policy' of universities 'can be explained or understood only as the outcome of those motives that appeal decisively to the 'discretionary officials' (1918 [1993, p. 178]). But Veblen stated that 'What those incentives may be' is 'not altogether easy to say' (1918 [1993, p. 174]).

Our first task is to establish the identities and motives of the 'discretionary officials.' We begin by examining the two conflicting value systems that shape those motives. Those value systems give rise to two different views on the purpose and functions of universities. To a substantial degree, the 'motives' of individuals in positions of some influence on academic policy tended to be influenced by one or the other of the value systems, or occasionally, both.

Conflicting Value Systems

The traditional view of universities rested on social values that were associated with the instincts of idle curiosity and workmanship and had been sanctified by popular opinion. By this view, the university is the institution of higher learning, embodied in the group of scholars and scientists that constitute the faculty. Academic policy, including the management of material equipment and technical staff, is seen as subordinated to facilitating scholarly and scientific research and the teaching of the next generation of scholars and scientists.

The newer view reflected the influence of business values outside the realm of business activities. By this view:

...the university is conceived as a business house dealing in merchantable knowledge, placed under the governing hand of a captain of erudition, whose office it is to turn the means in hand to account in the largest feasible output. It is a corporation with large funds, and for men biased in by their workday training in business affairs it comes as a matter of course to rate the university in terms of investment and turnover (1918 [1993, p. 62]).

Under the older traditional view, the outputs of universities are not comparable to market concepts. The work of scholars cannot be quantitatively stated in a balance sheet, nor 'can that intellectual initiative and proclivity that goes in as the indispensable motive force in the pursuit of learning be reduced to any known terms of subordination, obedience, or authoritative direction' (1918 [1993, p. 63]). But under the new view, universities as competitive business houses are expected to achieve a 'voluminous turnover' (1918 [1993, p. 64]) as a proxy for the profits of business enterprise.

While the newer view has rapidly gained strength, the traditional view has not been completely suppressed:

. . . when all these sophistications of practical wisdom are allowed for, the fact remains that the university is, in usage, precedent, and commonsense perception, an establishment for the conservation and advancement of the higher learning, devoted to a disinterested pursuit of knowledge. As such it consists of a body of scholars and scientists, each and several of whom necessarily goes to his work on his own initiative and pursues it in his own way (1918 [1993, p. 62]).

As we will note later, some of the individuals who are 'discretionary officials' were influenced to some extent by both sets of values.

A number of Veblen's statements indicated that the 'discretionary officials' were only members of the governing boards and executive administrators. Similarly, his repeated statements that 'the present regime' is one of 'centralized autocratic rule' suggested that 'captains of erudition' unilaterally made all the decisions (1918 [1993, p. 62]). But the autocratic decision-maker model is actually superceded in Veblen's discussion by a pluralistic model in which some faculty become, at least in a limited way, de facto 'discretionary officials.' Hence, the values and motives of individuals in all three positions have to be considered.

Values and Motives of Members of Governing Boards

On one point there was definitely strong agreement between Smith and Veblen. Both expressed a negative view of control of universities by external authorities. Governing boards comprised of men from outside of academia legally controlled the American universities observed by Veblen. Those boards existed because the universities had emerged from the existing colleges, which being established largely for the preparation of clergy were governed by boards largely comprised of clergymen. The role of those clergymen had been to assure adherence to doctrine and to serve as 'sturdy beggars' for funds to support the colleges from the various church congregations (1918 [1993, p. 48]). In the case of 'university-grade schools,' over the years the governing body of these seminaries of learning underwent a transformation from a constituency of clergy to a board of businessmen. Businessmen lacked any knowledge pertinent to the higher learning, but their dominating presence on the governing boards reflected the habituation process in shaping public attitudes. The typical modern universities are corporations 'possessed of large property and disposing of large aggregate expenditures' (1918 [1993, pp. 46–47]), so the public perception was that men of substantial experience in financial and business matters should be in charge. Accordingly, responsibility to exercise full discretion in academic matters was passed to individuals whose success in business was taken as incontrovertible evidence of their competence to make decisions on affairs about which they had no special familiarity.

While 'discretionary control in matters of university policy' rested in the 'hands of businessmen' (1918 [1993, p. 46]), Veblen noted that the governing boards exercised little, if any, current surveillance of the affairs of the universities. Rather, the boards exercised only a directive oversight of the distribution of the universities' incomes over the several academic purposes. Permanent staff officials, e.g., fiscal officers and their clerical forces, were charged with the actual administration of the university's investments, income, and expenditures, with the boards, or their committees, formally reviewing balance sheets and vouchers submitted by the university's fiscal officers.

Even so, the board's pecuniary control was a substantial one since 'The academic staff can do little else than what the specifications of the budget provide for; without the means with which the corporate income should supply them they are as helpless as might be expected' (1918 [1993, p. 58]). Thus, while the board plays no effective role in the fiscal administration of the university, it exercises a discretionary control over the academic programs and activities through its control of the budget.

How the governing board utilizes its power-in-trust to influence the operations of the university reflects the motives of the members, which Veblen asserted were relatively easy to determine (1918 [1993, p. 174]). Individuals serving as trustees tend to have business values (even if they are politicians rather than businessmen). Veblen stated flatly that 'The fact is that businessmen hold the plenary discretion, and that business principles guide them in their management of the affairs of the higher learning' (1918 [1993, p. 57]).

The most obvious consequence of those business values is a preference for tangible assets, e.g., buildings, and quantifiable outputs. Veblen stated that 'There is, indeed, a visible reluctance on part of these business-like boards to expend the corporation's income for those intangible, immaterial uses for which the university is established' because those uses leave 'no physical, tangible residue, in the way of durable goods' (1918 [1993, p. 59]).

But the individuals who serve on the boards have more personal motives. Veblen remarked that 'it should not seem probable that motives of personal gain, in the form of pecuniary or other material interest, would have a serious part in the matter' (1918 [1993, p. 174]). But he hinted repeatedly that some members seek to utilize the financial assets of the university for their own pecuniary gain. In a footnote comment, he stated that:

> It may be added that now and again the discretionary control of large funds which so falls to the members of the board may come to be pecuniarily profitable to them, so that the office may come to be attractive as a business proposition as well as in point of prestige. Instances of the kind are not wholly unknown, though presumably exceptional (1918 [1993, p. 51, fn. and p. 49, fn.]).

Over and above any opportunity for personal pecuniary gain, there was a more basic motive of self-interest. People who serve on the boards have such 'a penchant for popular notability' (1918 [1993, p. 180]) that it was difficult to avoid the 'odiously personal interpretation' that 'these impassively purposeful men of affairs are greatly moved by personal motives of vanity' (1918 [1993, p. 174]). Veblen commented that:

> . . . election to one of these boards has come to have high value as an honourable distinction. Such election or appointment therefore is often sought

from motives of vanity, and it at the same time a convenient means of conciliating the good will of the wealthy incumbent (1918 [1993, p. 51, fn.]).

Thus, board members have a keen interest in activities that 'yield immediate returns in the way of credible publicity' (1918 [1993, p. 59]).

In addition to controlling the budget, the board also appoints the academic head of the university. In many cases, the alumni had much to say about the choice of the new academic head, but the sentiment among the alumni is essentially the same as among the members of the board (1918 [1993, p. 60]).

Values and Motives of the University Administrators

Veblen's analysis of the motives and behavior of administrators, i.e., presidents, was considerably more complex than his analysis of the motives and behavior of members of the governing boards. The university 'executive' appears both as an *institution*, i.e., a set of functions, duties, and powers, and as an *individual* with personal motives, and the distinction between the two (and whether there is a need to do so) is not always clear. At times, the 'executive' was described as being of the 'perfected type' of an autocrat in total congruence with the newer view of the university as a business house. But much of what Veblen said indicated the 'executive' existed in an imperfect form, having to observe to some degree both the traditional view of the university as an institution of higher learning and the new view. Some of Veblen's statements suggested that the behavior of the individual serving as the executive is institutionally determined, i.e., his behavior becoming habituated by the duties of that position. But other statements indicated some range of discretionary decision making, within which the executive's behavior is guided by motives of self-interest.

The 'Perfected Type' of Executive

The university executive of the 'perfected type' (1918 [1993, p. 69]) is autocratic and bureaucratic, having evolved from the administration of undergraduate colleges that Veblen likened to penal institutions. The person serving as the executive is simply an agent whose behavior is determined by the 'circumstances' (1918 [1993, p. 70]) of the position.

> In this episode of institutional growth, plainly, the executive head is the central figure. The light falls on him rather than on the forces that move him, and it comes as a matter of course to pass opinion on the resulting incidents and consequences, as the outcome of his free initiative rather than of the circumstances whose creature he is. No doubt, his initiative, if any, is a powerful factor in the case, but it is after all a factor of transmission; for he is

chosen for the style and measure of initiative with which he is endowed, and unless he shall be found to measure up to expectations in kind and degree in this matter he will go to the discard, and his personal ideals and initiative will count as little more than a transient obstruction. He will hold his place, and will count as a creative force in his world, in much the same degree in which responds with ready flexibility to the impact of those popular forces of popular sentiment and class conviction that have called him to be their servant. Only so can he be a 'strong man'; only in so far as, by fortunate bent or by its absence, he is enabled to move resistlessly with the parallelogram of forces (1918 [1993, pp. 70–71]).

Under the 'circumstances' in which the 'perfected type' executive is a creature, autocratic powers that are formally vested in a business-oriented governing board are delegated to the academic executive. Members of the board view the university 'as a business house dealing in merchantable knowledge' to be 'placed under the governing hand of a captain of erudition, whose office it is to turn the means in hand to account in the largest feasible output' (1918 [1993, p. 62]). They expect the executive to behave much like the executive head of a competitive business concern whose duties 'are of a strategic nature, the object of his management being to get the better of rival concerns and to engross the trade' (1918 [1993, pp. 65–66]). The executive head of the university must be a 'strong man' with a free hand to appoint, command, and discipline the academic personnel (1918 [1993, p. 60]).

One exercise of the controlling power of the 'perfected type' of academic executive is to select a group of advisors and agents, e.g., deans. While they hold administrative titles, their qualifications are complete and unquestioning sympathy for the executive's ideals and methods and an unreserved subservience. Hence, they scarcely count as 'discretionary officials.'

The Imperfect Case

Veblen noted, however, that the institutional 'circumstances' requisite for the 'perfected type' of executive had not yet fully emerged. The popular view that the true social function of the university is to serve as 'an establishment for the conservation and advancement of the higher learning, devoted to a disinterested pursuit of knowledge' (1918 [1993, p. 62]) still had some (although diminishing) influence. And in conjunction with this traditional popular view, there was still the academic tradition of the faculty being the keeper of the academic interests of the university, with the conduct of the academic affairs vested formally in the president, with the advise and consent of the faculty or senior faculty.

These institutional 'circumstances' require that the university 'make good both as a corporation of learning and as a business concern dealing in standardized erudition, and the executive head necessarily assumes the responsibility of making it count wholly and unreservedly in each of these divergent, if not incompatible lines' (1918 [1993, p. 64]). The executive administrator appointed by the board is to 'govern the academic personnel and equipment with an eye single to the pursuit of knowledge, and so to conduct its affairs as will most effectually compass that end' (1918 [1993, p. 63]). In all official pronouncements, these traditions must be duly observed and 'the scholastic purposes that notoriously underlie all university life' must be rigorously adhered to (1918 [1993, p. 68]).

The executive operates within a 'parallelogram of forces' (1918 [1993, p. 71]). The:

. . . 'exigencies of a businesslike administration demand that there be no division of powers between the academic executive and the academic staff,' while at the same time the 'exigencies of the higher learning require that the scholars and scientists be left quite free to follow their own bent in conducting their work' (1918 [1993, p. 71]).

This places the executive in an ambiguous position 'since the discretionary power of use and abuse is indispensable to the business-like conduct of the enterprise, while the appearance of scholarly co-partnery with the staff is indispensable to that prestige on which rests the continued exercise of this power' (1918 [1993, p. 191]).

A number of Veblen's statements about the academic executive as an individual suggested that his values and motives were exactly the same as those of the members of the governing board. Veblen repeatedly stressed that 'Where the power of appointment lies freely in the discretion of such a board, the board will create an academic head in its own image' (1918 [1993, p. 59]), and 'when and in so far as a businesslike governing board delegates these powers to the university's academic head, who is somewhat pre-emptorily expected to live up to the aspirations that animate the board' (1918 [1993, p. 61]). But a principal-agent problem for the board was clearly indicated by other statements. To be appointed to a high academic administration post, a candidate must show qualifications that will be viewed by the board members as being serviceable to their own goals (1918 [1993, p. 180]). But once he takes the office, it is a 'difficult question' as to what the appointed executive will do 'with the powers and opportunities so devolved on him' (1918 [1993, p. 61]). That question can only be answered 'in terms of the compulsion of the circumstances in which he is placed and of the moral wear and tear that comes of arbitrary powers exercised in a tangle of ambiguities' (1918 [1993, p. 61]).

Hence, the executive will enjoy some range of discretion within which his actions will reflect his personal motives. The extent of that discretion is, however, somewhat ambiguous. An important limiting factor is the specifications of the budget. Veblen noted that the 'permissible deviation in that respect are commonly neither wide nor of a substantial character' (1918 [1993, p. 59]). A wider range of discretion is created by the 'tangle of ambiguities' that arise from the dual nature of universities as institutions of both higher education and higher learning, and from the lack of knowledge on part of members of the governing boards about what universities actually do. This results in a version of the principal-agent problem for the governing board. Veblen observed that 'It is not an easy matter even for the most astute body to businessmen to select a candidate who shall measure up to their standard of business-like efficiency in a field of activity that has substantially nothing in common with that business traffic in which their pre-conceptions of efficiency have been formed' (1918 [1993, p. 60]). Since the executive is responsible to the board primarily in his observance of the pecuniary specifications of the budget (1918 [1993, p. 59]), he has discretionary choice over what will be done specifically within those specifications.

Given that the executive can exercise some discretion in deciding the types of academic policies to pursue, how will he act? What path will he choose to pursue within the 'tangle of ambiguities?' In a number of statements, Veblen suggested that the duties of the institution of the executive will shape the behavior of the man holding that position. For example 'The discipline of executive office will commonly shape the incumbent to its uses' (1918 [1993, p. 192]), and 'It is the duties of the office, not a run of infirmities peculiar to the incumbents of the office, that make the outcome' (1918 [1993, p. 197]). In a similar vein, Veblen commented that since scholarly activity does not produce a 'business-like showing' of 'large turnover and quick returns' it can wait, 'and it readily becomes a habit with the busy (academic) executive to let it wait' (1918 [1993, p. 64]). In speaking of the waste from competitive publicity, e.g., Veblen stated that 'the academic executives under whose surveillance this singularly futile traffic is carried on are commonly men of commonplace intelligence and aspiration, bound by the commonplace habits of workday intercourse in a business community' (1918 [1993, p. 172]).

Thus, despite Veblen's repeated claims that the point of the discussion was not the 'personal characteristics of the typical executive' but rather the 'run of events, and the conditions which determine them' (1918 [1993, p. 270]), the university administrator clearly emerges as an individual who pursues purposive behavior in utilizing the discretion which he enjoys, and his purposive behavior is guided by his own motives. What were those motives?

Veblen indicated that the motives of the academic executives were more 'obscure' than the motives of the members of the governing boards (1918 [1993, p. 174]). But clearly a strong element of self-interest is present that is visibly exhibited in a process of self-selection. Those who rise to the chief executive position are frequently ambitious men who have actively sought election to high office (1918 [1993, p. 179]). The executive understands that the university 'is to make good both as a corporation of learning and as a business concern dealing with standardized erudition' and 'necessarily assumes the responsibility of making it count wholly and unreservedly in each of these divergent, if not incompatible lines' (1918 [1993, p. 64]). However, his first concern will always be to 'take care of those duties that are most jealously insisted on by the power to whom he is accountable, and the due performance of which will at the same time yield some sufficiently tangible evidence of his efficiency' (1918 [1993, p. 64]). An efficient competitive market situation is suggested in Veblen's comment that if the administrator fails to do so 'His place would then be supplied by an incumbent duly qualified on this score of one-eyed business sagacity, and who would know how to keep his scholarly impulses in hand' (1918 [1993, p. 175]). This would seem to suggest that boards' principal-agent problem would be held in check.

But Veblen also described administrators as being energized by personal motives of 'vanity' (1918 [1993, p. 174]). The 'typical traits of the academic executive' (1918 [1993, p. 196]) included a strong desire for personal prestige. The class of people from whom members of the board and university executives are drawn are animated by an 'appetite for popular prestige' (1918 [1993, p. 203]), and have a propensity for 'self-aggrandizement' (1918 [1993, p. 204]). The university executive 'in his own right more readily appreciates those results of his own management that show up with something of the glare of publicity' (1918 [1993, p. 65]). In order to serve the dual masters of board and personal glory, each executive conducts 'meticulous manoeuvres . . . to enhance his own prestige and the prestige of his own establishment' (1918 [1993, p. 41]). Thinly veiled threats are issued as challenges to all administrators, faculty and staff that the traffic in merchantable instruction must be enhanced (higher rankings achieved, better academically qualified students enrolled); and, a "junta" is formed that is loyal and sympathetic to the agenda of the chief academic officer. Such policies make it clear to all university constituencies that the academic strongman means business and intends to provide the governing board with the immediate results and short-term returns that are imperative to them.

Values and Motives of Faculty Members

If institutional 'circumstances' made possible the 'perfected type' of academic executive so that autocratic centralized control existed, the values and motives of faculty members would have no relevance since academic policy would be entirely a matter of executive command. That was the case for 'the precarious class of schools made of the lower-grade and smaller . . . colleges' (1918 [1993, p. 109]). But the faculty of 'university-grade schools,' at least the senior-level faculty, retained some influence, in part as a general phenomenon because the tradition continued that the faculty is the keeper of the academic interests of the university (1918 [1993, p. 68]).

True Scholars/Scientists vs. 'Official' Scholars/Scientists

Veblen divided the faculty members into two groups – the true scholars/scientists and the 'official' or 'quasi-' scholars/scientists (or 'scholars by appointment') (1918 [1993, p. 189]). The values of the first group hold the higher learning in the highest esteem, and their motives were purely those pertaining to scholarly and scientific research. At one point, Veblen described them as being 'addicted' to the pursuit of knowledge (1918 [1993, p. 125]).

In contrast, the values and motives of the 'official scholars' or 'quasi-scholars,' whose eminence was based on common notoriety, i.e., 'the estimate of the unlearned' (1918 [1993, p. 131]), and sanctioned by administrators, were very similar to those of administrators and members of the governing boards. They often serve as advisors and aides to the executive, and as such must necessarily hold 'high (putative) rank as scholars and scientists' (1918 [1993, p. 69]). But their scholarly/scientific reputations are with the 'unlearned laity,' not with their peers in a seminary of higher learning. Their qualifications for being members of the executive's select group of advisors and agents are sympathy for the executive's ideals and methods, and an unreserved subservience. As individuals, they are motivated by the high academic rank and higher pay that comes with the positions of 'coadjutors and vehicles of the executive policy' (1918 [1993, p. 69]).

The 'official' or 'quasi-scholars' were most likely to be found in 'the humanities and the so-called moral and social sciences' (1918 [1993, p. 131]), including economics. In these fields, 'a clamorous conformity to current pre-possession, particularly the conventional pre-possessions of respectability, or an edifying and incisive rehearsal of commonplaces, will commonly pass in popular esteem for scholarly and scientific merit' (1918 [1993, p. 129]). Those in the social sciences 'who are by common notoriety held to be the leaders in this field of learning, and who therefore are likely to be thrown up by official preferment, are such as enlarge on the commonplace and the aphoristic wisdom of the laity' (1918 [1993, p. 133]). In particular, the 'official' scientists/scholars are most likely to defend the convictions of the well-to-do potential donors. 'One who purports to be a scientist in this field can gain popular approval of his scientific capacity, particularly the businessmen's approval, only by accepting and confirming those elements of the accepted scheme of life with which his science is occupied' (1918 [1993, p. 132]). Recall that Mill described the 'amateurs' in literary work as seeking 'celebrity' and avoiding the 'hard and troublesome' work of writing for newspapers in part because it did not provide celebrity status.

Students, Alumni, and the Laity

Students in *The Higher Learning in America* were portrayed as having any influence on academic policies in only one respect. That was in the discussion of vocational training and electives, where Veblen clearly disagreed with Smith and sounded much like Mill.

> Under the elective system a considerable and increasing freedom has been allowed the student in the choices of what he will include in his curriculum; so that the colleges have in this way come to refer the choice of topics in good part to the guidance of the student's own interest. To meet the resulting range and diversity of demands, an increasing variety of courses has been offered, at the same time that a narrower specialization has also taken effect in much of the instruction offered. Among the other leadings of interest among students, and affecting their choice of electives, has also been the laudable practical interest that these young men take in their own prospective material success. So that this – academically speaking, extraneous – interest has come to mingle and take rank with the scholarly interests proper in shaping the schedule of instruction. A decisive voice in the ordering of the affairs of the higher learning has so been given to the novices, or rather to the untutored probationers of the undergraduate schools, whose entrance on a career of scholarship is yet a matter of speculative probability at the best (1918 [1993, p. 143]).

Thus, students influence universities' behavior through an element of Smith's student-consumer sovereignty as universities compete for students by offering what students want.

The laity influenced universities' decision making very marginally through the academic executives. An important activity for the executives' publicity campaigns was speaking to groups of the laity. Those in self-selected attendance were largely 'the class of moderately well-to-do and serious-minded women who have outlived the distractions of maternity, and so have come to turn their parental solicitude to the common good, conceived as the sterilization of the proprieties' (1918 [1993, pp. 189–190]). In speaking frequently to such groups, the executives:

> . . . just as happens in all competitive retail business that has to deal with a large and critical constituency . . . find themselves constrained in their

management of the affairs of learning to walk blamelessly in the sight of this quasi-public spirited wing of the laity that has by force of circumstances come to constitute the public, as seen in the perspective of the itinerant *philanthropist* (1918 [1993, p. 190], emphasis added).

Veblen coined the latter term to describe the personality of the archetypical successful university executive who courts goodwill by a heavy schedule of public speaking (1918 [1993, p. 187, fn.]). Those wealthy few that are potential donors of endowments will be catered to, but their values and their views of what universities should do are the same as the members of the governing boards.

MODELING INSTITUTIONAL BEHAVIOR

With decisions about university goals, academic policies, and internal resource allocations made by the 'discretionary officials,' the nature of those goals, policies, and allocations will reflect what will satisfy the motives of those who function as 'discretionary officials.' The analysis is complicated by the rather shifting nature of the membership in that group. Much of Veblen's commentary suggested that only members of governing boards and presidents were 'discretionary officials.' He repeatedly described the political and economic positions of many members of university faculties as being highly marginal. In the 'perfected type' of autocratic centralized bureaucratic system, the faculty is viewed as 'hired men' who are expected to owe the president a 'hired man's loyalty' (1918 [1993, p. 184]). Poorly paid and with insecure tenure, faculty are forced to submit to the interests of administrators and trustees. They resist organizing as trade unions, and frequently settle for higher academic rank in lieu of higher incomes in bargaining on an individual basis (1918 [1993, p. 118, fn.]). Outside work engaged in for extra pay reduces their productivity as true scientists and scholars 'Like other workman, under the pressure of competition, the members of the academic staff will endeavour to keep up their necessary income by cheapening their product and increasing their marketable output' (1918 [1993, p. 121]).

If the 'discretionary officials' included only administrators and board members, university policies would be those that satisfy the common motives of these individuals. This explains the overriding importance of competitive prestige as the de facto goal of universities. The common element of vanity that appears in the motives of both university presidents and members of the governing boards explains the emphasis on *institutional prestige*. 'The incentives that decide the policy of publicity and guide its execution must accordingly be such as will appeal directly to the sensibilities of the academic head and the members of the governing board' (1918 [1993, pp. 173–174]). The prestige enjoyed by individual 'discretionary officials' derives from the prestige of the institution. In the case of the president, Veblen remarked that 'notoriety and the academic executive' are 'the two foci about which swings the orbit of the university world' in which the 'chief ulterior purpose' of university operations is 'the prestige of the university or of its president, which comes to the same net result' (1918 [1993, p. 167]).

The influence of business values on the motives of both the executives and board members explains the nature of the type of prestige that is sought as well as a good part of the competition among universities. The two converge nicely, with prestige serving as the strategic competitive factor. Barber (1988) has explained that the geographical dispersion and mushrooming growth of American institutions of higher education in the 19th century, making America 'a land of neighborhood colleges,' was largely due to long distances and difficulties in travel (p. 4). Veblen acknowledged that 'Critics of the present regime are inclined to admit that the colleges of the land are in great part so placed as to be thrown into competition by force of circumstances' (1918 [1993, p. 65, fn.]), and conceded 'though with doubt and reservation' that this might be true for colleges (1918 [1993, p. 65, fn.]). But he insisted that for universities no other motive had as much to do with shaping academic policy as competition that reflected the habits of thought induced by business experience being uncritically carried over into academic affairs. Veblen declared that 'there is no visible ground of such rivalry, apart from unreflecting prejudice on the part of the laity, and an ambition for popular acclaim on the part of the university directorate' (1918 [1993, p. 65, fn.])

The institutional prestige that satisfies the personal vanities of the members of the boards and administrators is largely with the 'unlettered' and well-to-do laity. Prestige of this type is associated with notoriety and publicity, phenomena of the influence of business values. Such prestige serves as the 'good will' of the university as a business house (1918 [1993, p. 98]), quantitatively based in a system of 'scholastic accountancy' in terms of 'academic bullion' (1918 [1993, pp. 76–77]). Competitively oriented, 'prestige value' is the product of salesmanship, the creation of an illusion of superior worth (1918 [1993, pp. 98–99]).

Yet, the prestige value of the presidential office comes from the illusion, rooted in the tradition of the office as it evolved from the American college president, that the president is the senior faculty member in a community of scientists and scholars devoted to the higher learning. Even as business values influence the view of the university as an competitive enterprise producing merchantable outputs, it is 'of the utmost moment to keep up, or rather to magnify, that appearance of scholarly competence and of intimate solidarity with the corporation of learning' before the laity (1918 [1993, p. 183]).

For a university, prestige for the university does not bestow the pecuniary gains that its counterpart 'goodwill' does for competitive business enterprises. *Prestige serves a pecuniary end only in the way of impressing potential donors*, which Veblen described as 'a highly speculative line of enterprise, offering a suggestive parallel to the drawings of a lottery' (1918 [1993, pp. 100–101]). There is a habituation element involved in universities' pursuit of competitive prestige that overrides pecuniary logic. Even the most well-endowed universities engage in the competitive quest for prestige, and universities pursue publicity well past the point justified by any comparison of gains from donors and the costs of publicity.

The thinly disguised personal vanities of board members and administrators are a large reason why universities engage competitively in conspicuous production of programs and courses, with heavily advertising of the numbers of students and courses offered (which is most easily applied to undergraduate programs). Physical facilities also lend themselves to publicity that evinces the size of the university's assets and the business-like efficiency in the management of those assets. 'These architectural vagaries serve no useful end in academic life' but 'they spread abroad the prestige of the university as an ornate and spendthrift establishment; which is believed to bring increased enrollment of the students and, what is even more to the point, to conciliate the goodwill of the opulent patrons of learning' (1918 [1993, p. 106]). A blending of the feudalistic pageantry of the ancient universities with the modern business reliance on notoriety and publicity leads to conspicuous 'exhibitions of quasi-scholarly proficiency and propagandist intrigue' (1918 [1993, p. 124]). 'Official scientists' with high reputations among the well-to-do and unlettered laity serve the need for 'advertising value' (1918 [1993, p. 129 and p. 134]).

Yet, as we noted above, the 'perfected' case of university governance by absolute authority of the chief administrator has not yet materialized in the real world. Consequently, the 'perfect scheme of low-cost perfunctory instruction, high-cost stage properties and press agents, public song-and-dance, expensive banquets, speech making and processions, is never fully rounded out' (1918 [1993, pp. 124–125]). Since administrators are still forced to at least pretend that university policy is based on the profitless quest for knowledge, the faculties of the 'university-grade schools' as keepers of academic interests are not entirely without influence. The public – the 'unlearned laity' – can easily be duped on that score by the 'pomp and circumstances, social amenities and ritual dissipation, quasi-learned demonstrations and meretricious publicity' that features the president and the 'official scholars' among the faculty. But a substantial number of the faculty may retain some conviction that the university exists for the pursuit of knowledge. The scholarly purpose of university work is never quite lost sight of since 'the general body of the academic staff is still made up largely of men who have started out with scholarly ideals' (1918 [1993. p. 126]). Indeed, there are some faculty members in whom the 'addiction to the pursuit of knowledge is too ingrained' (1918 [1993, p. 125]).

Balanced against this, however, is at least one suggestion that the faculties have a proclivity for the activities of pomp and demonstration attendant to the prestige based on notoriety and publicity.

> As bearing on this whole matter of pomp and circumstance, social amenities and ritual dissipation, quasi-learned demonstrations and meretricious publicity, in academic life, it is difficult beyond hope of a final answer to determine how much of it is due directly to the masterful initiative of the strong man who directs the enterprise, and how much of it is to be set down to an innate proclivity for all that sort of thing on the part of the academic personnel (1918 [1993, pp. 122–123]).

Veblen suggested that it might well be quite a bit of the latter, although the initiative and countenance has to come from the former (1918 [1993, pp. 121–122]).

But in relation to the quest for prestige, there is an important reason why those faculty members who are true scientists may have to be included in the group of 'discretionary officials' because their motives influence academic policy. The collective prestige of the university is made up in large part by the prestige of the various individuals attached to the university (1918 [1993, p. 78]). Although the prestige of the executive person was particularly important, 'the appearance of scholarly co-partnery with the staff is indispensable to that prestige on which rests the continued exercise of this power' (1918 [1993, p. 191]). Like the prestige of the executive, the prestige of the 'official scientists' was that of notoriety and publicity among the unlettered laity who are potential donors. But true scientists have a meritorious prestige earned by reputation: 'it is the work of science and scholarship, roughly what is known in American usage as graduate work, that gives the university its rank as a seat of learning and keeps it in countenance as such with laymen and scholars' (1918 [1993, p. 73]). Veblen remarked that 'the presence of scholars and scientists of accepted standing is indispensable to the university, as a means of keeping up its prestige . . . [the need is for] a man [who] achieves such notoriety for scientific attainments as to give him a high value as an article of parade' (1918 [1993, p. 128]). Such individuals usually hold scientific inquiry above business principles and will:

... in a measure, bend the forces of the establishment to a long-term efficiency in the pursuit of knowledge rather than to the pursuit of a reputable notoriety from day to day. To the enterprising captain of erudition he is likely to prove costly and inconvenient, but he is unavoidable (1918 [1993, p. 128]) . . . . Those scientists who have done great things have a business value to the captain of erudition as a means of advancing the university's prestige. In some measure the scientific men so intruded into the academic body are in a position to give a direction to affairs within their field and within the framework of general policy. They are able to claim rank and discretion, and their choice, or at least their assent, must be consulted in the selection of their subalterns, and in a degree also in the organization of the department's work (1918 [1993, p. 129]).

On the whole, the motives of administrators and members of the governing boards dominate, but incompletely, over the motives of the true scholars and scientists on the faculty, who are likely to be senior-level faculty, so that academic policies are inevitably biased toward the competitive quest for institutional prestige. Veblen noted that this applied also in the internal allocation of resources. Academic departments compete for the custom of students in much the same way that universities compete. Failure not only brings official discredit to the chief of the department but also 'wounds his self-respect' (1918 [1993, p. 82]). Here again the two types of prestige come into play. The undergraduate program is favored because it lends itself to promoting the prestige based on notoriety and publicity. The prestige of the graduate programs is based on reputation of the true scholars and scientists on the graduate faculties. The dominance of the administrators and board members in the 'discretionary officials' assures a preference for popular prestige, and that results in less for graduate programs where reputation for first-class scholarship and science is earned (1918 [1993, pp. 92–93]). Even within the graduate program, however, some activities lend themselves to popular prestige and notoriety, and administrators and trustees will favor these over the others.

INSTITUTIONAL DRIFT AND 'PROPOSALS' FOR REFORM

At times, Veblen suggested that an institutional drift toward the ideal university as a seminary of higher learning was dominant in the long run. But for the most part, he declared that the intrusion of business values and practices were certain to dominate, as demonstrated by the examples of two major universities – one in the Middle West (obviously Chicago, but perhaps Johns Hopkins) and one in the Far West (obviously Stanford). Both were established 'under conditions as favourable to the cause of learning as the American community may hope to offer' (1918 [1993, p. 193]). Both were sufficiently endowed 'to be adequate to the foundation of an effectual university, sufficient to the single-minded pursuit of the higher learning, with all the 'modern appliances' requisite to scientific and scholarly work' and the 'directive' heads were 'men who, at one point or another in their administration of academic policy, entertained a sincerely conceived ambition to create a substantial university, an institution of learning' (1918 [1993, pp. 193–194]). One favored the pursuit of scholarship, while the other favored the pursuit of scientific knowledgeable and serviceability. Both administrators had 'been selected by individual businessmen of the untutored sort' and allowed 'an unhampered discretion in their autocratic management of affairs' (1918 [1993, p. 194]). The outcomes were the same:

> Under pressures of circumstances, in both cases alike, the policy of forceful initiative and innovation, with which both alike entered on the enterprise, presently yielded to the ubiquitous craving for statistical magnitude and the consequent felt need of conciliatory publicity; until presently the ulterior object of both was lost in the shadow of these immediate and urgent maneuvers of expediency, and it became the policy to stick at nothing but appearances . . . . Both establishments have come substantially to surrender the university ideal, through loss of effectual initiative and courage, and so have found themselves running substantially the same course of insidious compromise with 'vocational' aims, undergraduate methods, and the counsels of the Philistines (1918 [1993, pp. 194–195]).

There was 'no longer a reasonable chance of their coming to anything of serious import in the way of the higher learning, even, conceivably, under the most enlightened management in the calculable future' (1918 [1993, p. 196]).

'Reform Proposals'

Veblen stated that 'from the point of view of the higher learning, and disregarding considerations extraneous to that interest, it is evident that this run of events, and the conditions which determine them, are wholly untoward, not to say disastrous' (1918 [1993, p. 198]). He also stated that his 'inquiry' was 'nowise concerned to reform, deflect, or remedy this current drift of things academic away from the ancient holding ground of the higher learning' (1918 [1993, p. 198]). But to avoid the appearance of merely offering 'negative criticism and citation of grievances' for the purpose of irritation, and 'as a means to a more adequate appreciation of the rigorous difficulties inherent in this current state and drift of things,' it was not 'out of place to offer some consideration of remedial measures that have been attempted or projected, or that may be conceived to promise a way out' (1918 [1993, p. 198]).

Veblen's presented proposals for reforming universities in both Chapter One and Chapter Eight of *The Higher Learning in America*. Those presented in Chapter One were written later, during the war, and were expressed in more diplomatic terms. More stridently radical proposals were presented in Chapter 8, where the tone is much different. Clearly, Veblen had no intention of suggesting 'reforms' that would be socially acceptable. Rather, his intent was obviously to infuriate those readers who might be supporters of the current system. We will address those 'reforms' first.

In his discussion of the governing boards, Veblen stated that:

> So far as regards its pecuniary affairs and their due administration, the typical modern university is in a position, without loss or detriment, to dispense with the services of any board of trustees, regents, curators, or what not. Except for the insuperable difficulty of getting a hearing for such an extraordinary proposal, it should be no difficult matter to show that these governing boards of businessmen commonly are quite useless to the university for any business-like purpose. Indeed, except for a stubborn prejudice to the contrary, the fact should readily be seen that the boards are of no material use in any connection; their sole effectual function being to interfere with the academic management in matters that are not of the nature of business, and that lie outside their competence and outside the range of their habitual interest (1918 [1993, p. 48]).

The only function served by these boards was 'a bootless meddling with academic matters which they do not understand' (1918 [1993, p. 48]). Their only reason for survival appeared to be 'an unreflecting deferential concession to the usages of corporate organization and control, such as have been found advantageous for the pursuit of private gain by businessmen banded together in the exploitation of joint stock companies with limited liability' (1918 [1993, pp. 48–49]).

Veblen also recommended dispensing with the academic executives who are largely responsible for directing university activities through the triad of 'visible magnitude, bureaucratic organization, and vocational training' (1918 [1993, p. 184]). He noted that that the American university president had institutionally emerged from the American college president who had originally been the senior member of 'a corporation of scholars' who was competent to serve as the faculty spokesman and to chair their deliberative assemblies. Veblen remarked that the office of university president was uniquely American, with no counterpart to be found in other countries because the typical universities in other lands had not grown out of underlying colleges (1918 [1993, pp. 182–183]).

The more statesman-like consideration of possible changes in Chapter One were written after the United States entered into World War I, and apparently after Chapter Eight recommendations had been formulated. Veblen noted the negative effects of the war on the communities of European scholars and scientists, including the loss of confidence in German scholars and scientists who had 'earned much of the distrust and dispraise that is falling to their share' (1918 [1993, p. 36]). Under the existing circumstances, America was in the best position to protect and expand knowledge. Veblen called for a beginning in the form of 'a joint enterprise among American scholars and universities for the installation of a freely endowed central establishment where teachers and students of all nationalities, including Americans with the rest, may pursue their chosen work as guests of the American academic community at large, or as guests of the American people in the character of a democracy of culture' (1918 [1993, p. 39]). He suggested that 'Measures looking to this end might well be made, at the same time, to serve no less useful a purpose within the American academic community' (1918 [1993, p. 39]). He noted the 'extensive and wasteful competitive duplication of plant, organization and personnel among the American universities, as regards both publications and courses of instruction,' particularly 'in respect of that advanced work of the universities that has to do with the higher learning' (1918 [1993, p. 39]), and the current pinch for funds these universities were experiencing due to wartime inflation. Pooling of common issues would offer relief. Since the 'competitive animus' runs deep in the habitual outlook of American schools, the practical solution would be to create additional 'extra-academic foundations for research' such as the Carnegie Institution. The increased productivity achieved during the war provided the ability to fund such institutions. He even suggested that there was 'at least a fighting chance' that members of the governing boards and executives might rise above their parochial interests to allow the seminaries of learning to 'turn their best efforts to their ostensible purpose, "the increase and diffusion of knowledge among men," and to forego their habitual preoccupation with petty intrigue and bombastic publicity' (1918 [1993, p. 42]).

While it might appear that Veblen was advocating research institutes, it is clear that he was not from his criticism of research institutes that had emerged in response to the failures of universities. He observed that 'one line of aggressively remedial action' was being tried as a means of 'relieving' universities of 'work which they are no longer fit to take care of. It is a move designed to shift the seat of the higher learning out of the precincts of the schools' (1918 [1993, pp. 198–199]). He was referring to the recent founding of 'certain large establishments, of the nature of retreats or shelters for the prosecution of scientific and scholarly inquiry in some sort of academic quarantine, detached from all academic affiliation and renouncing all share in the work of instruction' (1918 [1993, p. 199]). While many of Veblen's critics may have expected that he would have strongly endorsed these 'establishments of research,' he argued that they were capable of competently 'serving only one of the two joint purposes necessary to be served by any effective seminary of the higher learning; nor can they at all adequately serve this one purpose to the best advantage when so disjointed from its indispensable correlate' (1918 [1993, p. 199]). That one purpose was research, but effective research requires teaching. Veblen noted:

> . . . [t]his cuts out of their complement of ways and means one of the chief aids to an effectual pursuit of scientific inquiry. Only in the most exceptional, not to say erratic, cases will good, consistent, sane and alert scientific work be carried forward through a course of years by any scientist without students, without loss or blunting of that intellectual initiative that makes the creative scientist. The work that can be done well in the absence of that stimulus and safeguarding that comes of the give and take between teacher and student is commonly such only as can without deterioration be reduced to a mechanically systematized task-work, – that is to say, such as can, without loss or gain, be carried on under the auspices of a business-like academic government (1918 [1993, p. 200]).

Research institutes must depend upon scholars and scientists trained at universities, frequently as the type of individuals which the universities find to be of little use, not being suitable 'for the academic purposes of notoriety' (1918 [1993, p. 200]). But when this source dries up 'as it presently must, with the increasingly efficient application of business principles in the universities,' research institutions may be placed under 'pressure of instant need' to 'turn their forces to instruction as well as to inquiry' (1918 [1993, p. 200]). But if they do, the research institutions 'would incontinently find themselves drifting into the same equivocal position as the universities, and the dry rot of business principles and competitive gentility would presently consume their tissues after the same fashion' (1918 [1993, p. 200]).

Veblen's economic model of university behavior illuminates the motives for academic policy and its development and implementation. Although the pursuit for competitive prestige frequently exceeds the justification by any comparison to gains from donors or students, it becomes an end in itself in direct proportion to the vanity of the captain of erudition. The academic bullion or benchmark of scholastic accountancy is the comparative ranking of university programs. Since high relative standing in the academic market place requires superior salesmanship and the creation of an illusion of superior worth, resources are unavoidably misallocated and university corporations are subverted from the true mission of scientific and scholarly work and, thus, precluded from becoming seminaries of higher learning.

7. Riesman on Veblen and Modern Universities

David Riesman, a Harvard Law School graduate who became a sociology professor at the University of Chicago and then Harvard University, is included in this study of economic perspectives on universities' behavior for two reasons. The first is his sharp, at times almost bitter, criticism of Veblen's views on American universities. Riesman acknowledged that Veblen provided some unique insights into the institutional behavior of universities. But he disagreed with Veblen on the institutional functions of universities, and especially on the motives and roles of administrators and faculty members as 'discretionary officials.' Particularly interesting was his argument that Veblen's 'legend' that was based on *The Higher Learning in America* had exerted a negative influence on the behavioral tendencies of deans and university faculty members.

The second, and fundamentally more important, reason is Riesman's own behavioral analyses of American universities and colleges in the post-World War II era. In his introduction to the 1993 reprint edition of Veblen's *The Higher Learning in America*, Ivar Berg commented that most of the books on American higher education that have appeared since the 1960s will soon be forgotten. One of the few exceptions that Berg cited was Riesman's writings (in Veblen 1993, pp. xii–xiii). Those writings merit consideration because while Riesman did not attempt to formally develop an economic model of university behavior, his analyses of data generated through participant observation and survey research emphasized the fundamental importance of supply and demand trends in higher education. Moreover, he essentially adopted Veblen's approach of relating universities' behavior to the motives or interests of those in positions to wield some degree of 'discretionary authority.' In his perceptions of the motives and relative influence of the parties involved, Riesman frequently disagreed with Veblen. But Veblen's emphasis on universities' competitive quest for institutional prestige remained much in evidence.

Riesman's interpretations of the evolutionary institutional changes in higher education are particularly interesting. In *The Academic Revolution* (1968), Riesman and his co-author Jencks argued that in American universities faculties had achieved dominance over trustees, administrators, and students in the 1950s. John Kenneth Galbraith's depiction of the role of the 'educational estate' in *The New Industrial State* (1971) presented a somewhat different, but essentially complementing, view of the new power of the faculties of universities. Only twelve years later, Riesman reported in *On Higher Education* (1980) that what he and Jencks had interpreted as a permanent change in the relative bargaining position of university faculty had turned out to be only a short-term development. As a result of subsequent changes in supply and demand conditions in higher education, the faculty hegemony was eroding and a form of student-consumerism was emerging as the dominant influence on university decision-making. (Hence, the subtitle *The Academic Enterprise in an Era of Rising Student Consumerism*.) On the surface, at least, that seems to suggest that Veblen's ideal situation had actually evolved, only to be quickly replaced with the student-consumer sovereignty that Adam Smith had advocated.

RIESMAN'S CRITIQUE OF VEBLEN AND THE HIGHER LEARNING

Riesman's stated purpose in *Thorstein Veblen* (1953) was to develop a 'critical interpretation' that would expose the ambiguity and internal contradictions of Veblen's social theory and his critiques of institutional values and systems (1953, p. vii). It is often difficult to separate his attempts to objectively argue that Veblen failed to understand the institutional situations and his overtly subjective attacks on Veblen's personal character. Those attacks took the form of psychological analyses of character flaws that served to create motives for Veblen to produce ('with sly aggression') flawed social theories and invalid criticisms of institutional systems and values. According to Riesman, Veblen lacked 'conventional masculine prowess' and hid 'like a court jester behind a "masculine" façade of science and objectivity' (1953, pp. 41–42). Rather than being 'a victim of academic Babbittry,' Veblen 'conspired in his own exploitation' by 'subtle and unconscious ways,' actually wanting to be underpaid and denied promotion to higher rank in order to create an atmosphere in which little would be expected of him (1953, p. 11). An example of Riesman's psychological analyses was his explanation of the reported practice of giving blanket grades of 'C' to undergraduates as covering Veblen's fear of any one person taking precedence over another ('invidious distinction of persons') by repressing all equally (1953, p. 13). It also covered his fear of face-to-face meetings with individual students, and allowed him to avoid competing with other faculty members for students and the disappointment of seeing students choose other instructors (1953, p. 13).

In that manner, Riesman's critical evaluation of *The Higher Learning in America* was loaded with charges that Veblen failed to understand or appreciate the institutional nature of universities and sharp attacks on Veblen's personal character. But there were also some rather grudging acknowledgements of Veblen's unique insights into the world of higher education. Riesman described *The Higher Learning in America* as 'Veblen's wittiest book, the one where his shafts of satire, based on the closest observation of every scabrous detail, penetrated furthest; as an effective caricature of academia it has not been equalled' (1953, p. 100). In contrast to having only 'second-hand' knowledge of business and factory life, Veblen had done 'field work' for this book as a 'participant-observer,' which 'appears to be reflected in the effectiveness of the attack' (1953, pp. 100–101). But Riesman insisted that effectiveness was largely due not to its validity, but rather to the sly manner in which Veblen cleverly mounted the attack.

Defense of University Presidents and Competitive Publicity

Riesman seemed to agree with Veblen on the role and behavioral tendencies of businessmen-trustees. His main criticism was aimed at the accuracy of and the personal motives behind Veblen's portrayal of the role of university presidents as the 'captains of erudition.' He lamented the willingness of readers to be taken in by Veblen's devious misrepresentations and especially his pretence at being a moralist.

> Our willingness to let Veblen punish us for our sins is heightened by another stylistic device of his. As in a morality play, he dramatically sharpens the conflict of good and evil by personification: in academic life, the good guys are the faculty, the bad guys the president and trustees (1953, pp. 79–80).

In deriding Veblen for hiding behind the façade of a 'moralist' in his sly attacks on university presidents (and on businessmen), Riesman stated that his own biases would be perfectly plain to his readers (1953, p. 81). Those biases were very clearly indicated later in *On Higher Education* (1980):

> . . . my own observations led me to believe in the 'great man' (today we would say 'great person') theory of academic change or reform. Although individual faculty members might seek to make changes, they were almost invariably unsuccessful without support from the top, and it was often in fact the academic leaders, especially those in an earlier era who had authority and long tenure, who had a view of the whole and wanted to leave their stamp on an

institution as well as to keep up with its rivals and thus were less provincial than their faculties (1980, p. 293).

In conjunction with his criticism of Veblen's views on university presidents, Riesman also disagreed with Veblen's argument that the university is a specialized institution whose only functions are to conduct research purely for its own sake and to teach graduate students to become the scientists and scholars of tomorrow. Riesman rejected Veblen's call for institutional specialization. What Veblen termed 'the university corporation' had necessarily evolved as an institution to serve useful purposes ranging from teaching undergraduates to utilitarian training and public service. The fact was that viable institutions must serve a number of functions, including some which may be 'accidentally' linked by history without any logical connection (1953, p. 108).

Riesman argued that Veblen's 'habit of dramatic abstraction' produced a world history of predation in which in every social era is dominated by a different set of men gifted in exploit or selling 'specious but respectable intangibles.' In that context, Veblen's comparisons of what was honorable and respectable in modern civilization with barbaric behavior in previous eras were more 'witty than revealing' (1953, p. 101). But in his comparison of university presidents with the 'Captains of Industry' of the 19th century, Veblen revealed some original insights about the nature of entrepreneurial activities in American life. Riesman described, with obvious approval, the executive administrators of universities in the 1950s as having inherited much of those entrepreneurial energies, having taken over much of the spirit and drive of the early captains of industry. In contrast, modern businessmen had become rather cautious and anemic heirs of those early entrepreneurs (1953, p. 101). Veblen would view that development as an unequivocal victory by business enterprise, as its methods, morals, and models having captured the 'holy places' of American culture (1953, p. 101). But Riesman interpreted it as a clever academic resistance to the intrusion of businessmen by a 'partial incorporation' of the business model, effectively turning business methods against the businessmen. The 'overly cynical observers' who viewed the University of Chicago as one of Rockefeller's 'false fronts' were wrong. In actuality, Rockefeller was being victimized by William Rainey Harper's ability as a salesman, an ability that was acquired by many non-businessmen in a business culture (1953, pp. 101–102).

Riesman conceded that Veblen's portrayal of Harper as president of the University of Chicago was more or less accurate, but argued that Veblen failed to take in the whole picture. He saw the university president in only one of his several roles, 'the salesmanship of the university's intangible assets in the marketplace and conversely his efforts as face-lifter within the academic walls in order that there be something to sell' (1953, p. 105). At the time Veblen was writing *The Higher Learning in America*, university faculties were becoming stronger and more outspoken and critical, which generated pressure against them from the business community (p. 104, fn.). In arguing that even a good and honest scholar would become corrupted by the institutional system upon being appointed university president, Veblen failed to appreciate the possibility that presidents, who were coming from faculties rather than the clergy, were playing a double game. As internal academic leaders, they were fostering scholarly research. As external leaders, they were protecting university scientists and scholars, rather than jeopardizing their research, by public relations work vis-à-vis the trustees, alumni, and the community at large. Veblen was unable to see (or refused to admit) that a president might employ his parental bent in fostering scholarship rather than in sabotage of it, that non-scholarly morale factors in the control of an academic administrator might lead to an increase in genuine research (1953, p. 105).

Rejecting Veblen's criticism of competition among universities, Riesman defended Harper's extensive reliance on competitive publicity. The reality was that as a new midwestern school, the University of Chicago had to compete with the wealthy universities of the Eastern Seaboard. Harper had to engage in high-pressure promotion because the university could not count on loyal generations of alumni who part with their sons and testamentary trusts on the basis of unshakable tradition. Rather, Chicago and other newer institutions had to appeal to 'new money' by advertising, naming buildings, and all the other things that attract favorable notice (1953, p. 103). As an illustrative case, a later Chicago president, Robert M. Hutchins, shared Veblen's views on the need to separate graduate level research from undergraduate and vocational education and from all student entertainments, such as football and fraternities. Academically, Hutchinson actually implemented 'the essentials of a Veblenian program' at Chicago. But his approach was the same as Harper's, using his 'very creative energies' to 'take power and prestige away from the faculty and (whatever his personal selfishness) made use of it in the national market for students, funds, and veneration' (1953, p. 102).

In defending university presidents, Riesman attacked Veblen's views on who would be included in the university faculty and restricting university students to serious mature people bent on becoming scientists and scholars. Veblen was 'vain-gloriously impractical' in his concept of the ideal university, posing as an academic conservative who preferred 'a must Oxford to a bustling, vocationalist American state university' (1953, p. 103). The true impracticality of *The Higher Learning in America* was Veblen's 'insistent assumption that an autonomous faculty, free of any bureaucracy, would return to a primal state of disinterested, generous, and collective pursuit of idle curiosity' (1953, p. 104) and universities could run themselves once the trustees and presidents had been removed. (But here again, Riesman accused Veblen of playing a sly game as his belief in the innate seriousness of faculties was only 'assumed as a polemical device to sharpen his attack on presidents and governing boards' (1953, p. 105).)

While seeming to concede that Veblen's economic model of 'discretionary officials' pursuing their vested interests had some explanatory power, Riesman criticized it as being too narrowly focused. In suggesting that the academic struggle among the 'discretionary officials' for dominance was between the administration and the faculty, Veblen failed to see that vested interests were numerous within the university. The vested interests of the president are countered by the vested interests of their faculties, comptrollers, deans, and various groups in the support staff. Within faculties, different individuals and groups have vested interests in fields or methods, in what counts as research, and what the curriculum should include. Each of these has some opportunity to act as a 'discretionary official' because to some extent each has the ability to exert at least a negative impact on consensus decision making, if only by passively withholding their efforts (1953, pp. 76–77). (One is reminded here of the ratifying power of each type of specialist in Galbraith's 'technostructure' in the *New Industrial State*.)

Riesman's criticism of Veblen's views on teaching and students was more personal (disguised as psychological profiling) than analytical in orientation. He recounted the popular anecdotes about Veblen's indifference to teaching, and criticized Veblen's contention that university-level students and teaching are different from students and teaching in undergraduate colleges and professional/technical schools. Rather than giving Veblen credit for editing the *Journal of Political Economy*, Riesman described that work as a way to avoid accepting 'the slightest drudgery connected with the curriculum.' Veblen was unable to 'muster the energy to cope with the diurnal routines of teaching, any more than, in his later years, of housekeeping and the most elementary attention to his own affairs' (1953, p. 106). Veblen had a negative reaction to students because of 'his uneasiness in the presence of the energies of adolescence, whether these were devoted in the more typical fashion of the day to football and dissipation or to an idealistic search for the true, the beautiful, and the good' (1953, p. 107). He 'liked children (at least in small doses), hated and feared adolescents, and admired those who had put childish things away' (1953, p. 107). Hence, Veblen developed a social theory in which the peaceful savagery of primitive cultures is glorified as the childhood of man, militant barbarism from feudalism through the modern business enterprise culture is lampooned as the all-too-prolonged adolescence of mankind, and the industrial society (with scholarship and science as counterparts in education) is the freedom from 'adolescent muscularities, rivalries, and illusions' (1953, p. 107).

The Effects of Veblen's 'Legend'

In what was perhaps his most bitter attack on Veblen's character and motives in writing *The Higher Learning in America*, Riesman charged that he was a sneaky, cowardly 'academic wobbly,' a slyly effective saboteur of university administrators (1953, p. 107). Riesman's extreme bitterness toward *The Higher Learning in America* appears to be have been due to a perception that Veblen's 'academic legend' (1953, p. 107) had had a negative influence on the American academic culture. That influence was partly due to Veblen's ability to vocalize and rationalize his 'uneasiness vis-à-vis students' and his desire for 'an 'ideal' student who would be all help and no trouble to anyone' (1953, p. 107). But mainly, it stemmed from Veblen's insistence that the true university had only one function (1953, p. 107). Riesman contended that 'academic people' are particularly receptive to the argument that institutions should return to their single original function, and readily accept the notion that their only function should be doing research, not counseling the young, reforming the cities, or engaging in academic politics and publicity (1953, p. 107).

Riesman argued that Veblen failed to realize (or refused to admit) that every viable institution serves a congeries of functions, some without any logical connection. In that manner, universities have survived by catering both to apprentice-level scholars and scientists and to gilded youth seeking appropriate rites of passage (1953, p. 108). In multi-function universities, some operations will bring prestige, while others will be the 'dirty work' that has to be done. Riesman declared that Veblen's influence contributed to increasingly highest status accorded to research and the lowest to 'bureaucracy' and 'politics.' He compared the continuing influence of Veblen's belief that university bureaucracy is not necessary to the way in which 'the analogous Manchesterism hangs on among opponents of "government intervention"' (1953, p. 108). That attitude had contributed to the creation of obstacles to doing the routine tasks needed in any large enterprise (1953, p. 108).

It had also contributed to building up fierce suspicions at the least signs of a parental bent on part of university administrators (1953, p. 108). In a curious footnote statement, Riesman seems to blame Veblen for administrator's negative dealings with faculty members. University deans had become unconsciously hamstrung by a 'bad conscience' that Veblen had helped create by arguing in *The Higher Learning in America* that their usefulness to the true function of the university was nil since they were no longer scholars. Because deans envy faculty members who are still scholars and feel that their own share of the total multiplicity of university functions is inferior, they are unable to be more generous and helpful (1953, p. 108, fn.).

Riesman blamed the influence of *The Higher Learning in America* and Veblen's 'legend' for helping to generate 'many guardedly inefficient academic bohemians,' who are proud of their inability to perform routine teaching and service duties or write memoranda 'not tainted by irrelevance' (1953, p. 109). At the same time, however, he made a partial concession to the accuracy of Veblen's analysis. To some degree, that 'cult of incompetence' was a reaction against the earlier type of 'Philistine businessmen' who scorned those who had not 'met a payroll,' and also against 'the strident joviality of many vulgar, still-adolescent men who were adepts of academic intrigue' (1953, p. 109). Thus, *The Higher Learning in America* had served to encourage a useful counter-style among academicians (1953, p. 109). But Riesman contended that Veblen went too far, and actually encouraged a type of academic snobbery, a hierarchy of rankings in which research activities were at the top. Themes and phrases from Veblen's book have helped in the United States, along with many more important influences, to nourish and sustain 'academic complacencies' within the universities (1953, p. 109).

Riesman argued that ironically while Veblen thought universities were succumbing to businessmen, just the reverse was occurring. The prestige of university careers was now luring young men into natural or social sciences rather than banking or other business careers. The growing competitiveness in academic careers and loss of gentility was due more to the entry of these young men than to businessmen as trustees. But through it all, Riesman conceded one of the major points in Veblen's positive analysis of universities' behavior, namely that universities' pursue in a competitive fashion the institutional goal of prestige. Riesman argued that the greater prestige of universities was luring the young because they also were seeking prestige. At the same time, being university scholars and scientists satisfied motives that had been heavily influenced by Veblen's criticism of businessmen and business values. Holding university positions 'allowed them to pose as gentlemen amiably superior to business-like conduct both within and without the ivied halls' (1953, p. 109).

RIESMAN ON MODERN UNIVERSITIES: AN ERA OF FACULTY DOMINANCE

Despite Riesman's criticism of Veblen and *The Higher Learning in America*, his own analyses of modern universities essentially followed Veblen's approach of explaining institutional decisions and performances as reflecting the relative power of the groups with an interest in university policies. But he not only disagreed with Veblen on the motives and functions of university administrators, he offered two different interpretations of who constituted the dominant 'discretionary officials.' In this section, we examine the argument presented in *The Academic Revolution* (1968) that university professors had achieved 'faculty hegemony' by the 1950s. The major points in that analysis were that university faculty: (1) had become professionalized; (2) had gained dominance; and (3) had implemented a 'meritocracy' that emphasized research. That would seem to suggest an institutional blending of Smith's faculty-dominated universities and Veblen's ideal of seminaries of higher learning.

How University Faculties Gained Dominance

As an evolutionary development, the professionalization of university professors began with the rise of American universities in the late 1800s. That led to the growing importance of granting Ph.D. degrees and having faculty member with earned doctorate degrees. By World War I, several dozen major universities had emerged, and the number had grown only slightly by the 1950s. A relatively high degree of uniformity developed among institutions, academic staffs, and academic programs. Institutionally, all of the major universities were placing high importance on producing Ph.D. degrees in more or less standardized programs of classes and research activities. As fields of study became more specialized, those earning the Ph.D. in each field had similar ideas about what the field covered, the correct pedagogical methods, and how the frontiers of knowledge should be advanced through research. That did not mean complete uniformity and standardization within the academic profession. Rather, when contrasted with other interested parties in the affairs of universities – trustees, administrators, parents, students – the outlook of Ph.D.s in a given discipline seemed quite uniform. For those working in scholarly and scientific pursuits, that uniformity was maintained as academic disciplines established professional associations that held annual national and regional meetings, published national journals that reported research results in every specialized subject, and established an informal national system of job placement and replacement. By the 1950s, Ph.D.s had come to regard themselves almost as independent professionals like doctors or lawyers, responsible primarily to themselves and their colleagues rather than to their employers, and committed to the advancement of knowledge in their specific academic fields rather than any particular institution (1968, pp. 13–14).

As professionalism spilled over into the administration of universities, one important effect was a diminished role of trustees (1968, p. 15). In

Veblen's era, the basic issue was whether the president and trustees or the faculty would determine academic matters such as the curriculum, content of particular courses, or the use of particular books (1968, p. 15). While individual faculty members lost battles (Veblen was cited as an example), the faculty as a whole ultimately won the war. In modern universities, faculty, as professional scientists and scholars, have control (on a departmental basis) over curriculum matters, degree program requirements, courses, and teaching methods that is rarely challenged. In principle, ultimate control still mostly remained with the presidents and trustees as budgets and personnel decisions formally remained subject to 'higher' review (1968, p. 16). But relative to their counterparts in Veblen's era, modern trustees had become 'permissive' and 'more sensitive to individuals and groups unlike themselves' (1968, p. 16). Drawn largely from the 'upper-middle class,' modern trustees exhibit that class's general tendency to want to avoid 'trouble' of any type. Hence, they will usually go along with any 'strong internal pressure for a given course of action' (1968, p. 16). On most matters, trustees seek to avoid complex issues that can not understand, and delegate authority to college presidents who as Ph.D.s can claim professional expertise.

In a Veblenesque statement, Jencks and Riesman commented that 'One reason boards spend so much time on buildings and grounds is that trustees feel at home in this area, presidents regard it as useful occupational therapy for them, and usually the decisions on these matters can wait (1968, p. 16). (The latter part of the statement contrasts with Veblen's observation that presidents could let the scholarly issues wait.) With admitted exceptions, Riesman and Jencks perceived the overall trend as being toward moderation and an increasingly ceremonial role for trustees. Beyond ceremony, they can be useful as buffers to cope with legislators, potential donors, and other pressure groups, giving legitimacy to the institution and its activities that would otherwise be hard to achieve' (1968, p. 17).

An unusual aspect of the transfer of power from boards of directors to administrators in the universities was the extent to which the presidents, while nominally acting in the interests of the board, were actually representing the interests of the faculty to the governing boards and to external world (1968, p. 17). Usually beginning as members of professionalized faculties, presidents inevitably become somewhat 'deprofessionalized' after becoming administrators. Nevertheless, they generally still see the universities primarily as an assemblage of scholars and scientists, each of who is doing his own work in his own way' (1968, p. 17). The typical university president's greatest ambition is usually 'to "strengthen" his institution, and operationally, this usually turns out to mean assembling scholars of even greater competence and reputation than are now present' (1968, p. 17). University presidents often have to make compromises that offend faculty, and they serve as convenient scapegoats for faculty (especially 'weak' faculty who are not productive researchers). While they are more responsive to students than most faculty, their greatest concern is with keeping faculty happy (1968, p. 18). Thus, a faculty that is unified (often not achieved) has an informal veto at most universities and colleges' (1968, p. 15).

Professionalism was only part of the equation that led to the power of faculty to do what they wanted, namely, to engage in research. Ultimately, the most important development was one of simple economics – an imbalance between demand and supply that had occurred largely in the post-World War II era. With the swelling numbers of students enrolling in universities, the demand for university services increased faster than the supply of institutions and Ph.D.s to do the teaching. But the really critical development was the large amount of research funds that were made available by the federal government. The result was to further enhance the status of the scientist/scholar as a prime fund raiser for the university. Since the amount of research support had grown much faster than the number of competent researchers, qualified scientists and scholars were in very short supply. Thus, they could use their market power to command rapidly rising salaries and the freedom to set their own working conditions.

The Effects of Faculty Dominance

The new faculty power had been used to impose an academic 'meritocratic system,' with new faculty members chosen on basis of their output and professional reputation and graduate students chosen on basis of similar criteria – the ability to write good examinations and do good academic work (1968, p. 19). The results were a rapid decline in teaching loads for productive scholars, an increase in the ratio of graduate to undergraduate students at the institutions where scholars are concentrated (Veblen's 'university grade' schools), 'the gradual elimination of unscholarly undergraduates from these institutions, and the parallel elimination of unscholarly faculty' (1968, pp. 14–15). The power of faculty led to departments and whole institutions seeking '. . . to become more distinguished by using the expansion of their student enrollments to recruit more faculty members than would have been necessary on the basis of earlier teaching loads and student/faculty ratios, thus allowing the build-up of graduate and research programs, which grew even more rapidly than undergraduate enrollments.' Distinguished faculty members were recruited 'who could make use of graduate teaching assistants to spare the faculty members the "handicraft labor" of working with any but the most committed and adept undergraduates' (1968, p. 2).

Jencks and Riesman argued that the effects of the dominance of a professionalized faculty of Ph.D.s on undergraduates were not felt until the 1950s when the number of young people applying to college increased steadily. This gave colleges a choice between expansion and greater selectivity. Faculty preferred the latter, and the result was that the leading undergraduate colleges began demanding higher academic aptitude and more proof of academic motivation. This increased the attractiveness of the academic profession and the proportion of undergraduates wanting to go on to graduate study increased. Pre-World War II undergraduates were described in more Veblenian terms, and as generally being not very vulnerable to faculty pressures (1968, p. 23). As more students wanted graduate school admission, they became more concerned about grades to win acceptance. The 'university college' emerged primarily to prepare students for postgraduate work – a de facto prep school for a small number of graduate professional schools (1968, p. 24).

Through the process of emulation, non-university colleges (Veblen's 'lower schools') began hiring Ph.D.s and recruiting faculty members in national markets. In turn, the new and better-trained faculty helped to propel the colleges to recruit academically-able students. Riesman and Jencks argued that even administrators and trustees seemed to be more often chosen according to the criteria of achievement, competence, and judgement that prevailed in established universities with national reputations (1968, p. 25). Presidents less often thought of themselves as presidents of special-interest colleges, e.g., to prepare public school teachers, but rather as presidents of academically first-rate, second-rate, or third-rate institutions (1968, p. 25). One consequence of the established national institutions of higher education was to make higher education look like a fairly effective instrument for sorting and grading of future employees of other established national institutions – public and private (1968, p. 26). Jencks and Riesman declared that the 'university college' had become the model for the future, and the result was likely to be a continuing trend toward meritocracy (1968, p. 27).

For Veblen, the true university was the graduate program, and his normative analysis was couched in terms of how that level of research and education was affected by institutional practices. In last chapter of *The Academic Revolution*, entitled 'Reforming the Graduate Schools,' Riesman and Jencks emphasized the importance of graduate programs under the professionalism installed by the new faculty hegemony. But whereas Veblen lamented the contaminating effects of undergraduate colleges (along with technical and professional schools) on graduate level work, Riesman and Jencks expressed concern about the influence of graduate schools over undergraduate education. They declared that:

If this book has any single message it is that the academic profession increasingly determines the character of undergraduate education in America. Academicians today decide what a student ought to know, how he should be taught it, and who can teach it to him. Not only that – their standards increasingly determine which students attend which colleges, who feels competent once he arrives, and how much time he has for non-academic activities (1968, p. 510).

It must be noted, however, that what Riesman and Jencks included as graduate level work included much of what Veblen would view as professional and technical schoolwork.

Riesman and Jencks argued that undergraduate students were now better, well prepared, and interested in academic work. While research had distracted some able senior faculty from undergraduate teaching, there was still some prestige among scholars (as opposed to engineers, businessmen, or school administrators) in teaching. And since undergraduates were more competent, sophisticated, and mature than they once were, colleges were treating them more and more as they have traditionally treated graduate students (1968, p. 513). Faculty were less inclined to see themselves as policemen. Evidently, the 'academic bohemians' who had been encouraged by Veblen's book and 'legend' that Riesman had complained about in 1953 disappeared from the scene in the era of faculty dominance.

The American graduate school has become the envy of the world, and one of the central institutions of American culture, with both the worst and the best in undergraduate education emanating from it. Riesman and Jencks sounded almost like Veblen in stating that 'the overall quality of American intellectual life depends on it than on any other single institution' (1968, p. 514). What is defined by graduate schools as research is what will get done, while what they exclude will likely languish. Graduate schools have achieved 'an essentially emperial relationship' with undergraduate colleges, importing the colleges' gifted graduates and training them as scholars. They keep the best for themselves and export the rest to teach the colleges to become teachers. They maintain their empire by keeping order and maintaining standards (1968, p. 515).

Riesman and Jencks went into lengthy discussions of perceived problems of this 'graduate emperium' and offered suggestions for reform. That which is interesting within the context of this study has to do with who decides the proper subjects of research and how those decisions are made. The 'academic profession' seeks to ensure that everyone will draw up his research agenda to please his colleagues by making the test of good research the influence it has on other scholars. This is the 'pure' work, on which basis promotion and tenure decisions are made by departments. But government and major foundations that provide research funds are primarily interested in non-academic problems. Hence, their funds go to those engaged in applied research. The methodologies, however, are the same. Applied research is desired largely because the funders are impressed by the methodological competence of university professors, but want to redirect it in new areas (1968, pp. 516–517).

Galbraith's Educational and Scientific Estate

A complementing view of the importance of research activities of university faculty was presented in Galbraith's 1967 book, *The New Industrial State*. In briefly tracing the development of higher education in the United States, Galbraith drew on Veblen's account of businessmen attempting to impose pecuniary values on the academic community, but argued that the 'doctrine of financial paramountcy' was not fully accepted by that community (1971, p. 286). The conflict between academics and business communities was aggravated by the role of colleges and universities as a principal source of social innovation, which was often opposed by conservative businessmen (1971, p. 287). While Galbraith accepted that Veblen was correct in asserting that academic expression was often accommodated to the conservative wealthy middle class's values, he argued that the academic community might well have given more than it received in the conflict by virtue of its capacity for social invention.

But the relations between those associated with economic enterprise and the academic community underwent a radical transformation with the emergence of the new industrial state. The technostructure is deeply dependent on the educational estate for its supply of trained manpower, and its needs to maintain a close relationship with the scientific sector of this estate to insure that it is safely abreast of scientific and technological innovation. The mature corporation is much less troubled by the social inventiveness of the educational estate. Two social innovations in the field of economics were particularly important for planning and thus the success of the technostructure – regulation of aggregate demand and the more tentative steps toward stabilization of prices and wages (1971, pp. 290–291). As the decisive factor of production has become the supply of qualified talent, a similar complex of educational institutions has come into being to supply this need. Attitudes accordingly changed, and education (rather than thrift to accumulate capital) has now the greatest solemnity of social purpose. The educational estate has acquired prestige from the productive agent it supplies, and that potentially at least is a source of power (1971, pp. 283–284).

The business executive no longer sits on the college board as a source of worldly knowledge and a guardian against social heresy. Rather, his presence provides him with an opportunity to maintain closer liaison with sources of talent or to keep more closely abreast of scientific and technological innovation. While the corporation president has become increasingly a traditional or ceremonial figure in his association with education, the modern scholar of science, mathematics, information systems, or communications theory is ever more in demand to guide the mature corporation through its besetting problems of science, technology, and computerization (1971, p. 292). A member of the technostructure who might criticize university discussion will be warned by colleagues that he was making life unnecessarily difficult for those who visit campuses to recruit talent and that he risked having his more distinguished academic consultants take their knowledge and their possible secrets to some less vocal leadership (1971, p. 293).

RIESMAN'S 'ERA OF RISING STUDENT CONSUMERISM'

Riesman's 'faculty hegemony' thesis was quickly replaced with a new thesis. In *On Higher Education*, subtitled *The Academic Enterprise in an Era of Rising Student Consumerism*, published in 1980, Riesman admitted that he and Jencks had misinterpreted trends in the 1950s and early 1960s. The increase in the demand for faculty, and hence in their bargaining power which they had thought was a permanent development turned out to be only a temporary spurt (1980, p. xx). During that time, higher education in America, at least in the top-ranked national universities, was at the very peak of undiluted meritocratic competitive pressures. But the supply and demand conditions that gave rise to faculty dominance quickly reversed. By the 1970s, the combination of a declining demand for universities' services and a rising supply of those services favored the 'student consumers.' Accordingly, the relative power shifted from the faculty to the students, explaining the subtitle of the book, *The Academic Enterprise in an Era of Rising Student Consumerism*.

The rise of student consumerism was attributed in part to demographic developments. There was a reduction in the population from which college students could be drawn. In the middle 1970s, enrollments began to taper off, with enrollment among white males actually falling (1980, p. 9). At the same time, the number of colleges and universities had increased, with an even larger increase in the number of programs offered. An increased supply in Ph.D.s relative to faculty positions available weakened the bargaining position of faculty members even further.

Given those demographic changes, the more important factor in changing the demand equation was what Riesman termed 'the counterculture.' The role of 'student subcultures' in the era of faculty dominance had been discussed in *The Academic Revolution* in terms of a 'war between generations' (Riesman and Jencks, 1968, Chapter 2). Students were described as accepting, up to a point, subordination to professional faculty. While Harvard Law School was cited as a prime example, it also applied to students in graduate schools. The nostalgic view that in the 'good old days' colleges were small, and faculty and students interacted on a daily personal basis was only a myth (1968, p. 35). Actually, faculty and students were historically hostile, with faculty incompletely in domination, seeking to impose rule and order for the purpose of 'improving the social and moral character of the young rather than of their intellectual attainment' (1968, p. 38). In the modern era, professors at the better universities are scholars (or at least pseudo-scholars) who are only interested in a minimal way in the academic development of undergraduate students (1968, p. 38). Many professors and administrators no longer believe in conventional views of what students should be or become (1968, p. 39). Jencks and Riesman described the situation as one resulting in many faculty and administrators developing a 'Veblenian ideal,' i.e., wanting undergraduates to act like graduate apprentices, both socially and intellectually, and to dismiss those who do not as not belonging at a university (1968, p. 39). The faculty and its apprentices were regarded as the heart of the university, and 'the still uncommitted undergraduates as an expendable penumbra' which should be left free to go its own way as long as it did not interfere with the true work of the university (1968, p. 39).

Most of the students, feeling that they could not compete with their professors and could not relate to them in any other way, retreated into their own world. Traditionally, this had been the world of fraternities and football, as described by Veblen. But by the 1960s, more students were joining the 'counterculture' that rejected both the 'adult world of big business and bureaucracies' and the 'traditional juvenile counterpart, the formally organized extra-curriculum' (1968, p. 45). Graduate students were described as forming a 'semi-stable occupational group' unable to see any prospect of changing their status. Students with a 'white-collar mentality' expected to gain jobs by conforming to faculty demands, while a minority with 'blue-collar mentality' expected no jobs and wanted to improve current conditions (1968, p. 47).

A different situation was described in *On Higher Education* (1980). During the 1970s, the student 'counterculture' had come to rest on an ideological movement toward freedom from all restraints on individual behavior (1980, p. 6). With help from sympathetic faculty members and administrators, student activists generated student attitudes that were channeled into behavior that challenged 'meritocracy' in higher education. As applicant pools for most institutions were not large enough to permit a high degree of selectivity, student insistence on freedom – 'the student as customer' – gained overwhelming strength (1980, p. 9).

The Consequences of 'Student Consumerism'

In analyzing student impacts on the curriculum and on universities as institutions (1980, p. 105), Riesman distinguished between student *influence* and student *market power* (1980, p. 277). Students have always had influence, if only because professors do care to have bright student disciples to carry forward their ideas (1980, p. 277). Riesman again cited 'Professor Thorstein Veblen's contumacious disregard for undergraduates,' suggesting that it was perhaps a defense against the threat of being disappointed by students' lack of interest in what he cared about. That is the kind of disappointment that professors continually receive from students, who may unaware they are inflicting it. Students exercise this influence continuously in a number of ways – by the level of effort they put forth in class, by their responsiveness to what interests them, and by their indifference or even disappearance when they are bored. This is an outcome that students almost never feel reflects on themselves, but only on the teacher or the subject matter' (1980, pp. 277–278).

In contrast, the new market power of students rests in their decisions of whether they want to attend college and if so, which college to attend. These are individual choices influenced by family economic factors as well as other factors. In contrast to Adam Smith's vision of rational student-consumers, Riesman described modern student-consumers as having 'wants' that differed from their 'needs,' choosing colleges and universities in haphazard and ill-informed ways. Often they were misled in making their choices. Colleges and universities seek in various ways to position themselves to attract students. In the best of cases, the intent is to try to influence student choices for the sake of the students themselves, i.e., satisfy their needs rather than their wants. But in many cases, the institutions were simply responded to market forces by the various strategies colleges had found that will retain some members of their old clientele while inviting new ones to fill up the vacancies' (1980, p. 105). In this regard, Riesman discussed students 'as more or less autonomous units, exercising their power through the market, by choosing to attend one college and not another, to stay or drop out or to transfer' (1980, p. 136).

Institutions of higher education were competing frantically for 'full time equivalent students.' Riesman sounded almost like Veblen in warning that the frantic competition among institutions for 'full time equivalent students' was having a negative effect on academic quality. Both faculty members and administrators were reluctant to demand that students meet rigorous academic standards from fear that they would go where standards were easier. But Riesman argued that student-power had induced some beneficial expansions of curricula, although the examples that he gave would hardly be appreciated by Veblen as university-level studies – (1980, p. 136), with women's studies, black and ethnic studies, and 'third world' studies as examples.

The new situation was very similar to what would be expected in markets characterized by monopolistic competition. Universities and colleges act like monopolistic competitors, reluctant to depart from offering what consumers want but seeking some small product differentiation as a basis for advertising as a means of claiming a share of the mass market (1980, p. 197). Student-consumers are reluctant to get too far out of line and will respond only to minor variations in standardized products (1980, p. 197). For that reason, he argued that the 'marginal differentiation' type of competitiveness among universities had the consequence of diminishing the educational curriculum options for students, although any particular institution will offer a variety of paths (1980, p. 198). State universities will have less leeway to offer marginal differentiated programs (1980, p. 198).

At the same time, 'the free market is not as free as it might appear', i.e., students are prevented from making full use of their market power because 'partial oligopolies' exist. A few institutions, largely limited to medical schools, continue to experience excess demand for admission (1980, pp. 210–211). That was not the case with Ph.D. programs, where the supply of programs was far greater than the demand (1980, p. 212). Hence, this is not a significant thwart to student consumerism. Riesman also discussed 'viscosity in student attitudes,' which means that students often act with very little information and make little effort to become better informed (1980, p. 213). One behavioral tendency of an economic nature was the tendency to view a price difference in the short-run rather than amortized over a lifetime (1980, p. 216).

While Riesman's student-consumers were not as rational in their behavior as Smith argued they would be if given the freedom to choose, there are shades of agreement between Riesman and Smith. Smith was a staunch advocate of setting standards through examinations. Riesman criticized the 'consumerist onslaught' on standardized testing by the Educational Testing Service, maintaining that students had failed to realize the advantages of standardized testing as sources of information for their own decision making (1980, p. xvii). He also spoke against government regulations to protect students and in favor of strengthening regional accrediting agencies, improved high school counseling, and centers for information and advice. But he also argued that the 'wants' of students are different from the 'needs' of students, and there is danger in institutions competing for students by catering to those 'wants' (1980, p. xiv).

Riesman sought to avoid over-generalizations, having realized his previous errors in mistaking short-run developments for long-run trends. He offered few 'prescriptions' and no panaceas, expressing a belief in 'incremental improvements particular to a time and a locale rather than in packaged reforms applicable anytime everywhere' (1980, p. xix)

Ultimately, Riesman acquiesced to a fundamental tenet of Veblen's positive analysis of university behavior – universities pursue the pre-eminent institutional goal of prestige through competitive behavior that emulates successful business practices. Riesman's disagreements with the Veblenian caricature of students and administrators had much to do with his distaste for Veblen's personal and professional habits and reflected six additional decades of evolution in higher education.

8. The Buchanan–Devletoglou Economic Model of Universities

In *Wealth of Nations*, Adam Smith presented a very positive view of university students as serious individuals who genuinely want to be taught and will show great respect to those who seriously attempt to teach them what they need to learn. He placed great confidence in the ability of students to choose courses of study and teachers, so much so that market-like payment of teachers and institutional competition for students was the recommended solution to failures of the English universities. Two centuries later, Riesman argued that a form of student consumerism was becoming the dominant influence on universities' curriculum and academic policies. But ten years earlier, radical student activism that included episodes of terrorist-type violence was creating stresses on universities. In *Academia in Anarchy* (1970), Buchanan and Devletoglou developed an 'economic diagnosis' of the behavior of universities in that era of student radicalism.

As was the case with Smith and Veblen, the analysis presented by Buchanan and Devletoglou was prompted by a perception that universities were failing in their institutional functions. But in this case, the failures were seen as approaching a crisis point as 'university chaos' created by radical student terrorism was threatening to destroy the traditional academic heritage of universities. Since campus disturbances by radical student activists essentially ended with the end of the Viet Nam War, our interest is primarily in the general economic model of behavior of universities which they developed in Part I of *Academia in Anarchy*. Buchanan and Devletoglou specified that their model was not time-constrained. It was just as applicable to universities in the earlier, more tranquil period of the 1950s (1970, p. 89).

In their positive analysis, Buchanan and Devletoglou utilized the same approach as Smith and Veblen, explaining institutional behavior in terms of the self-interests of those in positions to influence decision making. Curiously, there was no reference to either Smith or Veblen on universities' behavior. But the Buchanan–Devletoglou economic model of universities was essentially a *partial* version of Veblen's 'economic model,' although the roles of the 'discretionary officials' were quite different. Their normative critique of university behavior and the institutional structure that gave rise to that behavior, however, was essentially a modern version of Smith. Buchanan and Devletoglou seemed to see the primary function of universities as educating undergraduates, although unlike Smith they did not suggest what the curriculum or teaching methods should be. As in Smith's analysis, the institutional failures were attributed to universities not responding to student-consumer preferences, and the remedies were essentially to make universities act more like competitive market suppliers. Oddly, on some points, the normative analysis was also suggestive of Veblen's (and Mills') views on university-level education.

But where Smith and Veblen both focused on universities as non-profit (private) institutions, the Buchanan–Devletoglou model was of a public university financed largely by taxes, with students paying little or no tuition. While the analysis was very much within the context of Buchanan's public choice approach, it was argued that the model was generally applicable to private universities as well. The economic analysis of universities' failures centered on three curious institutional characteristics of universities. Those were: (1) taxpayers who finance universities' operations do not control what the universities do; (2) students who consume the educational services do not pay and have no control over the quality or variety of services received; and (3) faculties who produce the educational services do not sell those services.

In the second part of *Academia in Anarchy*, Buchanan and Devletoglou applied their economic model of universities' behavior to explain the attacks on universities by radical student activists in the late 1960s and the responses of universities to the demands of the radicals. Interestingly, an argument that universities produce, or at least conduce, radical social activism had been presented earlier by Joseph A. Schumpeter in *Capitalism, Socialism, and Democracy,* first published in 1942. In the first part of this chapter, we examine his thesis that universities in the 20th century were over-producing intellectuals who become radical agitators against capitalism, and then devote the remainder of the chapter to the Buchanan–Devletoglou economic model. It is appropriate to combine Schumpeter and Buchanan in this topical manner. Schumpeter's discussion of democracy and the political process in *Capitalism, Socialism, and Democracy* could be regarded as the beginning of the modern approach of applying economic theory to the political decision-making processes, generally known as public choice, for which Buchanan received the Nobel Prize in Economic Sciences. Moreover, there are strong elements of Schumpeter's view in their charges that 'liberal intellectuals' on university faculties were partly responsible for the radical disturbances on university campuses.

Schumpeter on Universities and Radical Intellectuals

Adam Smith argued that so many men had been able to receive a university education that the supply of teachers had pushed the market wage almost to the poverty level. In *Capitalism, Socialism, and Democracy*, Schumpeter presented a different view of 'over-production' of university-educated people, albeit with some similarities. In several of his writings in the 1930s and early 1940s, Schumpeter identified a number of cultural, social, political, and economic factors that were allegedly eroding the institutional supports that capitalism required for its survival. One of those was the presence of frustrated and alienated 'intellectuals' who acted as articulate advocates of hostility to the capitalist system. By aligning themselves with various groups who felt deprived or exploited by the capitalist system (in particular, such groups as labor organizations), the 'intellectuals' would serve as the catalytic agents bringing on political action of a devastating character so far as entrepreneurial capitalism was concerned. Such a role was made more effective by the rising levels of economic output generated under capitalism, and by liberalism in government, which not only transferred political power from the bourgeois class to the non-bourgeois masses but exposed all existing institutions to the scathing attack of rational inquiry.

Essentially, those 'intellectuals' were the surplus production by modern universities. One of the distinguishing features of the later stages of capitalism was the vigorous expansion of the educational system, particularly at the college and university level. To some extent, that expansion was an inevitable development, like that of large-scale enterprise. There is, however, an important difference. Expansion of capitalistic enterprises will always be limited by market conditions. Firms will expand until the economic incentive to do so has been eliminated by falling prices on the demand side and/or by rising costs on the supply side. But educational expansion had not been subject to natural limits imposed by economic market conditions. Rather, it had been pushed further by public opinion and public authority than it would have done under its own steam. Whatever the precise causation of that expansion, and whatever may be thought about it from other standpoints, it had several consequences bearing upon the size and attitude of what Schumpeter termed 'the intellectual group' (1950, p. 152).

Under the heading of 'The Sociology of the Intellectual,' Schumpeter described 'intellectuals' as a certain group of people who belong to no social class as agitators of hostility toward the capitalist system (1950, p. 146). Never one to accept the assumption of rational consumers who signal to business firms and entrepreneurs what they want produced, Schumpeter argued that the masses of people are incapable of developing any opinions or initiating action on their own. Instead, they only choose to follow, or not follow, group leadership whose function is to 'work up and organize resentment, to nurse it, to voice it, and to lead it' (1950, p. 145). It is the institutional nature of capitalism that it 'invariably and by virtue of the very logic of its civilization creates, educates, and subsidizes a vested interest in social unrest', which was what Schumpeter labeled the 'Sociology of the Intellectual' (1950, p. 146).

Schumpeter conceded that it is difficult to define 'intellectuals,' who do not comprise a social class. Rather, they rather come from all classes, and spend much time fighting each other and in forming the spearheads of class interests not of their own. In that capacity, they are important because they have influence over group attitudes and group interests.

While 'intellectuals' cannot be defined simply as people who have had higher education, anyone who does is a 'potential intellectual' (1950, p. 146). Nor are professions such as law and medicine necessarily peopled with intellectuals. While journalists largely belong in the intellectual domain, the members of all professions have the opportunity of becoming 'intellectuals,' and many 'intellectuals' take to some profession for a living. Schumpeter finally declared that 'Intellectuals are in fact people who wield the power of the spoken and written word, and one of the touches that distinguish them from other people who do the same is the absence of direct responsibility for practical affairs' (1950, p. 147). They lack first-hand knowledge that only experience can provide.

The bourgeois culture defended the freedom of intellectuals to criticize and agitate against the bourgeois society and capitalism because the capitalist mentality found the methods of controlling the intellectual sector uncongenial (1950, p. 151). With the expansion in colleges and universities, the number of people having attained higher education will exceed the need in the business sector. That results in a situation similar to that described by Adam Smith in *Wealth of Nations* in his discussion of the consequences of subsidized university study on the incomes of 'men of letters.' Schumpeter's intellectuals experienced sectional unemployment or underemployment or employment at wages viewed as undesirably low by the educated people (1950, p. 152). Their educational experiences render them 'psychically unemployable in manual occupations without necessarily acquiring employability in, say, professional work' (1950, p. 152). In an interesting choice of terminology, Schumpeter stated that:

> . . . ever larger numbers are *drafted* into higher education and as the required amount of teaching increases irrespective of how many teachers and scholars nature chooses to turn out. The results of neglecting this and of acting on the theory that schools, colleges and universities are just a matter of money, are too obvious to insist upon (1950, p. 152, emphasis added).

'Intellectuals' who are unemployed, or unsatisfactorily employed, tend to become instigators of radical criticism and activism (1950, p. 153), primarily in 'stimulating, energizing, verbalizing, and organizing' the 'raw material' of the general hostile atmosphere that surrounds the capitalist engine. 'Intellectuals' rarely enter professional politics and even more rarely hold responsible offices. But they staff political bureaus, write party pamphlets and speeches, act as secretaries and advisors, make the individual politician's newspaper reputation which, though it is not everything, few men can afford to neglect (1950, p. 154).

In *Capitalism, Socialism, and Democracy*, Schumpeter was not directly critical of the institutional behavior of universities, but rather of universities becoming to accessible to the masses. But his views on universities, university professors, and graduate students are rather well known. Clearly, he shared Veblen's view that a select few are both intellectually capable of being scholars or scientists and motivated by the instinct of idle curiosity to become university men, and he saw social value in leaving them free to pursue knowledge. In his own field, Schumpeter insisted that economists should be pure social scientists doing analytical work for its own sake, not policy advocates or advisors to political leaders. His complaint that Harvard University saddled graduate students with the tasks of teaching undergraduates when they really should be learning and researching echoed Veblen. Schumpeter believed that universities as institutions existed to serve professors who were doing analytical work, and that those on the faculties with no scientific talents to hone or work to do should serve the institution. He devoted attention to departmental and full professors' meetings because their work determined the economics curriculum and personnel.

Schumpeter's view of undergraduates seemed to match Veblen's. In his biographical work, Allen (1991) stated that:

> In his conception of the ideal university, no 'students' existed, only master scholars and apprentice scholars working together in a more or less medieval arrangement. As the masters and apprentices educated one another, they mutually pushed forward the frontiers of knowledge. His university also had no room for those attending to please their fathers or satisfy family tradition. No babysitter or haven for growth between puberty and maturity, the university existed to serve the intelligent, the dedicated, and the scientific and intellectual worker.

The radical intellectuals in *Capitalism, Socialism, and Democracy* were those who had acquired a higher education, and presumably gained 'book knowledge,' and became instigators of hostile policies in their post-university life. Had Veblen been an activist, or even suggested reforms, he might have been the perfect example. But Riesman's claim that Veblen played the role of the sly academic wobbly who, in rather unmanly fashion, generated hostility toward administrators, and whose 'legend' continued to influence the behavior of faculty members suggests that he would qualify as being in the same family as Schumpeter's 'intellectuals.'

The Buchanan–Devletoglou Economic Analysis of Universities' Behavior

Buchanan and Devletoglou asserted that universities' behavioral tendencies could be explained through application of basic economic theory. An analysis of institutional behavior as shaped by the responses of individuals to incentives and penalties provided by institutional structures, the distribution of exclusion rights, and competitive pressures (or lack thereof) would reveal that an institutional structural stagnation was the normal state of modern universities. Moreover, they claimed that the traditional academic heritage was verging on collapse as the weaknesses were exposed by attacks from radical student activists (1970, p. 92).

Like Smith, Buchanan and Devletoglou seemed to see the primary social function of universities as providing 'university education' to undergraduates. But they recognized that faculty members also teach graduate students, conduct research, publish papers and books, and perform various types of extra-curricula services. Unlike Smith and Veblen, Buchanan and Devletoglou were not concerned with the specific attributes of 'good' university education, curriculum, or teaching methods. The alleged failures of universities were in the nature of market failures of the institutional system to achieve allocative efficiency. The institutional system of university education predictably failed to provide quantity, quality, and variety of output in response to the preferences of those who consumed (or were willing to pay to consume) those outputs.

Their purpose was not to specify what student-consumers' preferences would be. Rather, they simply focused on sketching a conceptual model of the institutional system of modern universities that had evolved over the centuries and the behavioral characteristics of those who finance, who consume, and who produce university services. Within this framework, the model explained that what will be taught, to whom, and how will reflect the preferences of those who produce – the faculties and administrators – rather than the preferences of those who consume (students or potential students) or the taxpayers who finance universities' operations.

The universities in the Buchanan–Devletoglou economic model were publicly funded institutions, with governments (taxpayers) imposing the ultimate economic constraints. The decision makers within universities are utility-maximizers who respond to the various incentives and punishments that universities place before them. The Buchanan–Devletoglou model differs from Veblen's 'economic model' in several notable respects. There is no explicit recognition of the institutional objective of maximizing prestige, although at one point faculty members are described as under pressure to develop prestigious reputations. As in the Riesman–Jencks model of faculty dominance, governing boards have become passive players. Taxpayers are the ultimate external authorities, but like the trustees who represent them, they tend to be very passive players. But perhaps the most striking difference is the absence of conflict between faculty and administration. Essentially, the faculties rule the academic aspects of universities and are joined with the administrators in a consensus relationship to form a 'hierarchy' of university staff that decides what universities will do and for whom.

University Education as an Economic Good

University education is an expensive *economic* good that requires economic resources with large opportunity costs. In explaining the nature of 'university education,' Buchanan and Devletoglou were primarily concerned with explaining why this particular economic good is viewed by the public as a free good, one which taxpayers willingly finance. But how they defined university education has special importance because it tended to place their pro-market remedies for universities' failure in some doubt.

Buchanan and Devletoglou essentially rejected Smith's view that universities should prepare students for the 'business of life.' Instead, they sounded somewhat like Mill and Veblen in distinguishing between 'university education' and professional training. If university education is investment in human capital in the form of professional training, as is often claimed, familiar efficiency norms of equating marginal benefit with marginal cost could be applied, and university education would likely be sold at a price. If university education is a form of consumption of leisure, the economic analysis would also be simple – organize the institutions to make students happy. Instead, university education has elements of both but also of something different. It is a life-changing experience, a one-way trip. The product is a process, a happening through time, to which the student submits in the knowledge that he will become and remain sensorily different from what he is. True education transforms, but the ultimate transformation is not known (1970, p. 13).

Financing by Taxpayers Who Do Not Control

The fundamental proposition underlying the Buchanan–Devletoglou economic analysis of universities' behavior is that that the public views university education as a free good. Hence, they developed a 'free tuition' model in which the financing of universities' operations is by taxpayers, an institutional system somewhat inspired by the California state system in the 1960s. In contending that the model was also applicable to private universities, they conceded that tuition was not low in private universities. But students in those schools pay less that the full cost (1970, p. 67), and modern private universities receive substantial support from public funds. Hence, universities in general are 'common property' in 'the domain of the commonwealth' that draws sustenance from 'the whole community' (1970, p. 62). Without massive and continuing financial support from the community at large, modern universities could not exist.

But those who are involved in financing, producing, and consuming university education do not behave as if the universities are 'public dependencies' (1970, p. 63). Rather, they act as if the universities are still self-supporting monastic communities of scholars. Buchanan and Devletoglou compared the financing and management of universities with the separation of ownership and control of business corporations (1970, p. 65). In a genuine sense, modern university management does as it pleases, paying little or no respect to the interests of the ultimate owners, the citizens of the community. Restrictions on university mismanagement and inefficiency are highly indirect and remote (1970, p. 66). Citizens can exert influence only very indirectly through the political process, and the politicians must act through 'inactive and cumbersome' governing boards. Universities are 'quasi-secret organizations' (1970, p. 66). Buchanan and Devletoglou noted the extent to which the world of higher education actually resembles a conglomerate corporation (1970, p. 66), a statement with which Veblen would most definitely agree.

Why do taxpayers accept paying the high costs of operating universities without exercising control? The persistence of the myth of independence of universities from those who pay for their operations is due in part to the payoff in technological progress. That is, the release of science from the straightjacket of church hierarchy facilitated much of the technological progress since 1543. But that is not a complete explanation, since the massive increases in government (taxpayers') support and students occurred in the post-World War II period, after the scientific and technological revolutions.

One reason is the free-rider problem in reverse. Because of the sheer sizes of political groups, a single individual's share is very small; hence, there is no incentive to initiate action (1970, p. 68). A second explanation is that taxpayers must think their tax efforts provide something in return (1970, p. 69). The rationale for governmental-taxpayer financing must be based on some presumed social or community value attached to the experience of becoming educated at the university level (1970, p. 69). Without mentioning Adam Smith's argument that education makes for better citizens, they essentially rejected it, noting that clichés touting better citizenry are impossible to quantify or objectify (1970, p. 69) as an explanation of taxpayers' behavior. On a more objective basis, modern economists have taken a capital investment approach, but private gains in expected future income streams provide no basis for such massive governmental financial support. At best, it could only lend strength to policy efforts aimed at guaranteed student-loan programs to offset repayment risks borne by private lenders (1970, p. 70). Thus, taxpayers must perceive some type of benefits external to those who consume university education services.

An alternative explanation is that the public values university education precisely because the benefits cannot be quantified. That is, a positive value is placed on taxpayer-supported university financing due largely to a certain mystique that causes individuals to look on education as an end in itself. While this may sound like Veblen's argument that the public places high value on its 'higher learning,' that is not the case. Rather, Buchanan and Devletolou compared paying taxes to finance universities' operations to the act of charitable giving (1970, p. 71). The valuation is in on the outlay and investment made, rather than on the actual output of university education. The act of giving is valued because financing or tax sacrifice is regarded as a 'moral act' (1970, p. 71), the performance of a 'duty' which yields value to the actor. That explains the taxpayers' relative lack of interest in the product itself or with the behavior of those who supply and consume it (1970, p. 72). (Like Smith and Veblen, Buchanan and Devletoglou tended to take an evolutionary historical view. In this case, they suggested that viewing the paying of taxes to finance universities as a moral act is due in part to the historical origin of universities in medieval religious orders. In the intense struggle between church and state, the universities were arms of the church and subject only to canon law. Even after the state assumed financing of universities, this independence was retained, with the university demanding the 'rights' to act in accordance with its own 'moral' law (1970, p. 74).)

THE TAXPAYERS' REPRESENTATIVES: GOVERNING BOARDS

Representing the taxpayers or citizens are the governing boards of universities. Buchanan and Devletoglou described the boards as being deliberately designed to keep taxpayers (and also 'financing angels,' i.e., large donors) from controlling universities through their elected representatives. To avoid subjecting the educational institutions to the controls of either political leaders or 'financing angels,' governing boards were established to act as buffers between these and the academicians

(1970, p. 75). In principle, universities are owned by the trustees or regents for the citizens of the states. But in part as a holdover from the medieval universities, the ownership rights as 'rights to exclude' are complex and inter-linking chains of rights, duties, and obligations that are claimed and exercised by several well-defined groups in a peculiar hierarchy. The allocation and understanding of those rights is based on long-established custom and tradition (1970, p. 82). The governing boards were conceived to serve the primary function of warding off external control, and not for imposing political control over internal behavior. In the post-World War II era, the boards existed for the purpose of providing a pretense that effective external control is being exercised on the internal authorities (1970, p. 76).

Universities' governing boards vary greatly in organization, functional detail, and the effective powers exercised. But they share several characteristics in common. Members are laymen who have established prominence in business or the professions, and have demonstrated interest in higher education, normally in particular institutions. For state universities, members are normally appointed by political leaders, their terms of office extend over several years, and they hold full-time positions in their other pursuits. The standard pattern is one-half day per month or eight days per year of trustee meetings. As a rule, the boards do not have their own staffs, and members rarely do more than participate in the actual meetings. Board members are expected to 'rubber-stamp' policy actions initiated by administrators and faculty.

STUDENTS AS CONSUMERS WHO DO NOT PAY

Given free tuition, students become consumers who do not pay. The behavioral characteristics of these student-consumers constitute an important part of the Buchanan–Devetoglou model in predicting how students will behave under the system of free tuition. Even more importantly, the pro-market remedies for the failures of universities rest on making universities more responsive to the preferences of these student-consumers. Here we are dealing with how students were described in the presentation of the general economic model of universities. Later we will note that Buchanan and Devletoglou at least partially contradicted that depiction of student behavioral tendencies in suggesting those remedies.

In contrast to Smith's view that students will be rational consumers of university education, Buchanan and Devletoglou argued that most high school graduates are irrational consumers of college-level education. The university student is a 'man-child.' Education choices for the 'child' are made by the parents who act as buyers of education, supplemented as required by taxpayers who share the public-goods benefits of common schooling. For the university 'child,' parents have less experience and knowledge because many never attended college. The university 'man-child' is launched into a world which he cannot possibly know or understand, playing the 'man' and expected to choose, to exert his own being, to select his own options among processes of transformation that must embody almost maximum uncertainties (1970, p. 15). Young people essentially have been conditioned to feel that they must go on to college, to regard university education as the only thing that matters, even though they are not familiar with the transformation process they are seeking. (1970, p. 17). The opportunities that must be foregone become subservient to this singular goal. Buchanan and Devletoglou declared that 'university education is surrounded by a much undeserved aura of importance as an essential step to a better life ahead' (1970, p. 32). The result is that 'In endless streams, the faithful massively converge toward every campus in the nation year after year' (1970, p. 17).

While social conditioning was mentioned, Buchanan and Devletoglou placed major emphasis on economic factors (e.g., free nominal tuition) as the primary reason for irrational behavior on the part of students. From a simple economic perspective, the increased demand for the services of universities in the post-World War II era combined with a price being held to nearly zero resulted in excess demand (1970, p. 18). When price is prevented from rising to an equilibrium level, there are two means of limiting demand. The available facilities can be allowed to become congested by increasing the quantity of students accepted for enrollment. That amounts to allowing the quality of education to fall (1970, p. 19). Alternatively, congestion may be avoided by resorting to some form of direct rationing. The latter is more likely be the option selected when the demands are for personal services. In the 1950s and 1960s, the excess demand for university services generated both responses. Physical facilities were allowed to become more congested, while admissions policies weeded out some of the potential demanders, primarily on a quantitative rather than qualitative basis (1970, p. 19).

CONTROL OF UNIVERSITIES BY FACULTIES WHO DO NOT SELL

With taxpayers and trustees playing passive roles and students unable to influence universities do by withholding payments, the academic operations of universities fall under the control of faculties. While acknowledging that decisions are often made by authoritative rather than democratic methods, Buchanan and Devletoglou assumed away any administrative authority so that university procedures could be evaluated 'in their revered and traditional setting' (1970, p. 53). That does not mean that administrators were left out of the picture. Rather, in sharp contrast to the dominant role of administrators as 'discretionary officials' in Veblen's model, there appears to be a convergence of interests between faculties and administrators. In the Buchanan–Devletoglou model, the two groups combine in the 'university staff' (1970, p. 35) that forms an 'administrator–faculty hierarchy' (1970, p. 65).

Free tuition combined with the lack of information about university education on part of students and the peculiar institutional structures of universities allow faculties to establish the criteria for selecting students and deciding the variety and quality of products to produce (1970, p. 41). The free tuition means that faculties are not subject to any market pressures in making their decisions. They produce university education but do not sell it. Whatever they produce will be 'demanded' by the students. Because of faculty dominance, universities are caught in a type of academic conservatism that is not of an ideological or philosophical nature. Rather, it stems from institutional structures and an academic heritage that have evolved over the centuries. The economic explanation of that conservatism by Buchanan and Devletoglou is very much in the nature of a modern version of Adam Smith's explanation of the indolence of English university professors.

In deciding what universities will do, faculty members are naturally guided by their own utility functions. The procedures for selecting, retaining, and promoting faculty members represent an important part of the quality of educational services that universities provide. With faculties determining procedures and methods of university operation, almost without outside control, job-security figures prominently in personnel policy (1970, p. 49). Hence, the tenure system is at the root of that academic conservatism. Under the security of tenure, economic theory predicts that the decisions about what faculties do and how they do it will be aimed at making the position of faculty-scholar as pleasant as possible. With salaries paid on an annual basis, no time clocks to punch, no reports of their own attendance, and nearly complete freedom to organize academic instruction as they desire, the positions of university scholars are highly esteemed. While faculty salaries fall predictably below comparatively trained personnel in non-university positions, that is because much of the rewards is made up of 'non-taxable, non-monetary perquisites of university life (1970, p. 51).

Given the 'man-child' nature of students, it is predictable that excessive power would be transferred to the academicians, who were rather sarcastically described as those 'experts' who maintain the citadels of learning, the university faculty and administrators who stand willing, perhaps eager, to pronounce to all concerned what process is 'good' for each and every one. Forced by institutional circumstances to make subjective or personal choices among potential customers, the faculty administrators will tend to make the choices of who will be admitted and what quality of services will be provided based on their own set of priorities. As producers who do not sell, university faculties are unique in their freedom to maximize their own utilities free of normal economic constraints (1970, p. 60). But while their preferences will be to choose what will enhance their own comfort (1970, p. 38), narrowly defined self-interest will not necessarily prevail. Faculty-administrators may choose what they consider to be 'reasonable standards' of discrimination.

But those standards will be based on their own preferences, not the preferences of students. Preferences will be for 'high quality' services with little or no variability in quality attributes, that reflects a certain Veblenian 'pride of workmanship' (1970, p. 40). Faculty members will generally prefer to work with good students as indicated by grades and test scores, with criteria based on some subjective representation that gives the appearance of 'scientific' criteria. But they may also set up entrance criteria to achieve social purposes, admitting those least able to meet the rigorous tests.

In the admission of students, faculties and administrators secure relatively little direct benefit from expanding the number of places. But indirectly, they do benefit from enlarged facilities. If faculty were in complete control, they would reduce the number of students to some ideal small number. Faculties complain of being 'overworked' and of 'over-crowded facilities,' but those are based on their own concepts of ideal situations. Once the educational mix is selected that will represent faculty preferences, curriculum, university organization, and teaching methods will remain essentially unchanged. It is costly for faculty members to change and there are few offsetting benefits. But faculty members do face constraints. In order to gain resources from the government, universities have to compete with other tax-financed activities, including the lower schools (1970, p. 32). Taxpayers and donors place importance on numbers of students, so the financial support of the universities depends on quantity of students. Even so, the compromise will typically allow the faculties to keep the number of students below capacity level.

THE NATURE AND CAUSES OF UNIVERSITIES' FAILURES

Buchanan and Devletoglou claimed that: (1) their economic model of universities predicted that institutional failures were inevitable; and (2) those failures were reaching a crisis point. In explaining the nature of the alleged failures, Buchanan and Devletoglou did not specify what universities should teach or how. Indeed, they explicitly expressed a lack of concern for what constitutes a 'good' university curriculum, instructional methods, and organization (1970, p.46). Rather, the failures were efficiency failures, defined as a lack of convergence between the quantity, variety, and quality of university education that the universities were supplying and the preferences of those willing (and able) to pay for university education. Universities were admitting fewer students than the capacity of universities to serve, selecting students by using of highly subjective (and inconsistent) rationing criteria, and supplying university education with quality/variety attributes that differed from what student-consumers prefer.

This was explained as the predictable result of the peculiar financing arrangements, institutional structures, and academic heritage that allow control of universities by faculty members who are largely free of any responsibility to either the student-consumers of the services produced or the taxpayers who own/finance the universities. Put more simply, the failures were the inevitable result of free tuition and the behavioral traits of the controlling faculties in a non-competitive institutional environment that does not change in response to economic pressures.

The Economic Effects of Free Tuition

Free tuition imposes the necessity of a rationing process that naturally enhances the discretionary power of administrators and faculty members who were responsible for choosing among the many applicants, and diminished the power of those who are successful in securing admission' (1970, p. 20). University education can be 'free' only in the sense that a pre-determined and limited number of university places are made available to certain students. The central questions are who those students will be and how their behavior will be affected by free tuition.

As free tuition singles out a particular group to receive a particular subsidy in a particular form, ambiguities are involved (1970, p. 23). It is not clear that all selected to receive should be subsidized to the same degree or why some of the student's expenses (tuition) should be subsidized but not others (such as books and housing). It is not evident that the subsidization of the student in higher education should take the particular form of direct financial support to the university as an institution. The alternatives would include making grants or loans directly to the students (1970, pp. 23–24). Much of the 'loose philosophizing in favor of free tuition stems from a failure to distinguish two altogether different economic magnitudes: wealth and current earnings' (1970, p. 25). In terms of current earnings, all prospective students are poor. But if wealth is the present value of future earnings, all students become rich relative to those who cannot qualify for admission to universities. In this sense, the subsidy they receive amounts to a transfer of wealth from the poor to the rich, which is the reverse of ordinary standards of justice or equity. Free or nominal tuition would seem to make the final distribution of income and wealth more unequal, not less (1970, p. 25).

To salvage free tuition from such logical attacks, universities began implementing certain new programs in the 1960s. Studies by economists revealed that lower income groups were providing the universities with a smaller proportion of students than taxes, so that the whole program of free tuition was subsidizing students with wealthy parents at the expense of lower income taxpayers, naively transferring wealth from the poor to the rich. The universities' response was to modify the standard rationing scheme by moving rapidly to implement exceptions for special groups of poor students. Buchanan and Devletoglou argued that it would have been more efficient 'to reduce the perverse distributive impact by installing a system of tuition charges based on scholarship loans or grants made directly to the students from poor families' (1970, p. 26). Since any system of subsidies will have some perverse distributive effects because the gifted will be favored, arguments for student loans rather than student grants carry more weight (1970, pp. 26–27). While faculties will generally prefer to work with good students as indicated by grades and test scores, with criteria based on some objective representation that gives the appearance of 'scientific' criteria, they may also set up entrance requirements to achieve social purposes, admitting those least able to meet rigorous tests. In the 1960s, universities reflected a combination of both, exposing the personal and non-objective aspects of the present rationing process (1970, pp. 41–42). In shifting from one rationing scheme to another the 'myth of objectivity' was exposed, and faculties faced increased criticism from disappointed applications (1970, p. 42). The subjectively discriminatory admission process would naturally create resentment on part of those who were denied admission while others with lower qualifications were admitted under lower standards. Those admitted under the ordinary standards would resent the admission of those under the special lower standards, viewing that as a diminishing of the quality of university education they would receive.

On a more general basis, free tuition had a negative effect on the behavior of those students who survived the initial rationing process. Since they did not have to pay, students would the university, faculty, and facilities as having little or no value (1970, pp. 27–29). Obviously, that argument reinforced the view of the student-consumer as irrational 'men-children.' Rational consumers value their consumption opportunities based not on the prices but on the potential utility gains, and will act to maximize utility gains from exploiting those opportunities. Rather than treating universities, faculties, and facilities as having little value, students who were rational consumers under a zero-price arrangement would consume those services up to the point that the marginal utility of the incremental unit would be zero. That is quite a different proposition than regarding the entire consumption opportunity set as having little value.

Effects of Behavioral Characteristics of Faculties

With demand exceeding supply, the faculties select those who will be admitted as students in a discriminating fashion. Given the 'man-child' nature of students, it was predictable that excessive power would be transferred to the academicians. These were sarcastically described as those 'experts' who maintain the citadels of learning, the university faculty and administrators who stand willing, perhaps eager, to pronounce to all concerned what process of education is 'good' for each and every one. Here, Buchanan and Devletoglou injected a commentary on human nature that does not necessarily derive from economic theory. The power to ration 'embodies the power of man over man,' and 'individuals enjoy power,' relishing 'opportunities to control the lives of others' (1970, p. 36). Predictably, there will be a loss of humility, as the producing faculty members begins to think of themselves as omnipotent, in unique possession of the relevant criteria for good judgement (1970, p. 36). Since an expensive good is being given away, the quality of product deteriorates as 'suppliers begin to take on the arrogance of despots.' Such a deterioration in quality of product contradicts the prediction that faculty members will have a bias for quality over quantity, preferring good students taught in small seminars, etc.

Because the suppliers of university education (faculties) do not personally bear the costs, they disregard for cost reduction and efficiency in operations. In choosing quantity to be supplied, i.e., the number of students to admit, producers will restrict the level to below capacity based on their own priorities for 'orderly' operation. If faculties could convert reduced cost of facilities into salary increases, facilities would be more fully utilized and faculties more occupied with instructional duties (1970, pp. 45–46). But Buchanan and Devletoglou argued that 'syndicalist pressure' would prevent any experiments along those lines, a reference to the role of accrediting agencies (1970, p. 46).

Since the educational mix will represent faculty preferences, the curriculum, university organization, instructional procedure will all remain almost immune from student-consumers' tastes. Predictably this results in stability, with little innovation. While faculty members are not concerned about the operational costs of what they produce, they are keenly concerned about costs to themselves. Buchanan and Devletoglou asserted that faculty members will be moved to action only when something they value is threatened. Since it is personally costly to change and there are few offsetting benefits, quality standards will be customary ways of doing traditional things. Once particular programs are started, those offerings will be almost impossible to discontinue. New programs and methods will be resisted, primarily because they offer little reward rather than on basis of plausible arguments in favor of the established procedures.

While faculties control universities' admission policies, curriculum, and general academic policies, the actual control falls by default into the hands of the least qualified faculty members. Providing high-cost university education with general tax revenues was possible only by forcing down costs at the expense of all those involved in university education. Pay scales for university staff are artificially fixed as a result of the government's interest in keeping costs within some limits, which further intensifies the usual effects of price control leading to deterioration in quality of product. Either inferior staff remains full-time at the universities to carry out their everyday operations, or the better staff seeks additional income elsewhere, taking a less direct interest in the affairs of the university. The indiscriminate treatment of better and worse staff built into the structure of higher education further accelerates this process. The inferior staff reaps 'rents' and remains full-time on staff. The better can command higher rewards elsewhere. The result is that the decisions on university entry-study-graduation stands are more and more determined by less qualified people (1970, p. 31).

Faculty democracy contributes further to the problem. Since not all those affected by the group decisions are allowed to participate, i.e., the students are excluded, decisions reached democratically by faculties can be equally or even more oppressive to the persons thereby affected than those reached by authoritarian administrators (1970, p. 54). But while all faculty participate, some participate more fully than others. Those who value teaching and research will find serving on committees highly costly, while the 'faculty drones' will find committee work more rewarding that their colleagues. Economic analysis based on utility maximizing individuals predicts that faculty committees will, in normal circumstances, be staffed by the less imaginative members of the university community' (1970, p. 55). With the more 'pedestrian members of academia' dominating faculty control, the inherent inflexibility is even more extreme. Innovation will be resisted because those who are effective in making final choices generally fail to sense new concepts and methods that are proposed (1970, pp. 55–56). Policies dominated by faculty mediocrities will establish curriculum, rules, procedures, and methods that naturally reflect their particular preferences. The university as an established and going concern will thus cater to the desires of the unimaginative faculty members, with little expression of the preferences of top-quality scholars or teachers (1970, p. 56). Veblen would obviously agree with that argument.

LACK OF COMPETITION

On the subject of competition, Buchanan and Devletoglou essentially reiterated (albeit without any reference to) Adam Smith's arguments about 18th century English universities. They charged that there is too little competition among separate faculties of the universities. Competition among universities would involve competition for students (also between schools within a university) and for faculty members. Even if tuition was zero, universities could have to compete by offering packages that attract students. But any shift toward making the university more attractive to students involves costs to faculties, as they find their own satisfactions reduced. To the extent possible, they will resist such shifts, and seek out ways to reduce competition to minimal levels. Collusion is predicable. Agreements among universities will emerge to limit sharply the degree of university differentiation of product. As universities reach broad agreement through accrediting bodies on standard criteria for admissions, numbers accepted, and quality of university services, there is little incentive for students to shop around (1970, p. 58).

Smith and Veblen restricted their analyses of competition among universities to students and (in Veblen's case) donors. Buchanan and Devletoglou extended their analysis to include competition among universities for faculty, which they argued was more effective than competition for students. Universities must make opportunities attractive for the more productive scholars and teachers they hope to employ. Here is an interesting contrast with Smith's claim that university professors who controlled universities and received fixed salaries would become indolent. Buchanan and Devletoglou did not explain why faculties who had been described as being concerned with maximizing their own comfort would want the universities to hire more productive scholars and teachers. The competition for such faculty members did serve to reduce somewhat the dominance of the mediocrites in faculty committee government, but it still left students' preferences unconsidered. It was also argued that attempts had been made to stifle inter-institutional competition for faculty through 'cartel agreements,' e.g., the University of California system (1970, p. 59). Thus, while competition may mitigate to some extent the starkness of the predictions made about university structure, the essential features remain unchanged. Faculties control universities more or less as free-floating islands, moored neither in the demands and desires of those who consume their product, the students, nor to the demands and desires of those who supply the resources, the taxpayers. But it hardly seems likely that the creation of large university systems was initiated by the faculties. That suggests more involvement of external authorities than the model specified.

There were other inconsistencies to be noted. In Part II of *Academia in Anarchy*, Buchanan and Devletoglou indicated that faculty roles were changing. The effects on teaching undergraduates were consistent with the earlier arguments, but the image of faculties looking after their own comforts largely disappeared. As the major accrediting institution of society, the university was increasing in importance as a center of influence and power. Faculties were now described as being under greater pressures to do research, to publish, and to take part in extramural activities, at the expense of being instructors. Research-oriented faculty gave more attention to graduate students. The increased involvement of the faculty in a national and international prestige system (based on evaluations of their scholarly achievements or extramural activities), together with a sharp rise in their income (partly from extra-university employment), meant that teaching was no longer the fundamental aspect of being a university professor. Faculty members consequently found themselves in a highly competitive situation in which they are judged on basis of the national and international celebrity ratings. Most cannot compete in the 'supra-university struggle for scholarly status' and fall into an inferior status (1970, pp. 107–108). There is also competitive pressure on administrators. Administrators were also being subjected to competitive pressures. Because of the financial structures of universities, administrators spend most of their time in fund raising, lobbying public officials, handling research contracts, or recruiting 'prestigious faculty' (1970, p. 107). Hence, there was a general administrative indifference to students, especially to the large numbers of undergraduates. But the existence of those pressures on faculties and administrators was essentially incompatible with the model in which faculties are in control and are concerned with maximizing their own comfort.

THE CRISIS ON CAMPUSES

In Part II of *Academia in Anarchy*, Buchanan and Devletoglou argued that attacks on the universities by radical student extremists were putting the traditional academic heritage at the crisis point. The weaknesses of the peculiar institutional systems of universities had been critically exposed under pressures from a rapid increase in young people seeking admission to universities and a much slower increase in faculties. Student frustration had mounted to the point that a minority of radicals was able to disrupt campuses, sometimes through violence, while the majority of the students remained apathetically uninvolved. At the same time, the behavioral characteristics of those who controlled the universities led them to capitulate to the demands of the radical minority. The Buchanan–Devletoglou analysis of the crisis on campuses was not completely out of keeping with Schumpeter's concept of 'intellectuals' as anti-capitalist agitators. Indeed, as Leathers (1971) noted, it seemed at the time that the mutual interests binding university faculties and industrial corporations in Galbraith's 'new industrial state' might well become a victim of anti-capitalist intellectual activism on university campuses.

By rejecting change over many generations, by the age-long independence from the creative evolutionary force that had swept through all other institutions more responsive to economic pressures, universities were on the threshold of collapse. Their structural stagnation was more apparent in an environment of dynamic change and especially in a period when a quantum increase in the demands for higher education was occurring. The radical protests on campuses were part of a larger social development. But the ability of the militant minority to created chaos in the university community was a direct consequence of the highly traditional, almost feudal, university system failing to adapt itself to the desires of a society caught in a process of continuous transformation. Students, whose preferences were ignored, were frustrated. A variety of faculty behavioral traits had led to a progressive deterioration in the quality of the educational offering. A minority turned to radical attacks on universities, while the bulk of the students were apathetic.

Tenure allowed faculty members labeled 'pseudo-scholars' to engage in propagandizing their own personal or party values in university environments (1970, p. 49). There is a curious mirror-image relationship between these 'pseudo-scholars' and Veblen's 'official scholars.' While the latter were conservatives who supported the conventional business enterprise values and the universities' presidents and boards of trustees, the former deliberately departed from the traditional role as a 'detached truth-seeker' to advocate left-wing ideas and policies. Since tenure basically was a means of making life easy for faculty members with both good and bad consequences, and student terrorism did not threaten incomes or pension rights, faculty members could be Schumpeterian intellectuals if they wished or simply capitulate to the demands of radical students (1970, p. 50).

But there are inconsistencies in the Buchanan–Devletoglou analysis of the confrontation with what they had argued in developing their general economic model of the behavior of students and faculty members. Initially, the portrayal of student 'men-children' as irrational consumers continued. The large increase in their numbers had led to deterioration in their influence on academic programs. Young people tend to be immature and inexperienced. They readily accept radical ideas; their actions are seldom tempered by the ethic of responsibility. They have little thought of the consequences of their actions, and they have low opportunity costs by dropping out. Their emotional stability is seriously affected by the relative aggressiveness of competitive modern society. As students, their insecurity had been increased by the deterioration in their influence on academic programs as the numbers of students increased relative to faculty. They suffered from less faculty attention and 'repressive' university-wide congestion. They lacked a clear-cut sense of their personal future. The loss was even greater since attending university had ceased to be an elite activity. An additional factor was the rising social tendency to idolize youth and deprecate age, so that accepting the social and political views of the youth was the 'in thing.' Their elders were no longer training young people in decent conduct. Sounding very much like Schumpeter, Buchanan and Devletoglou observed that modern *liberal* society treat the young as morally superior, more idealistic, and better motivated, with absolute rights.

But Buchanan and Devletoglou subsequently argued that while most university students were apathetic and inactive, they are largely like everyone else – interested in money, prestige, promotion, opportunities, and security. They compete for resources as much as businessmen do, and when resources are scarce they are as fierce and conservative (as opposed to being wasteful) as anyone else. Observations of students' competitive behavior for limited classroom space during periods of registration suggest that students can also be cunning and manipulative. The majority of students are rational, hardworking, and purposeful (1970, pp. 173–174). This revised portrayal of students was, as we will explain shortly, critical to their pro-market remedies for the failures of universities.

A major factor in the apathy of the majority of students stemmed from changes in the role of the faculty. With increasing size and greater pressures on faculty to do research, publish, and take part in extramural activities, the result was poorer instruction, more faculty aloofness, and great administrative indifference to students. But Buchanan and Devletoglou argued that faculties and administrators had responded to the threats of radical student activism in ways that were decreasing their own power. While the university structure was the root cause, they largely blamed intellectual liberals on faculties and those faculty members who were unable to compete for prestige as scholars and scientists for encouraging student militancy. Curiously, after arguing that universities had ignored student-consumer preferences, they then asserted that universities had become hypersensitive to student demands, at least to demands by the radicals (1970, p. 93).

Remedies for Universities' Failures

Fundamentally, Buchanan–Devletoglou economic diagnosis was that universities were failing due to the inability of student-consumers to compel via market means universities to supply what they most prefer. Because of free tuition, they could not reveal their preferences through demand curves. But even if they could, the institutional structures of universities essentially encourage collusion rather than effective competition for students. Choices had been reduced by the standardization of the higher education process. Universities had failed to exhibit the orderly process characteristic of commercial dealings. The remedies were very much in the competitive market tradition of Adam Smith, although Smith's idea of making professors' incomes dependent on student fees was at best only hinted at in rhetorical questions. Essentially what was needed was 'some shift toward greater inter-university competition which would embody more usage of market-type adjustments' (1970, p. 33).

Buchanan and Devletoglou argued that there is no incentive for students to avoid wasting university resources since they have no conception of the cost of those resources. Again, this raises the question of inconsistency in the analysis and the prescriptions derived therefrom. Their analysis emphasized that faculties restricted the admitted number of students to levels below capacity. Thus, exactly how students waste scarce resources was not made clear. But the proposed remedy was to alter loan programs to allow the student rather than the university to receive loans. That would induce more rational behavior as the student would have a sense of his own property being used, and thus think more seriously about the opportunity costs involved and the scarcity value of a university education (1970, pp. 27–29).

In viewing free tuition as an obstacle to progress, Buchanan and Devletoglou presented an argument that was reminiscent of Adam Smith's criticism of scholarships and fellowships that tied students recipients to particular colleges in English universities. By turning students into consumers who do not buy, free tuition stifles any tendency toward inter-university competition (1970, p. 30). The result is less efficient allocation of scarce university resources. If students themselves were financed, the universities would find it necessary to compete to obtain their resources. Instead, universities receive subsidies from governments and make the students compete for limited places. Under the free tuition system, students have to accept an educational offering which is determined by the highly subjective traditions built into the bureaucratic decision processes of universities (1970, p. 30). Students are thus severely limited in their effective ability to shop around in the expectation that competition will produce products suited to their own tastes and needs. The system makes universities accountable to politicians rather than to the consumers of their services. If forced to compete for students to obtain their financing, universities would have to put emphasis on satisfying their student-customers or at least explaining to them why they ought to be satisfied with what is being offered.

In comparing universities with corporations, Buchanan and Devletoglou asked what could be predicted if shares in corporations could be traded (1970, pp. 66–68)? The answer was that the prices would plummet, forcing a change in management or a takeover. They spoke of possible private innovations (1970, pp. 173–177) with private universities emerging that put maximum emphasis on satisfying the customer and the community. They conceded, however, that the relatively uninformed buyers would not sense the differentiation of products, at least not immediately, and sounded like Adam Smith in arguing that the tuition-free state-finance universities and colleges would make it very difficult for innovators to successful establish independent universities. The product would have to be immensely differentiated to induce much of a switch of custom. But the turmoil of the 1960s seemed to create a more fertile ground, although the failure of the English universities in 1776 had not spawned any competitive rivals.

Some rather obvious weaknesses in the proposed remedies begin with how Buchanan and Devletoglou defined university education. Since there is no way of predicting the outcome, who can rationally exercise choice? The argument for assuring that universities respond to the preferences of student-consumers must be weighed against the statement that 'With university education . . . all prospective consumers find themselves in the curious situation of committing themselves in favor of a product they do not know' (1970, p. 13).

The Buchanan–Devletoglou analysis of economic institutions of higher learning enhances earlier models of educational behavior by developing a role for the rational student consumer. This allows for the somewhat tautological policy prescription of a student loan financed educational system. Economic logic suggests that if students are forced to carefully consider their opportunity costs that more rational choices will be made. However, the question remains as to the type and quality of university education that will be provided in a system guided by student consumerism.

9. Recent Economic Models of Higher Education

While the Buchanan–Devletoglou economic model of universities had Smithian antecedents, other economists were developing formal (i.e., quantifiably testable) economic models of non-profit institutions that had even stronger Veblenian antecedents. Several general economic models used hospitals as case examples, but were intended to apply to non-profit universities as well. In the first part of this chapter, we briefly review the distinguishing Veblenian features of the models presented by Newhouse (1970) and Lee (1971).

In the second part of the chapter, we examine the economic model of universities' behavior presented by Garvin (1980). While Garvin did not acknowledge Veblen's earlier work, his model is essentially a neo-classical version of the 'economic model' of 'discretionary officials' that we examined in Chapter Six. Universities' behavior is explained as satisfying converging elements in the utility functions (Veblen's 'motives') of individuals in positions to influence institutional decision making. As in Veblen's 'model,' institutional prestige is the common element in the utility functions of the decision makers, and the pursuit of that prestige occurs within a competitive environment.

We will also note significant differences between normative aspects of the modern economic models and Veblen's perception of institutional failures of American universities. In the modern models, decision makers' utility functions are simply taken as given, with no links to the conflicting value systems as in Veblen's institutional theory. In contrast to Veblen's evolutionary approach, the modern models are static, taking the institutional environment as given. To the extent that normative analyses are involved, the criteria applied are much different than Veblen's concept of the functions of the true university. The normative basis for the prediction of institutional 'failure' in Newhouse's general model is the neo-classical concept of allocative efficiency, defined as what consumers would prefer if they were purchasing the products in a perfectly competitive market. In that regard, the modern models are more in keeping with Smith's normative approach than with Veblen's.

In his economic analysis of universities' behavior, however, Garvin presented an entirely positive economic analysis, choosing to focus on 'not how institutions should be making decisions, but on how they actually behave' (1980, p. xi). Still, there was the implied purpose of providing information about how universities behave that would contribute to knowing how to improve resource allocations within universities and how to develop external policies to achieve 'sensible programs of financial aid, sponsored research, and government appropriations' (1980, p. xi).

While most of the economic models of universities have dealt with non-profit universities, a model has also been developed that explains the behavior of public (state-supported) schools using a similar approach. State universities rank prominently among the research universities, and have played major roles since about 1890, as Goldin and Katz (1999) have explained. While those 'university grade' schools do operate much like non-profit universities, their behavior is also significantly influenced by a partial dependence on legislative appropriations. Hence, we close out this chapter with a review an economic model of public enterprises as it applies to public universities. Here again institutional behavior is explained as reflecting an outcome that satisfies converging elements in the utility functions of the individuals involved in making the decisions.

ECONOMIC MODELS OF NON-PROFIT INSTITUTIONS

The economic models of non-profit institutions that were developed in the early 1970s tended to utilize the non-profit hospital as an illustrative example. While modifications must be made in applying these models to universities, the general features remain essentially the same. In the absence of a proprietary interest, the motivation of the decision makers can not be that of profit maximization. Institutionally, non-profit institutions have considerable freedom to set and pursue their own priorities, and are relatively insulated from market pressures and consumer preferences. The decision-making process involves a collective entity consisting of individuals in several different positions or roles – as members of the boards of trustees in which control is formally vested, as administrators appointed by the boards, and as members of the professional staffs.

Those who receive the services provided by non-profit institutions, e.g., patients in the case of hospitals and students in the case of universities, have less influence on institutional behavior than do customers of profit-seeking enterprises. In the aggregate, students might have more influence than do hospital patients who have essentially delegated their consumption choices to their physicians. But since college students do not pay the full cost of attending universities, follow prescribed courses of study to receive degrees, and rely heavily upon the advice of academic counselors in choosing major fields of study and elective courses, they may be expected to be less price sensitive than consumers of other economic goods and services.

Although the profit motive is missing, the behavior of the individuals with some influence on the institutional decisions can still be explained in terms of each individual seeking to maximize its utility from the institution's behavior. Personal utility functions contain a number of elements, some pecuniary and others purely psychic. Since the utility functions of the individuals comprising the three principal parties – trustees, administrators, and professional staff members – are different, decisions are explained in terms of a convergence of elements in those utility functions.

In the models developed by Newhouse (1970) and Lee (1971), the prestige of the institution is identified as a common element in the utility functions. Trustees derive utility from the personal prestige that comes from serving on boards of prestigious institutions. Administrators' salaries, promotions, and perquisites of office may be enhanced by maintaining or increasing the institution's prestige. Moreover, administrators gain professional status in the social community and among their peers from being associated with prestigious institutions. Individual members of the professional staffs also derive utility from the prestige that goes with being on the staff of a prestigious institution. That association may yield only psychic benefits, e.g., the respect of peers or of the wider community, but may also yield pecuniary gains. Physicians with staff privileges at prestigious hospitals may attract more patients and be able to charge higher fees for their services. Professional staff members may realize greater opportunities for grants, fees for consulting, and/or royalties from published works.

To the extent that the preferences of individual consumers of the services (patients or students) have any influence, the prestige of the non-profit institution may also be important for both pecuniary and non-pecuniary reasons. Prestige is highly associated with quality, and quality is associated with effectiveness of medical care and educational services. For students, degrees from prestigious schools are expected to result in better job opportunities, higher incomes, more rewarding career paths, and higher social status.

Both the Newhouse and the Lee models of non-profit institutions predict a bias in institutional decision-making processes toward activities expected to maximize prestige within the exist constraints imposed by such factors as budgets and mandated missions. Prestige is closely linked with quality, so the bias toward prestige is also a bias toward quality. The normative conclusion is that the quality/quantity mix of output that will be selected will contain more quality and less quantity that would be preferred by the patients if they were purchasing hospital services in a competitive market. But the Lee model of non-profit hospitals as seeking status through *conspicuous production* of outputs associated with institutional status brings competition among non-profit institutions more fully into play. Curiously, while Lee stated that his concept of conspicuous production was borrowed from Veblen's concept of conspicuous consumption, he gave no formal citation of Veblen's *Theory of the Leisure Class*. The appropriate citation, of course, would have been to *The Higher Learning in America*, where conspicuous production for universities played a prominent role.

GARVIN'S ECONOMIC MODEL OF UNIVERSITY BEHAVIOR

In *The Economics of University Behavior*, Garvin (1980) proposed to develop an economic model that explained how universities' actually behave, as opposed to how they should behave (p. xi). Thus, his analysis of university behavior was virtually void of any normative assessments. The book was aimed at two audiences. For the benefit of economists, Garvin's analysis incorporated a number of theoretical and econometric models. To render the work useful to administrators and policymakers, who would be interested in the descriptions of institutional decision-making and changes in the market for higher education, Garvin sought to minimize technical terms. In the first part of the book, he reviewed non-economic models of universities' behavior from other disciplines, described the market in which universities compete, and developed a formal model of universities as organizations that seek to maximize institutional prestige. The work here was largely theoretical. In the second part, his work was largely empirical, testing his economic model and considering several extensions that might help to explain the behavior of the university community as a whole.

Non-Economic Models versus Economic Models

Garvin began with a brief critique from an economic perspective of models of the organizational features of universities that had been developed by sociologists, political scientists, and public administration experts. In *collegial* models, which emphasize an absence of hierarchy, decision-making by consensus, and shared values. Because of the importance of professional values, the expert faculties cannot take orders from any superior in the official sense of the term. Hence, universities are governed by faculty groups, e.g., committees, senates, that share power widely. The faculty-dominance model presented by Riesman and Jencks (1968) might well fall into that category. *Bureaucratic* models emphasize the degree of centralization of power, and explore how variations in bureaucratic traits, such as the degree of administrative centralization, affect university policymaking, conduct of research, and other aspects of academic life. *Political* models emphasize conflicts that arise between various groups within the university – faculty members, students, and administrators – who have different ideas about the purposes of universities and the appropriate policies for achieving those goals. This approach recognizes the development of internal factions and focuses on how internal conflicts are resolved as the keys to understanding university behavior. *Organized anarchy* models view universities as having three special characteristics. Preferences are problematic, technology is unclear, and participation is fluid. As a consequence, it is critical to understand the process of choice, because how the various choices are presented to the decision makers have important effects on outcomes (Garvin 1980, pp. 3–4).

From an economic perspective, these models share three important limitations. First, the focus is exclusively on internal decision-making rules and procedures, with inadequate attention given to the environments in which universities operate. Second, the omission of important details makes the models difficult to test on an empirical basis. Third, the motivations of administrators and faculty are insufficiently addressed and explained (1980, p. 4). As a complement rather than a substitute for these non-economic models, Garvin's *economic* approach differed from those models in three ways.

First, there is the assumption of purposive behavior on part of those who participate in the internal processes of institutional decision making. Administrators and faculty pursue their own self-interests, which define the goals they seek for the institutions and consequently, the behavior of the institutions. Second, the entire analysis is set in a market context to emphasize the importance of the competitive environment in shaping university behavior. This applies to both internal resource allocation and strategies developed for the purpose of competing in the higher education market with other universities. Third, rather than focusing on the social and structural characteristics of universities, the economic characteristics of universities and the behavioral implications of different sources of revenue and costs are illuminated (1980, p. 5).

In Garvin's economic model of university behavior, universities are utility-maximizing organizations that are governed by consensus between utility-maximizing decision makers. But his model is a more truncated version of Veblen's 'model,' in that only utility-maximizing faculties and utility-maximizing administrators are involved. Trustees are omitted. The faculties are organized into utility-maximizing departments. The Veblenian precedent is revealed in that institutional prestige is the primary contributor to utility at all levels, along with quality and quantity of students. An important constraint on what universities do is their ability to compete in the market for higher education, which is essentially competition for students, again reminiscent of Veblen's 'model.' Garvin, however, more formally develops a 'market' for institutional prestige, in which universities attempt to improve or at least maintain their prestige. In addition to explaining his model of university behavior in conceptual terms, where the parallels with Veblen's conceptual model are rather easily noted, Garvin developed a formalized theoretical model using neo-classical economic theory.

THE UNIVERSITY AS AN ORGANIZATION: THE PRESTIGE OBJECTIVE

As an organization functioning in the higher education market, what is the objective function of the university? The fact that tuition is less than costs for both public and private universities indicates that universities are not profit-maximizers, that excess demand exists, and that a non-price rationing approach is used. A queue of students seeking admission insulates universities from market discipline and permits greater latitude in decision-making (1980, pp. 17–18). That allows universities to exercise considerable discretion in the admission of students and to pursue their own priorities without fear of losing students. The excess demand may also create pressures for expansion. Heavy reliance on outside sources of finances to avoid deficits is also indicated (1980, pp. 17–18).

After reviewing the rapid expansion in enrollment in institutions of higher education in the post-World War II era that was substantially aided by increased public expenditures at both the state and federal levels, Garvin posed three questions: 1) How in such an environment universities would be expected to respond? 2) Can the desires of both faculty and administration be captured in a simple analytical model? 3) To what extent has university behavior been shaped by market forces (1980, p. 21)?

Within the general framework of utility-maximizing individuals and a utility-maximizing institution, Garvin explained university behavior in terms of the pursuit of self-interested goals by the individuals who influence university decisions and competition among universities in the market for their services (1980, p. 5). His model essentially is a somewhat truncated version of the general non-profit models, with only two groups of individuals involved – administrators and faculty members (1980, p. 21). Members of boards of trustees are omitted. Unlike Veblen's 'model,' faculty members are major 'discretionary officials' in Garvin's model. Garvin explained these two parties as representing two distinct lines of authority in the internal organization of universities in which there is no simple hierarchy of authority. The administration is largely responsible for financial matters and exercises authority over the academic elements through budget control. The departmental faculty controls the academic decisions, including selection of students and new faculty members as well as course offerings within the budget constraint.

The assumption of 'purposive behavior' on part of both administrators and faculty means that each pursues goals consistent with their own self-interests (1980, p. 5). Policies of the universities are then explained in terms of 'goal consensus' (1980, p. 21), i.e., goals shared by the administrators and faculty. Considerations of organizational survival also come into play – those activities that enhance the university's survival as an organization are most likely to be pursued (1980, p. 22).

Garvin postulated that the major element in the utility functions of individuals, whether as administrators or faculty, is prestige. Institutional prestige enhances the market value and reputations of all associated with the university (1980, pp. 22–24). Citing Jencks and Riesman (1968), Garvin declared that for administrators, the prestige of the institution as a whole is of prime concern, along with cost efficiency. Hence, given administrators' authority over budget control, budgeting will reflect those concerns (1980, p. 55). Individual faculty members seek to enhance their personal prestige for reasons of self-interest, e.g., increases in their market values, salaries, promotion opportunities, increased ease of getting grants. Personal prestige is closely aligned with departmental prestige, so for faculty the prestige of their individual departments is of prime concern. Garvin argued that 'the pursuit of prestige – of recognition by one's academic and scholarly peers – is deeply ingrained in most faculty members and reflects the norms and standards they have internalized after years of training. As such, prestige is an essential feature of the social system of the scientific and academic community' (1980, pp. 22–23). Since overall prestige is important to administrators and department prestige is important to faculty members, Garvin assumed that the institution's overall prestige is a positive function of the prestige of the separate academic departments (1980, p. 23).

By being a functional adaptation, prestige contributes to survival of the university. By developing a reputation as a prestigious institution, the market area is expanded, and the queue of students increased. Increased quality also reduces elasticity of demand for some students with respect to higher tuition and fees. The greater the institution's prestige and the more renown its faculty, the better is the opportunity of gaining contract research that is peer-reviewed, and increased appropriations from legislatures whose members are responsive to prestige of state schools (1980, p. 24).

An important difference between Garvin's treatment of prestige and Veblen's is the latter's distinction between the earned prestige of scholars and scientists among their peers for meritorious scholarly and scientific work and the publicity-oriented prestige from the lay groups. There does, however, appear to be an implicit assumption in Garvin's model that prestige is largely based on recognition by faculties based on research and publications. This is reflected somewhat in that quality and quantity of students are closely related factors in the university's utility function are the quality and quantity of students. The interest of faculty and administrators in student quality closely parallel their desire for institutional prestige, since higher quality contributes to the reputation of the university and enhance its standing in the larger academic community (1980, p. 24). Faculty members may also derive personal utility from dealing with good students for several reasons. Such students, especially graduate students, may become research assistants, willing to accept wages considerably below their marginal products. Faculty members may gain considerable esteem when their students become recognized scholars (1980, p. 25), and good students are simply more enjoyable to teach.

But there is a quality/quantity trade-off involved. Many universities are committed to a service philosophy, and administrators are interested in keeping enrollments as high as possible. This is especially true in the case of state universities. Administrators may also pursue expanded enrollments because they lead to increased salaries. Academic departments have an interest in larger total enrollments. They expect that the number of students in their fields will increase as the aggregate enrollment increases, which will enhance the opportunities for promotion and additional facilities/resources. At some point, a trade-off is reached between increasing quantity and maintaining quality (1980, pp. 25–26). How that trade-off is made depends upon the relative importance to the institution of quantity of students versus quality of students, very similar to the trade-off between quantity of medical care and quality of that care in Newhouse's hospital model.

The process of maximizing institutional utility in choosing quality/quantity combination has to conform to budget constraints. Revenues for universities come from a variety of sources, including tuition, grants, state appropriations, alumni gifts, and sponsored programs. Costs fall into two major categories: those relating to the educational functions, which vary with student enrollment, and those resulting from research and scholarly activities of faculty (1980, p. 26).

Internal Organization

Seemingly echoing Veblen's earlier depiction of universities, Garvin stated that 'At one level, universities can be viewed as multiproduct firms, transforming their inputs via a production function' (1980, p. 40). Inputs are faculty, students (both undergraduate and graduate), and capital facilities. Outputs are educated individuals and research. In theory, those production relations can be specified and estimated, as they are for business firms. But the internal organization of universities is quite different from business firms, and plays a much more critical role.

Whereas most business firms have the simple hierarchy, universities operate with two distinct lines of authority – the administration and the faculty (1980, p. 40). The administration is responsible for financial matters, exercising direct authority over departments through budgeting procedures, and controlling departmental growth through the annual allocation of funds. It also plays the major role in fundraising, as well as controlling undergraduate admissions. On the other hand, admissions of graduate students, selection of new faculty members, and the choice of course offerings are generally departmental decisions. Within these academic areas, departments are relatively independent, constrained only by their annual budget allocations. Departments, then, are important decision-making units of the university, and there is often conflict and competition among departments (1980, p. 41).

What are the department's goals? How do they behave within the university? What are the implications for the behavior of the university as a whole? Garvin postulated that academic departments are prestige-maximizing organizations, acting to improve their standing among academic and professional colleagues. Prestige is a subjective subject, difficult to define. But it is closely correlated with relatively objective measures of quality (1980, pp. 41–42). Those include the research accomplishments of the faculty and the strength of the graduate programs. Ph.D. programs are especially important, and departments seek to add, keep, and improve their doctoral degree programs (1980, p. 42). Upgrading to gain prestige is expensive, with funds coming either from the administration or outside sources (1980, p. 43). For most departments, internal funds are most important. How does a department convince administrators to provide additional funding?

Garvin postulated that 'considerations of equity' dominate the internal allocation process. That means that administrators attempt to treat all departments as equally as possible to minimize internal conflict (1980, p. 43). This introduces the political model, since the administrators view faculty to some extent as their 'constituents' who may leave if they become dissatisfied (1980, pp. 43–44). The 'equitable distribution' of faculty positions is largely based on 'teaching needs' of the departments. Hence, increased enrollments lead to more faculty positions. Departments want more faculty because they permit coverage of more sub-fields, attract better quality people, and serve generally to enhance departmental prestige

(1980, p. 44). Consequently, departments may seek rapid expansions in enrollments to increase faculty size. But undergraduate and graduate enrollments respond to different forces and require difference responses from a department.

Undergraduate admissions are controlled by the administration and departments have to compete for the incoming students. The choice of majors is far more responsive to broad socio-economic and cultural trends, which makes predicting the number of majors per department difficult to predict and subject to considerable uncertainty over time. But overall, departments face fewer risks of losses of popularity when aggregate enrollments are increasing. Similarly, administrators have more flexibility and face fewer risks when allocating faculty positions under those conditions. Thus, rising undergraduate enrollments are desired by departments because of their indirect contribution to departmental prestige from increasing faculty positions (1980, pp. 45–47).

Graduate admissions are more decentralized and subject to greater departmental control. Most departments have considerable leeway in determining the size of the graduate programs, constrained by availability of funds. The main difference between graduate and undergraduate enrollments for the department is the greater prestige production of graduate students. Placing its Ph.D. students on the faculties of well-respected schools enhances a department's prestige. Thus, departments struggle to minimize their output of low-quality Ph.D.s in order to gain reputation for quality outputs. But at the same time, larger graduate enrollments are important to increase shares of academic budgets. Most universities allocate more funds per graduate student, but the marginal cost of adding students may be quite low in many cases. Departments may see expanded graduate enrollments as a means of gaining funds in excess of increased costs, with the 'profits' used for expanded facilities, higher salaries, etc. (1980, p. 49). Graduate students also provide important services, e.g., as inexpensive classroom teachers and research assistants, because they can be paid less than the values of their marginal products (1980, pp. 47–49).

This explains why quantity and quality of students are important in the university's utility function. But what are the 'technical relations' governing departmental growth? The major constraints are the number of qualified applicants that can be attracted, the size of the teaching staff, and availability of financial aid for incoming students (1980, p. 49). The first depends on the prestige of the faculty, and the latter depends on 'several institutional factors.' Some departments can grow faster because of outside funds available to provide financial aid in the form of fellowships, research assistantships, and teaching assistantships. For humanities, increased undergraduate enrollments may be the key to gaining graduate assistantships, which requires graduate programs. In science and engineering, outside funds for research may be the key, with those funds going to the departments with highest prestige (1980, p. 51). Science and engineering departments of high prestige often see no reason to expand departments to increase prestige, but do so because sponsored research requires more research and teaching assistants. Less prestigious departments build up graduate programs to enhance their prestige. Their behavior can be viewed as a form of 'competitive emulation – an attempt to duplicate the activities of the more prestigious departments and institutions' (1980, p. 52). Departments that successfully increase their prestige are able to acquire more sponsored funds, and use those funds to enhance the quality of their students rather than the quantity.

But administrators have other considerations than just equity in allocating faculty positions and funds. Efficiency and prestige are the two most important concerns. The administration is responsible for protecting the financial health of the university and often pays special attention to containing costs (1980, p. 54). Measuring and monitoring efficiency in the absence of any tangible outputs and making inter-departmental comparisons are extremely difficult. But certain visible cost differences in upgrading departments gain administrators' responses. Other things being equal, a department that can be upgraded more cheaply will get the approval of administrators. That tends to favor science and engineering departments where outside funds reduce the need for additional internal funds (1980, p. 54).

But university budgeting is often guided by the administration's desire for institutional prestige (1980, p. 55). Like faculty members, administrators prefer to be associated with institutions of high reputations gained through graduate and professional programs of high quality. This is especially important in institutions already possessing high prestige and seeking to increase it. Prestige considerations may temporarily violate the usual standards of equity and efficiency.

In essence, the administration represents the supply side of the internal allocation process, while departments demand funds and attempt to convince the administration of the validity of their requests (1980, p. 55). Various political games will be played, e.g., departments must have some expectation of success in gaining funds because failure to do so causes them to 'lose face' and damage its reputation for reasonable requests (1980, p. 58). Accrediting organizations and professional visiting committees may also place additional constraints on departmental proposals to upgrade (1980, p. 59). Environmental circumstances may alter the relative weights, e.g., during periods of prosperity the efficiency standards may be given less weight. When funding is tight, state universities gain undergraduate enrollments, which provide impetus for larger graduate programs, more faculty members, and hence, increased prestige. Scale economies may come into play. Prestigious private universities will be able to increase tuition without losing students, thus attracting and retaining scholars of high quality (1980, pp. 60-1). Prestige maintenance is less costly and much easier to accomplish than institutional upgrading (1980, p. 62). (This makes it likely that the higher education market will become increasingly segmented, with the elite private institutions and best public universities likely to maintain high prestige. A number of state universities with growing enrollments will be able to sharply increase their prestige. The lower quality public and private schools, especially those in urban areas, will likely opt for emphasizing service strategy with less attention to prestige (1980, p. 62).)

Digression: A Property Rights Approach

Meiners and Staaf (1995) developed a somewhat different model based on a 'property rights' approach to examining the consequences of the nonprofit nature of universities. They argued that in the absence of profit motives, trustees and administrators have an incentive to be informed about university finances that are measurable (1995, p. 199) because they behave like other public bureaucracies in being concerned about increasing revenues, i.e., maximizing budget growth. The non-pecuniary benefits associated with the position of trustee or administrator, in whatever form they occur, are likely to increase with an increase in institutional revenues. Trustees evaluate administrators' achievements in increasing revenues in relation to other universities. But Meiners and Staaf included increasing institutional reputation as a reason for the concern over revenue growth. Trustees want to avoid deficits because that would create more demands on their time and lead to diminished individual reputations similar to those of a bankrupt corporation (1995, p. 199).

Competition in the Higher Education Market

Whether state or private, universities are non-profit organizations that usually operate within an economic environment in which they must compete with one another. Garvin argued that although market discipline is often weak (1980, p. 1), the concept of a market still applies. Understanding the characteristics of that market is essential to understanding how universities behave in an economic model.

Institutions of higher education fall into a number of general types, with universities in a separate category. The relative importance of each type in the higher education market differs and has shifted significantly over time (1980, p. 7). The market is segmented by geography, quality of institution, and highest degree offered, so competition varies accordingly. The relevant sub-markets are often so small that oligopoly prevails (1980, pp. 7–8). Market segmentation results from the special characteristics of student demand. Undergraduate demand is strongly affected by accessibility and institutional quality. Geographical proximity becomes important by directly reducing the cost of attendance, by affecting preferences, and because of the availability and quality of information. Hence, most undergraduate students consider schools within their own geographical area. Schools that draw most of their students from limited geographical areas find their markets limited to local or state boundaries. Institutions of high quality that have reputations for excellence operate in much larger geographical market spaces. Students of high academic quality often ignore local schools since their demand is heavily a function of quality. Quality and renown are probably the most important determinant of market area (1980, p. 10).

The number and types of degrees offered also confine institutions to particular sub-markets. At the Bachelor's degree level, colleges and universities compete somewhat more geographically than at the associate (junior college) degree level. But at the graduate degree level, the area is much wider, becoming regional or national in scope (1980, p. 11). Only those institutions offering higher degrees in the same fields are in competition with one another. For many doctoral programs, the market may include only a handful of large, broadly diversified public and private universities. Those correspond, of course, to Veblen's 'university grade' schools.

Over time, institutions may move from one market segment to another by creating branch campuses, new academic units in metropolitan areas, constructing dormitories and other facililties to attract non-residential students, and by expanding their academic offerings. This increases competition with the sub-markets (1980, p. 12). Much of the upgrading behavior can be viewed as a response to market pressure. But downgrading behavior is also possible. In some cases, schools offering graduate degrees opted to move to the less expensive Bachelor degree-only programs (1980, p. 14).

The Market for Prestige

Prestige plays a major role in market competition. Reputation and relative standings in the academic community are closely related to the range of degree programs offered (1980, p. 14). The addition of graduate degree programs, especially doctoral programs, is generally related to a desire for increased institutional prestige. Such expansions expand the pools of prospective students and enhance visibility and improve standings. Garvin drew a distinction between quality and prestige, arguing that an institution's actual quality tends to be less important that its prestige, because the reputation is what in fact guides the decisions of prospective students. Prestige can be equated with reputation for excellence, reflecting both relative and absolute standards. The absolute measures of quality come into play, with quality and prestige being closely related as the objective and subjective measures (1980, p. 15).

The existence and extent of graduate programs is one element of prestige. Others are the quality of faculty and caliber of student body. The three are closely related and tend to change over time. The higher the prestige, the greater is reputation, and that increases the geographical market area. The higher the prestige, the less elastic is demand for admission, and hence, tuition can be raised without decline in student quality. The trade-off of increased prestige – which is expensive – for high tuition while attracting sufficient numbers of high quality students is easier. Universities compete with one another in 'tuition-prestige' space, offering particular combinations of the two in an effort to attract students.

Aggregative Behavioral Tendencies

While most of Garvin's analysis modeled the micro-behavior of individual universities and departments, he also employed a higher level of aggregation, treating higher education as a single industry subject to shifting patterns of supply and demand. Within that framework, he considered two topics. The first concerned the translation of individual university's upgrading efforts into overall changes in prestige, in terms of differences among the various academic disciplines. A 'new theory' was required to account for variations in the performance of entire disciplines. The second issue dealt with the introduction of new doctoral programs during the 1960s and whether some disciplines exceeded others and what forces were responsible. His approach was to adopt a market framework, with the entire discipline (all departments within a field) as the level of analysis. This is a market for prestige in which the forces of supply and demand determine the amount of improvement likely to be achieved (1980, pp. 114-115).

The determinants of prestige begin with individual scholars as the building blocks of academic departments. Their prestige is reflected in departmental rankings, i.e., departmental prestige is a statement of what one's colleagues think of one's department, which mean they think of individual members of that department. The chief factors contributing to scholarly reputation and departmental prestige start with the quality of research accomplishments evidenced through publications. Quality is more important than quantity, and some sub-fields are more prestigious than others. Intellectual ability is important, with reputation based on channels of informal communication. An individual scholar's reputation may be enhanced by appointment to an especially prestigious department, the so-called 'halo effect' (1980, pp. 115–117). Since departmental reputations/prestige are sums of the individuals', the same factors determine departments' prestige. Quality of published research is the most important (1980, p. 118). But departmental size is strongly correlated with prestige. The importance of faculty backgrounds is unclear (1980, p. 119). Departments also enjoy a 'halo effect' with prestige being enhanced by being associated with a prestigious university (1980, p. 120).

Like more conventional markets, the market for disciplinary prestige is subject to the forces of supply and demand. Garvin began with a simple model of the academic labor market as a matching process that attempts to map a distribution of potential employees in descending order of quality with a distribution of jobs in descending order of desirability (1980, p. 121). The most prestigious departments have their choices of the new Ph.D.s entering the market. The process has important implications for the distribution of prestige by departments. If the supply of new Ph.D.s increases while demand does not grow, the overall rank order of quality faculty would not change but the spreads would narrow. Should demand rise, the quality distribution would depend upon which departments had the largest increase in demand and the reason why – increasing need for teachers or increased research support (1980, pp. 121–122).

The availability of complementary inputs, e.g., federal research funding, plays an equally important role in explaining prestige gains by discipline (1980, p. 123). If there are increasing returns to prestige improvements over some range of quality for some disciplines, departmental prestige gains would be accompanied by more than proportional increase in its research funding. Administrators would respond by pursuing prestige improvements in these fields, budgeting internal funds accordingly (1980, pp. 124–125). Universities, however, are limited in their ability to adjust faculty salaries in response to market forces, as a result of their emphasis on internal equity and the usual requirements that salary differentials between disciplines be kept as small as possible. Universities offer incentives in the form of relatively inexpensive perquisites, e.g., larger offices and reduced teaching loads (1980, p. 130).

Disciplinary improvements in prestige should be positive related to increases in the number of new faculty members entering the field, to increases in the complementary inputs required for research, to increases in the aggregate volume of sponsored research, to the wider distribution of research funds among departments, and to shifts within a discipline toward more prestigious sub-fields. They will be negatively related to increases in non-academic demand for specialists in the field (1980, pp. 131–134).

The introduction of new doctoral programs, an important element in prestige determination, was also explained by use of a market approach. An increase in undergraduate majors indicates an increased demand for doctoral training. If existing doctoral programs have inelastic supply curves, as may be the case for the most prestigious programs, new programs will be demanded. But whether university behavior will be influenced is not clear. There is limited consumer sovereignty in the market for higher education (1980, p. 141), with preferences of faculty and administrators dominating. Public universities and private service-oriented schools will tend to be more responsive. Administrative demand for new doctoral programs will be influenced by the availability of sponsored research which lowers cost (1980, pp. 141–142). The motivation to innovate, i.e., to start new doctoral programs, plays on the demand side, while faculty and administrative resistance (closely related to cost) is a supply constraint (1980, p. 158). Programs will appear where there are the greatest comparative advantages in attracting prominent faculty or research funds. But there are also the cases where it is thought that any good university should offer Ph.D. degrees in the basic fields of humanities and social sciences (1980, p. 159). The supply side is also affected by the interest of professional societies.

GARVIN'S FORMAL MODEL

Thus far, we have described Garvin's economic model in conceptual form. But he also formalized it in a neo-classical style of specifying elements in utility functions. In the university's utility function, several important features of university behavior are incorporated – both faculty and administrators wish to be associated with prestigious universities and administrators' desire to meet the educational needs of their communities and serve a large constituency of students (1980, p. 28). In some cases, the prestige variables with dominate while in others the service (enrollment) variable will dominate. (In aggregate enrollment, no distinction was made between undergraduates and graduate students (1980, p. 28).)

While departmental prestige is related to university prestige, the exact relationship is not entirely clear. But an increase in university prestige will result in some increase in departmental prestige (1980, p. 28). Departmental prestige is a function of prestige of quality and number of faculty members. Prestige must be produced, and is produced by research and publications of faculty members, and can been enhanced by increasing the quantity or quality scholarly output (1980, p. 28). It can recruit more highly qualified faculty who are productive scholars or increase the size of their departments (assuming that new faculty produce).

In this model, there is a clear analogy with the household production function approach to consumer behavior. Consumers derive utility from various goods and services that the households produce with goods purchased on the market. The demand for faculty members who generate scholarly output is derived demand. The utility that the university seeks is provided by institutional prestige, which cannot be purchased directly on the market. It is a function of the quality of inputs, principally faculty members who are capable of producing scholarly output that produces the prestige (1980, p. 29).

The rest of Garvin's model: (1) relates the quality of the students to the aggregate size and overall prestige of the university; and (2) an inverse demand function, with demand affected by both the price charged and the prestige of the institution. Increasing prestige can increase the supply of quality students and reduce the elasticity of the demand curve (1980, pp. 29–30).

The model assumes that the university wants to maximize its utility through its control over the prestige of its departments and the number (and quality) of students enrolled (1980, p. 30), subject to budget limitations that require revenues be equal to costs. The sources of revenues are tuition, research funds from grants and contracts which are department specific and positively related to department prestige, and student subsidies provided by outside sources, e.g., endowments. The constraint is the demand curve, which is affected by numbers of quality students, prestige of the university, and rate of tuition. Outside sources of revenue include research revenues and student subsidies from outside sources (1980, p. 30).

The two components of costs are the cost of acquiring faculty and cost of educating students, although that was recognized as being an artificial separation made for the purpose of simplifying the analysis. A hyperbolic cost function to capture the inter-dependence of faculty quality and size was defended on grounds that it made 'good economic sense.' An increase in average quality is more expensive for a large department and an increase in quantity is more expensive if the faculty members of are higher quality (1980, pp. 30-31). Per-student costs of education were assumed to be constant (1980, p. 31).

The university then attempts to maximize utility within the constraints imposed by revenues and costs involving quantity and quality of both faculty and students. Two different first order conditions can be derived. Taking those with respect to the utility-producing 'commodities,' (e.g., prestige of a given department and the number of students enrolled) yields the ratio of marginal utilities (MU) equated to their marginal costs (1980, pp. 31–32). (MU of increasing prestige of *ith* department/MU from increased enrollment.) Both have two components – affecting total utility directly by affecting institutional prestige and indirectly through the effect on quality of students. Both are positive in the case of the first, but positive/negative in the case of the second.

The ratio of marginal costs is the shadow price of increased prestige of the *ith* department (determined by the prices of various goods and their productivity in producing departmental prestige)/the shadow price of increased enrollments. Both have several components. In the numerator, the increased revenue from increasing the prestige of the *ith* department decomposes into two parts – the increased tuition revenues that can be collected due to the increase in the university's prestige, and the expanded research volume that flows to the *ith* department because of its higher prestige. The unit cost of increasing the prestige of the *ith* department is subtracted from the increased revenue to get the shadow price of increased prestige in the *ith* department. Similarly, the denominator is the increased revenues from expanded enrollment minus the net increase in cost that results (1980, pp. 32–33).

While this captures a number of important features of university behavior, it is only one of the optimization conditions that can be derived from the model. Taking the first-order condition with respect to all factors of production (i.e., the number of faculty and quality of faculty assigned to the *ith* department) yields the result which states that factors (quantity and quality of faculty) should be allocated so that the ratio of the utility value of their marginal products just equal the ratio of their factor prices. Again, the factors directly contribute to institutional prestige which provides utility, while improved quality of students indirectly contributes to utility (1980, p. 34).

The equilibrium conditions of the model summarize a number of important aspects of university behavior. The first shows how universities balance the quantity and quality of students of enrollments in determining the size and composition of their student bodies. It also illustrates the importance played by prestige variables in university decision making, and how the increased costs of prestige may be partially offset by an accompanying increase in tuition and research revenues. The second condition emphasizes that increases in the number and quality of faculty members may have very different effects on departments in different disciplines. In disciplines where coverage of sub-fields is especially important to prestige, departments will tend to be larger because of the high marginal productivity of increases in faculty sizes. Responsiveness of research revenues to increases the number of faculty in a department or to improvements in their quality might differ sharply among disciplines, providing an incentive through the effects on relative prices, to expand departments in some fields while upgrading those in other fields (1980, p. 34).

The equilibrium conditions also have implications for comparative statics. Any relaxation of the budget constraint will lead to an increase in university utility, with both income and substitution effects important.

Increased per-student subsidies will make it cheaper to increase the number of students. If government increases research funds available in a particular field, making it easier to secure those funds, the university will respond to the change in price by increasing the prestige of that department if departmental prestige is a normal good (1980, pp. 34–35). But the effects of these changes on institutional size can not be determined from the model alone. A decrease in the price of faculty in the *ith* department implies a loosening of the budget constraint, and the university could increase its utility by enrolling more students. But the shift in relative prices makes it more expensive to forego prestige improvements. If the substitution effect dominates, the institution will decrease enrollment in favor of increasing the quality or quantity of faculty in the *ith* department. If the income effect dominates, the number of students enrolled will increase (1980, p. 35).

Garvin claimed that his model was sufficiently general to incorporate the behavior of the whole spectrum of universities – from those largely concerned with institutional prestige and quality of students to those primarily concerned with maximizing enrollment, with some minimal level of quality standards (1980, p. 35). This was illustrated with different shapes of indifference curves, with quality of students and quantity of students as the trade-offs in one case, and institutional prestige and quantity of students in the other case (1980, pp. 36–37).

Within this model, the excess demand situation of the post-World War II period resulted in non-price rationing that allowed universities to put greater emphasis on quality and to allow faculty priorities to become more dominant over student preferences, trends reinforced by government grant funds (1980, p. 36). Hence, universities more closely resembled prestige-maximizing organizations (1980, p. 37).

Garvin noted that while the utility-maximizing model illuminates a number of important features of university behavior, universities may possibly be maximizing something else, e.g., profits or revenue, or they may be such complex organizations with multiple and possibly conflicting goals, that a unitary objective function gives misleading results. He considered the profit-maximizing and revenue-maximizing possibilities against real-world behavior, and rejected both on grounds of lack of any evidence of such behavior based on a lack of parties who would have an interest in doing so and the fact that tuition is set too low to maximize profit or revenue (1980, pp. 38–39). While the utility maximizing model is preferred to either, it treats the university as a 'black box' and ignores internal decision-making processes, paying little attention to how these decisions are made. This leaves unanswered the question of whether the university is too complex of an organization for a single objective model to apply.

Garvin argued that while the utility-maximizing model is quite abstract and necessitates a high level of aggregation, while the analysis of internal organization is more detailed and views university operations through a finer filter, they are complementary in a macro/micro sense (1980, p. 59). The technical relationships governing the internal allocation process involve a department's prestige, size of teaching staff, number of undergraduate and graduate students enrolled, and volume of sponsored research being closely connected (1980, p. 59).

Formal Model of Prestige Improvement

Garvin also developed a formal model of prestige improvement. A university has two ways of improving the prestige of its departments – by attracting more faculty members whose personal prestige translates into institutional prestige, and by increasing the average size of departments by hiring new faculty (1980, p. 64). The law of diminishing returns was assumed to apply for already prestigious departments (1980, p. 65). Garvin's model related changes in prestige to (1) changes in faculty salaries; (2) changes in the number of faculty members; (3) some measure of the university's prestige in an earlier period, and (4) a random disturbance term (1980, p. 65). Factors (1) and (2) are positively related to prestige, which (3) is inversely related. Such factors as increased enrollments and increased revenues result in larger faculties and also larger faculty salaries (1980, p. 66). There is some institutional control over revenues from students, i.e., increased rate of tuition because prestige increases or increased tuition because enrollments increased, as well as some control over student reenrollments (1980, pp. 66–67).

Garvin's economic model of universities is a truncated version of Veblen's in ways other than the restriction of the decision makers to administrators and faculty members. The model offers no explanation of the non-academic activities of American universities.

An Economic Model of Public Universities

Large research universities that are state universities tend to function much like non-profit universities. They are governed by boards of trustees, enjoy considerable independence from the state legislature, receive a large part of their funds from sources other than state appropriations, and the faculty and administration function in much the same way as those of non-profit universities. But our survey of economic perspectives on universities would not be complete without recognizing that a general economic model has been developed that explains the behavior of public institutions such as state colleges. This model is much more applicable to state colleges that are essentially undergraduate schools. But to the extent that state research universities continue to have a public institution character, that model is relevant in explaining their behavior.

Although Veblen's 'economic model' was of non-profit universities, a precedent for an economic model of public universities is not entirely lacking *The Higher Learning in America*. In fact, Lindsay's model of government enterprises essentially develops two observations made by Veblen. As we noted in Chapter Five, he briefly noted that state universities were managed by 'political masters of intrigue' seeking 'short-term political prestige' through the operations of these schools (1918 [1993, pp. 43–44]). The modern economic model of public universities recognizes and incorporates the political interests of members of the legislative body as a major component. Veblen's emphasis on the bureaucratic nature of the administration of the non-profit universities is paralleled and amplified in the model of public universities as the power of bureaucratic administrators to assure that the behavior of the public institutions they manage functions in a way that appeals to quests for 'short-term political prestige' by members of the legislature is the second major component.

The general model of government enterprises developed by Lindsay (1976) was illustrated with the specific example of Veterans' Administration hospitals. But Lindsay indicated the model was also applicable to explaining the behavior of public universities. Other than the United States military academies, there are no pure examples of public universities, which would require that an institution be totally dependent upon the legislature for funds, very much like most public schools. But there are many state universities that depend almost entirely upon appropriations from the state legislature along with tuition and fees paid by students. Moreover, even the large state 'university corporations' with substantial endowments and revenues from grants and contracts receive significant revenues from state legislatures.

The difference between the economic models of non-profit universities and Lindsay's model of public universities lies in the differences in institutional environments. Several parties are involved in decision making, and individuals comprising those parties attempt to maximize their own self-interest to the extent allowed by their influence over institutional decision making. Institutional constraints on the types of personal gains allowed may be more severe in the public sector. That is especially true for pecuniary rewards, so personal gains often must be in psychic form. The parties involved in the decision-making processes, however, are different from the non-profit model. The *legislature* as a body has the power to provide or withhold funds (including proscribing how the funds can be used), and has the responsibility to monitor the use of funds by the institutions. *Administrators* of the institutions have the responsibility of managing the operations, and for seeking funds from the legislature through the budgeting process. In the pure model, the professional staffs, i.e., the faculties, are employees who have little (if any) discretionary influence over institutional decisions. Students have no influence because they pay no fees for the educational services consumed, and they are not organized in an effective fashion.

Individuals who are members of the legislatures and individuals who hold administrative positions in the institutions are assumed to be utility-maximizers. The model explains a process of bureaucratic choice in which administrators seek to maximize the 'value' of institutional outputs, with 'value' interpreted as what is perceived by members of the legislature as serving their own self-interests. The legislature as a body consists of individuals whose utility functions are maximized by either gaining re-election or winning election to a higher office. They have little knowledge or direct involvement with most of the different institutions, programs, and agencies that are funded by the legislature. But each member wants to demonstrate effectiveness in those areas that are of particular interest to constituents. It is important to the office-holder that public institutions generate demonstrable evidence of legislative effectiveness, which can be used to visibly tout that member's claim of effectiveness as a representative agent of the voters/taxpayers. Although claims of qualitative attributes are important, such information is most impressive if it is in the form of quantitative data.

In the legislative process, the power effectively is vested in the various committees and sub-committees. Each member of the legislature will attempt be assigned to those committees and sub-committees that deal with the programs and institutions of greatest constituency interest. Given the general lack of knowledge on part of all members of the legislature, sub-committee reports and recommendations are usually endorsed by the whole committee, and subsequently accepted by the legislative body as a whole. Thus, the monitoring and appropriations functions are largely in the hands of the few members of the sub-committees. Those who are most interested in the public universities and colleges because their constituents have strong interests in those institutions, will be on the sub-committees dealing with those schools.

The administrators of the institutions have two functions. First, they administer the budgets appropriated, and report to the sub-committee that monitors the performances of the institutions. Second, they prepare budget proposals for the coming fiscal year and attempt to convince the sub-committee members to accept their proposals. Administrators will utilize their large discretionary authority over the management of the institution to make the institutions function in such a manner as to maximize their utility functions. Their utility comes from a number of sources, e.g., salary, fringe benefits, size of the institution, prestige, etc. But generally, the larger the budget for the institution, the greater will be the opportunity for utility in whatever form. Thus, the familiar budget-maximizing behavioral model comes into play.

A game of strategy emerges. The administrators provide information to the sub-committee members which they use to assess the effectiveness of the institutional performances. But that information is generated from the activities of the institutions, which have two general attributes – qualitative and quantitative. Qualitative often involves judgements of intangibles and high unit costs. While members of the sub-committees will want to be able to assure their constituents that the public institutions are providing high quality outputs, the intangibility of quality education makes it difficult to impress constituents with data. Members of the legislature will prefer information in the form of numbers that can be used to demonstrate how effectively they are managing the public's tax dollars. On that basis, administrators will realize that quantitative attributes such as numbers of students enrolled, number of degrees awarded, number of majors offered, etc., will be much more influential on legislative budgeting decisions. Hence, administrators will tend to bias the operations of the institutions toward those activities that generate such numbers or, as Veblen intimated, maximize the vendable and merchantable educational product for public consumption.

Lindsay argued that with excess demand for admissions because universities underprice, 'university managers' behave as the model predicts. The 'best qualified' are admitted because they are the least costly to teach. This allows the universities to maximize the easily monitored quantitative outputs – numbers of students, number of credit hours, and number of degrees awarded. In the allocative decision between teaching and research, there will be a bias toward teaching because it generates large numbers. While research offers more prestige, it is also more costly and the results are difficult to quantify and display. Thus, teaching which can be done in large sections and in a highly routine fashion, falls in the 'quantitative attributes' category while research falls in the 'qualitative' category.

Recent economic models of higher education in America have used neo-classical economic models to technically explain university behavior. Garvin's model adds some technical sophistication to the analysis of decision making within public universities the assumptions are Veblenian. Universities compete in an academic market for students and revenues by producing institutional prestige. Prestige increases the inelasticity of demand for higher education, allows higher tuition and generates more revenue for the never-ending pursuit of a better reputation.

Recently, the administrators, boards of trustees, and many of the faculty of Alabama state colleges and universities have attempted to employ a strategy of organizing into a voting block to put political pressure on members of the state legislature. Institutions that normally compete for state funds – the two doctoral universities (and their several campuses) against the state colleges that call themselves universities – have colluded to compete politically against the public schools for public funds.

10. Meeting the Challenge: Explaining the Emergence of 'Entrepreneurial Universities' and 'Academic Capitalism'

When Adam Smith wrote *Wealth of Nations*, universities were small collegial teaching institutions. When Thorstein Veblen wrote *The Higher Learning in America* in the early part of the 20th century, the large doctoral-degree-granting institutions had recently emerged, combining academic research and teaching at the postgraduate level. At the end of the 20th century, a number of higher education policy analysts were observing a second institutional change in progress, with research universities being transformed into 'entrepreneurial universities' engaging in 'academic capitalism.' According to those analysts, that transformation has occurred in two continuing phases.

FIRST PHASE

The driving force behind the first phase, which began in the mid-1970s, was the changing nature of university research and the intended use of the results. With substantial funding from industry and working in close collaboration with industry, an increasing number of major universities are engaging in research projects aimed at producing intellectual properties with high market values. Department of Defense funding was largely responsible for the original Internet. Corporations failed to see the importance of 'the information superhighway.' But now, with the Internet a key commercial component in new markets such as electronic commerce and information services, the commercial value of a much faster Internet is easily seen. Thus, corporations like Cisco Systems, Inc. have contributed nearly one billion dollars for the development of an Internet 2 by United States universities and research centers. One hundred universities are expected to participate in the Internet 2 project. The technologies and applications credited for the Internet 2 project can easily be spun off into lucrative markets an universities are anxious to exploit the opportunity to generate sizable revenues. Universities are actively seeking to commercially exploit their ownership rights to other properties, either by creating firms to do the marketing or by entering into contractual arrangements with business corporations. In the process, the character and missions of universities are being affected. Essentially, universities are being transformed into a new type of institution that closely resembles commercial enterprises. The emerging 'entrepreneurial universities' (Etzkowitz, et al. 1998, p. 16) have two new missions – a proprietary mission of generating institutional revenues through commercialized research, and a public mission of contributing to economic development. For example, the University of Michigan reported that during 1999–2000 the university received $23.1 million in royalties and fees which were primarily generated by rewards related to the development of an AIDS drug and the sale of Net Perceptions, a firm developed by a university professor in which the school had a financial interest. Critics argue that the traditional missions of teaching and research are being altered, as the shifts from basic research to commercialized research are affecting both the relationships between faculty and students and between students and the universities.

In part, the transformation to 'entrepreneurial universities' is in response to changes in government support of university-based research. Public funding of fundamental or basic research has been reduced. Instead, policies have been adopted that encourage universities to pursue research that contributes to national goals of economic growth, job formation, and the ability to compete in global markets. The types of research proposals favored under the new policies are those that are expected to result in successful market innovations. Faculty members and universities aggressively compete for government funds in much the same manner that they compete for corporate funding of research. The ability to do groundbreaking research is no longer sufficient. Now, professors must be entrepreneurs who are knowledgeable about the commercial valuation potential of their proposed projects, and they must be supported by a university system for capitalizing on the intellectual properties that are forthcoming. Dr. David Kemp, the Australian Minister of Education, who administers $1.4 billion in research funds, authored a white paper in which the following view of the entrepreneurial view of the University was articulated:

> The culture of university research also needs to better recognize and reward the partnerships made with other members of the national innovation system. . . . it should become more entrepreneurial, seeking out opportunities in new and emerging fields of research that will provide social, cultural and economic benefit. . . . An entrepreneurial approach is needed to harness the fully cycle of

benefits from their endeavours through commercialization, where appropriate. This culture of entrepreneurship needs to be the context for the training of our research students, and indeed all students. (Kemp 1999, pp. 4-5).

Because faculty and universities must now engage in market-like competition for funds from external sources, Slaughter and Leslie (1997) coined the term 'academic capitalism' (p. 11).

SECOND PHASE

The second phase is occurring in the instructional activities of universities, particularly at the undergraduate level, but also at the professional graduate degree level, e.g., the MBA degree. Instructional materials for courses are being transformed into digitized courseware that becomes commercially viable proprietary products that can be sold in the online market. According to critics such as Noble (1998), this is not just a technological transformation in pedagogy, nor is it aimed at extending educational access to those unable to get to campuses. Rather, it is the commercialization of higher education. Universities, in collaboration with for-profit business companies are forming their own for-profit subsidiaries, are producing and actively seeking to commercially market copyrighted videos, courseware, CD-ROMS, and Web sites. Noble (1998, p. 5) cited a report by the investment firm of Lehman Brothers that the educational market will eventually become dominated by 'educational maintenance organizations' as the parallel to 'health maintenance organizations' (HMOs) in the health care field. Ironically, the primary market for these products have been students on campuses rather than those involved in distance learning. Noble cited the Western Governors' 'Virtual University Project' as offering explicit stated intentions to commercial develop and exploit the marketplace for instructional materials, courseware, and programs using advanced communications technology, and noted the proprietary interests of large publishing companies in the project.

Critics such as Noble maintain that this second phase has been touted as the solution to a financial crisis that has been engendered by the first phase. Universities have been placed under financial stress by 'an expensive and low-yielding commercial infrastructure and greatly expanded administrative costs.' Their response has been to attempt to increase the efficiencies of teachers who are already overextended by the reallocation of universities' resources to the research function. By requiring that instructional materials be placed on-line, universities are seeking to profit by marketing those materials. Critics, such as Noble, maintain that the result will be to compound the problem, increasing rather than reducing the costs of higher education.

THE CHALLENGE FOR ECONOMIC MODELS OF UNIVERSITIES' BEHAVIOR

The challenge for economic models of universities' behavior is to be able to explain not only the behavioral tendencies of universities in a particular institutional environment, but also evolutionary changes in that behavior due to changes in the external environment or in the internal processes of institutional decision making. The emergence of 'entrepreneurial universities,' with a proprietary mission to generate income by functioning more as commercial enterprises, poses important questions about Garvin's prestige-maximizing model based on consensus among the utility-maximizing individuals in positions to have some influence over institutional decisions. That model incorporates the essential elements of Veblen's 'economic' model of 'discretionary officials,' but not his underlying evolutionary institutional framework. Rather, it is a static institutional model that cannot explain evolutionary developments such as the emergence of the 'entrepreneurial university.' To meet that challenge, the essential connections that existed between Veblen's 'discretionary officials' model and his evolutionary institutionalist framework must be re-established for the modern economic models of universities' behavior.

OVERVIEW

In the following section, we briefly review the argument that commercialized research and close relationships between universities and industry are transforming universities into 'entrepreneurial universities.' In the supporting studies (e.g., Etzkowitz, et al. 1998; Slaughter and Leslie 1997), universities have been portrayed as responding to pressures created by changes in external factors, primarily in government funding of research and new opportunities presented by the willingness of industry to fund university research of a particular nature. Behavioral models of universities have only been superficially employed, and those that have been used are static models. Relatively little attention has been given to the internal institutional decision-making processes that explain why universities would respond in this manner to the changes in the external sources of funding for research.

We then examine the emergence of 'entrepreneurial universities' from the perspective of Veblen's evolutionary economic model of universities' behavior with its focus on the continued intrusive influence of business values, principles, and practices into university decision making through the values and membership of the collective group of 'discretionary officials.' In that light, the transformation from research universities to 'entrepreneurial universities' appears to be a logical development in the continuation of the evolutionary process of change that Veblen analyzed in the early 20th century.

Finally, our study of economic perspectives on universities' behavior concludes on a normative note. While their positive analyses of universities' behavioral tendencies followed surprisingly similar approaches, Adam Smith and Thorstein Veblen held very different views on how far removed universities should be from proprietary business firms and the economic forces of market supply and demand. Taking those normative views in hand, we consider how each might regard the trend toward 'entrepreneurial universities' and 'academic capitalism.'

THE EMERGENCE OF 'ENTREPRENEURIAL UNIVERSITIES'

Paraphrasing Marx and Engels, et al. (1998) declared that 'There is a spectre haunting the academic world of *externally driven influence* upon the mission of universities' (p. 21, emphasis added). That 'spectre' is 'entrepreneurial science,' i.e., corporations funding university research aimed at producing commercially profitable intellectual properties, which they suggest is producing a second academic revolution (the first being the development of the modern research university).

Universities and colleges have become increasingly involved in a variety of commercial activities, ranging from operating book stores and marketing products bearing logos of athletic teams to joint ventures with business firms in property and commercial developments. A number of universities are using their endowments for venture capital projects where equity positions are taken. But those kinds of for-profit activities are largely extraneous to the academic activities that traditionally have defined universities as specialized institutions – faculty research and teaching. While it may be argued that universities' commercial activities have important spillover effects on the university as an institution, the evolutionary transformation to 'entrepreneurial universities' is directly related to changes in the kinds of research being done by university faculty members. These changes necessarily impinge on the relationships between faculty members and the university, the nature of graduate level teaching, the relationship between graduate students and their supervising professors, and the relationship between graduate students' research activities and the institutional missions of the universities.

Much of the collaboration between universities and industry is occurring in the areas of science, engineering, and technology. As universities have become more involved in the creation of science-based industries, the relationship between universities and corporations has become increasingly on a business basis. Until recently, most university–industry connections separated academic and commercial practices. Control over commercial opportunities of academic research was in the hands of industry, and control over the direction of research and choice of research topics was left to the academic researchers. That has changed. As universities have become principal players along with industry and government in the innovation system, universities have assumed entrepreneurial roles, establishing technology transfer offices to seek out and market intellectual properties (p. 6). What has been termed the 'capitalization of knowledge' by Etzkowitz, et al. (1998, pp. 11–12) has involved a three-stage process. First, universities secure legal claim to intellectual property through patents. Second, research groups are restructured to generate a large intellectual property base. These groups operate as 'quasi-firms' that become more and more dependent on commercial income. Third, corporate vehicles such as spin-off firms are established within universities to maximize the financial return on intellectual property.

THE CONSEQUENCES OF 'ENTERPRENEURIAL' RESEARCH BY UNIVERSITIES

The process of capitalization of intellectual properties is driving a number of organizational changes within the universities. Research teams must be organized on more of a 'quasi-firm' business firm basis, lacking only a direct profit motive to make them full-fledged firms. To accomplish the research and development and the commercialization of the products requires research groups to provide their own corporate development plans, operate on full economic cost accounting, secure their own patent rights, and engender a range of technological spin-offs from their continuing basic or strategic research.

Etzkowitz, et al. (1998) described how the traditional function of the universities to advance and disseminate knowledge through research and teaching is being affected by the shifts toward more commercial activities. Conflicts arise over ownership of intellectual properties that affect relationships between faculty members and the university, between faculty members and graduate students, and between graduate students and the universities. Individual faculty researchers may be more interested in capitalizing personally on knowledge gained from research under their direction by starting their own firms. Universities want to capitalize institutionally from entrepreneurial research, but they need faculty members to do that research. If faculty members are allowed to profit personally by starting their own firms, the university appears to be subsidizing private research. On the other hand, if the university attempts to appropriate all the profits, faculty members have an economic incentive to withhold their efforts. The inevitable compromise rewards those doing entrepreneurial research more highly than those who continue to do the traditional basic research.

University scientists' traditional mission of making public the results of their research is threatened by 'entrepreneurial science' which privatizes intellectual properties. Under the proprietary institutional mission of appropriating the market values of intellectual properties, professors are less willing to submit papers reporting the results of their research for peer review and less willing to collaborate with other researchers. The whole system of promotion and tenure based on peer review of academic work is affected, as are the relationships between faculty and graduate students. The traditional sharing of authorship of graduate students' work with professors who provided the infrastructure has less appeal as the opportunities for new Ph.D.s to find academic employment have declined. Now, pecuniary interests as well as reputational interests are involved. The role of graduate students as inventors has taken hold as administrators have recognized that their research produces intellectual property as well as the traditional research papers. A graduate student's best chance at a job and future career may be in starting a company on basis of the intellectual properties resulting from his research. But the universities claim ownership rights to those intellectual property, and faculty members may lay claim to co-inventor status in addition to co-authorship. (This, of course, is very similar to what has long been going on in football, where universities and coaches appropriate the pecuniary gains from winning programs.) As pay and status of graduate students has lagged behind the importance of their research contributions to 'entrepreneurial science,' either the sharing of profits will have to increase or fewer graduate students will make themselves available. The traditional feudalistic status of graduate students as apprentices will certainly change as their bargaining power is enhanced by the ability to inflict pecuniary losses on universities (and faculty members) by withholding their services as researchers.

The Australian National University's intellectual property (IP) guidelines illustrate the gray area between traditional research and proprietary research. 'The University encourages creativity, scholarship and innovation, and affirms the principle that knowledge and ideas should be available within the public domain for the benefit of the entire community. To this end, the results of University research should be published and widely disseminated' (1999, p. 3). But the guidelines immediately qualify that in the statement: 'Without resiling from this principle, the University continues to be prepared to protect University IP and encourage its commercial development when this could be of financial benefit to the University, its employees, and Australia.' (1999, p. 3).

As another example, the Arizona Board of Regents revised its intellectual property rights policy to enhance cooperation between the universities and businesses on joint and sponsored research. The policy revisions were in response to high-technology companies' request to own certain university-created intellectual properties in order to preserve their competitive positions. At the discretion of the university, businesses can obtain title to university-conducted research if they pay all direct and overhead costs incurred in developing the properties. The universities' technology transfer offices are allowed to work out the best arrangement with each participating company, in some cases transferring title, in other cases sharing ownership through licensing or royalty agreements. The board president lauded this practice as attracting more industry funds to universities over the long run, creating richer research experiences for undergraduate and graduate students.

In their study of how public research universities and their faculties have responded under government policies that forced universities to compete for more limited research funds, Slaughter and Leslie (1997) observed changes in the internal distribution of power. Central administrators both gain and lose power. Centers, institutes, and departments that generate research funds gain autonomy and their power increases, causing reduced power for central administrators. But the latter gain power by being able to use block grants and discretionary funds to reward and build up those internal units most likely to secure external funds. An analysis of the distribution of financial flows within universities revealed a growing share for central administration, resulting in the conclusion that central administrators are gaining power. The university governance system also is changing from collegial governance of academic work to management of entrepreneurial activities. Administrators are becoming more technocratic managers rather than academic leaders.

In the larger picture, the academic autonomy of university faculty is being diminished as academics and academic work is becoming marginalized. The internal complexity of universities is increasing in response to the complex sources of external funds and the highly specialized relationships that develop between faculty seeking funds and those in agencies providing the funds. The National Center for Policy

Analysis reported that even trustees are having trouble finding out what their university administrators are doing with endowment funds. The latter see their role as managers of large pools of investment assets who run educational institutions on the side. A similar development is occurring in the commercialization of intellectual properties created by professorial-directed, corporate-funded research.

Slaughter and Leslie (1997) suggested that undergraduate instruction is deteriorating in quality as less is being spent on instruction and more is being spent on research and service. They explain that as reflecting a convergence of faculty preferences for research over teaching and faculty reward systems that honor research over all other activities. Administrators and the collective faculties are signaling individual faculty members that they should increase their efforts to secure grants. Prestige and power are part of the reward system. Faculty members are rewarded most highly in fields close to the market. Salary differentials reflect labor markets for professionals outside the university as well as faculty potential to win external revenues for the university.

AN ALTERNATIVE VIEW

Whether the growing involvement in commercial research activities is actually transforming research universities into 'entrepreneurial universities' is subject to debate. The type of commercial activities involved are engaged in by only certain schools and departments within research universities, primarily medical and engineering schools, science departments, and graduate schools of business. An alternative view is that these developments are simply an extension of earlier patterns, without seriously impacting the traditional separation of academic research and commercial exploitation of the intellectual properties that result. This alternative view draws some support from the assessments of challenges to research universities presented in Noll (1998). While business corporations have become an increasingly important source of support for universities, their profit orientation is viewed as severely limiting the size and scope of support. Some universities are turning more vigorously to their traditional teaching mission as research funds become more difficult to obtain. University enrollments have increased, and international students in graduate science and engineering programs have supported the traditional graduate programs. Noll and others see the trends as leading to decreases in the quality of research and the complementary activity of educating students in the technical areas with the shrinkage in opportunities for training in university research labs. With increased student loans available and the federal tuition tax credit, American universities will be able to increase tuition and fees to offset reductions in other funds. Universities will use the new funds to compete for students by investing in educational activities. Moreover, the most prestigious universities will be able to continue receiving strong endowment support.

THE 'COMMODITIZATION OF INSTRUCTION'

Critics insist that the transformation of instructional materials for courses into digitalized coursewares that become commercially viable proprietary products in the online market is not just a technological transformation of the pedagogical method, nor simply an attempt to extend educational access to those unable to get to campuses. Rather, it is the commercialization of higher education in the form of turning coursework instruction into a standardized commodity that can be profitably marketed. This is apparent from the arrangements that are being made. Universities in collaboration with for-profit business companies, and in forming their own for-profit subsidiaries, are producing and actively seeking to commercially market for profit copyrighted videos, courseware, CD-ROMS, and Web sites. A report by the investment firm of Lehman Brothers that predicted the educational market will become dominated by 'educational maintenance organizations' in the same way that health maintenance organizations (HMO's) have in the health care field (Noble 1998). Noble cited the Western Governors' Virtual University Project as offering explicit stated intentions to commercially develop and exploit the marketplace for instructional materials, courseware, and programs using advanced telecommunications systems, and also noted the proprietary interests of large publishing companies in the project.

That this is the commercialization of higher education is also apparent from the parties that are promoting it. Whereas research professors must become entrepreneurs in developing intellectual properties that have market value, online instructional properties reduce the power of faculty over their own courses and reduce the need for their classroom services. Four groups have been identified as promoting online instructional properties. The first group consists of for-profit companies with direct business interests either in the properties or the delivery. Those include publishing companies who view education as their market, vendors of network hardware, software, and 'content' such as Apple, IBM, Bell, and cable company administrators. The second group consists of corporate training advocates who envision the transformation of the delivery of higher education as a means of supplying their properly prepared personnel at public expense. The third group is university administrators who see commercialized online instruction as yielding several benefits –

giving their institutions a forward-looking image, a means of reducing direct labor and maintenance costs by reducing the need for teachers and classrooms, and a share of the profits. Administrators are supported in this by a number of private foundations, trade associations, and academic-corporate consortia that are promoting the use of the new technologies with increasing intensity. The fourth group consists of the 'technozealots' who view computers as the panacea for everything. They make claims about enhancement of education through modern communications technology without providing any real evidence to support those claims.

Critics argue that faculty activities are being restructured via technology, in order to reduce their autonomy, independence, and control over their work, and that workplace knowledge and control is being placed as much as possible in the hands of administrators. Noble stated that 'As in other industries, the technology is being deployed by management primarily to discipline, de-skill, and displace labor' (1998, p. 11). Once faculty and courses go online, administrators gain much greater direct control over faculty performance and course content, and the potential for administrative scrutiny, supervision, regimentation, discipline and even censorship increase dramatically. At the same time, the use of technology entails an inevitable extension of working time and an intensification of work. Faculty struggle at all hours of the day and night to stay on top of technology and respond, via chat rooms, virtual office hours, and e-mail, to both students and administrators to whom they have now become instantly and continuously accessible. The technology also allows for much more careful administrative monitoring of faculty availability, activities, and responsiveness.

Once faculty put course materials online, the knowledge and course design skill embodied in those materials pass from their possession to the machinery and placed in the hands of the administration. The administration is then in a position to hire less skilled, and hence cheaper, workers to deliver the technologically pre-packaged course. It also allows the administration, which claims ownership of this commodity, to peddle the course elsewhere without the original designer's involved or even knowledge, much less financial interest. The buyers of the packed commodity, other academic institutions, are able thereby to contract out, and hence, out-source, the work of their own employees and thus reduce their reliance upon their in-house teaching staff. Faculties become redundant once their instructional materials have been turned into digitalized courseware. Noble cited the example of UCLA requiring that all course instructional materials – syllabi, assignments, lecture notes – be put online, at the disposal of the administration – to be used by the administration without asking who will own it or how it will be used and with what consequences. It is becoming common practice to pay flat fees to contracting Ph.D.s to develop a course, with the rights being claimed by the universities.

The commercialization of instruction is illustrated by EDUCOM, an academic-corporate consortium, doing a detail study aimed at breaking faculty jobs down into discrete tasks for the purpose of determining what parts can be automated or outsourced. EDUCOM believes that course design, lectures, and even evaluation can all be standardized, mechanized, and consigned to outside commercial vendors.

Noble claims that university administrators are coercing or enticing faculty into compliance, placing the greatest pressures on the most vulnerable – the untenured and part-time faculty, and entry-level and prospective employees. At the same time, they are mounting an intensifying propaganda campaign to portray faculty as incompetent, hidebound, recalcitrant, inefficient, ineffective, and expensive – in short, in need of improvement or replacement through instructional technologies. Faculty members are portrayed as obstructionist, standing in the way of progress and the knowledge revolution, forestalling the panacea of virtual education allegedly demanded by students, their parents, and the public.

That this is being driven by commercial interest rather than student needs and demands is evident in the lack of concern for growing student alienation and their preferences for teachers to talk with. As resources were transferred from the education function to entrepreneurial research function in the first phase, class sizes swelled, teaching staffs and instructional resources were reduced, curriculum offerings were cut, and costs to students increased. The shift to online instruction is supposed to cut costs (and hence generate profits for the universities by keeping fees high), but there is no evidence that computer-based teaching is less expensive. Witness the need for outside funding and the adding on of 'technology' fees for students. Nor can the argument be validated that universities are simply extending educational opportunities to those who are unable to attend courses on campuses since the real market for online instructional products is the campus.

Universities not only create the products, but in effect give value to those products. What students seek are degrees, not the knowledge from the courses. Because only the universities can award degrees, and because degrees are so important for employment and even social status, courses required or accepted by universities for degrees will be taken and those that are not accepted toward degrees will not be taken. Thus, making the course required for a degree can create demand for online academic courseware available only online.

EXPLAINING THE EMERGENCE OF 'ENTREPRENEURIAL UNIVERSITIES'

The case that 'entrepreneurial universities' are emerging has been articulated so effectively as to pose a challenge to economic models to explain how such an evolutionary change could happen. But primary emphasis in the supporting analyses has been on external factors that have altered the revenue sources for universities. Relatively little attention has been paid to the internal processes of institutional decision making. In identifying an externally driven influence upon the mission of universities as the 'spectre' which is haunting academia, Etzkowitz, et al. (1998) made the point that 'Change within universities has always been notoriously slow when driven from within' (p. 21). In their study, Slaughter and Leslie (1997) postulated that universities' behavior is subject to resource dependence theory, according to which the organization seeks to maximize and stabilize the flows of revenues needed for its survival. Stability is preferred, and when resource flows are altered, the organization responds by directing efforts at restoring stability. This is a passive model of institutional behavior, as revealed in the statement that 'resource dependence theory holds that internal behaviors of organizational members are understood clearly only by reference to actions of external agents' (Slaughter and Leslie 1997, p. 68).

At the same time, Slaughter and Leslie (1997) also viewed universities has pursuing the prestige objective, treating revenue generation as the means of achieving prestige for both the institution and individual faculty members. Research is the immediate source of prestige, but resources are necessary to conduct research. Thus, to maintain resources for research, faculty members and administrators will turn to whatever sources are available. Slaughter and Leslie (1997) claimed that professors continue to be selective in their pursuit of external research dollars. They continue to pursue basic or fundamental research with the same vigor as before. But they increasingly looking for commercial research funding for 'frontier' science and engineering projects that are tied to national policy initiatives, i.e. Internet 2, and are partnered by prestigious firms (1997, p. 17). Similarly, Etzkowitz and Webster (1998) noted that many of the industrial funding of university research has been with the most prestigious university centers, e.g., Harvard University is expected to soon receive about one-fourth of its research funds from industrial sources (p. 29).

Still, Slaughter and Leslie (1997) noted that commercialized funded research is somewhat at odds with the traditional status and prestige system of research universities that venerated basic or fundamental research (p. 137). They seem to suggest that stability may weigh heavily in the decisions to pursue the funds for entrepreneurial research. Such funds contribute to better relations with external bodies. Improvements in those relationships are desired by university faculty to alleviate disruptions caused by changes in resource patterns (1997, p. 137). Universities in the United States, Canada, and the United Kingdom are turning to private credit rating agencies such as Moody's and Standard & Poor's to help in their search for corporate investors as they try to widen and deepen their support from firms and foundations. Higher education credit ratings focus on an institution's revenue sources and debt position as well as its prestige and potential for attracting research sponsorship.

The utility-maximizing model of universities' behavior could easily explain why professors and administrators would choose to respond to changes in external sources of funding for research if it is specified that those pecuniary gains are prominent elements in the utility-functions of individuals in those two groups. It could perhaps even be argued that Adam Smith's general 'model' of income/leisure maximizing individuals would be compatible with this approach. Faculty members and administrators are simply adapting to new economic incentives. Professors choose to engage in entrepreneurial research ventures because they find it to be more financially rewarding, directly through the incomes gained and indirectly by the revenues the universities gain through commercial exploitation of the products generated. Administrators even more so would be expected to have direct pecuniary interests in the revenues generated.

But the resource dependence model represents the type of economic theory that Veblen criticized in his article 'Why is Economics Not an Evolutionary Science?' In rejecting the assumption of rational utility-maximizing individuals, Veblen stated:

> The hedonistic conception of man is that of a lightning calculator of pleasure and pains, who oscillates like a homogenous globule of desire of happiness under the impulse of stimuli that shift him about the area, but leave him intact (Veblen 1961, p. 73).

That criticism would seem to apply equally to the implicit assumption in the resource dependence theory that universities and faculty members as revenue-maximizers simply 'oscillate under the impulse of stimuli' in the form of changes in the external sources of revenues. Even Adam Smith stated that the natural employment of 'men of letters' is to be a teacher of science (1776 [1976, p. 812]). In any case, an individual faculty member's utility functions that fits the resource dependence theory would be at odds with the utility functions that have shaped the acceptance of universities' missions as performing research purely for the sake of advancing knowledge and sharing that knowledge through publication and teaching students.

From the perspective of Veblen's evolutionary economic model, the changes observed in universities' behavior must be explained in terms of the 'motives' or utility functions of the 'discretionary officials.' A change may have occurred in the membership of the collective group of 'discretionary officials,' with the dominant group consisting of individuals whose 'motives' are satisfied by universities' engaging in commercialized activities. As we will see, this easily applies if administrators are making the decisions. But the situation is more complex because faculty members and graduate students conduct research that produces new intellectual properties. The pecuniary importance of their research necessarily makes research professors important members of the 'discretionary officials.' There is the obvious possibility that their 'motives' as faculty members have changed, but the more challenging task is to explain why they would now be satisfied with pursuing commercialized research whereas in the past they preferred to do pure scientific research.

An explanation was recently proffered by Michael Shattrock, registrar of Warwick University, who stated 'A pound note looks the same whether it comes from government, a venture capitalist or a company'. (Ben Russell, 'Turning Bright Ideas into Pound Notes,' *The Independent* (London) 26 March 1998).

A VEBLENIAN PERSPECTIVE

From a Veblenian perspective, this is simply a continuation of the process of evolutionary change that was analyzed in *The Higher Learning in America*. The influence of the pecuniary values of business enterprise society has continued to penetrate deep into the universities, reinforcing the utilitarian mentality of the technical and professional schools. Indeed, the 'second revolution' in universities being wrought by 'entrepreneurial science' (Etzkowitz, et al. 1998, p. 21) has been described as occurring in a most Veblenian evolutionary manner. In Chapter 5, we noted that Veblen described the evolutionary transition of universities from professional training institutions to institutions for the conservation, advancement, and dissemination of knowledge for its own sake, as occurring surreptitiously. University men concealed their disinterested searches 'that had no bearing on any human want' under the guise of some ostensibly practical line of inquiry. In his analysis of the failures of American universities, Veblen noted that the traditional view of the university as the academy of higher learning devoted to profitless pursuit of knowledge by scientists and scholars had not been fully eroded. There are echoes of both of those observations in the recent critical analyses of the 'entrepreneurial universities.' In their 'Foreword' to *Capitalizing Knowledge*: New

Intersections of Industry and Academia, Etzkowitz, et al. (1998) commented that the creation of closer ties of industries and government to university research 'has emerged behind the façade of universities viewed as the locus of curiosity-driven research conducted by individual investigators' (p. xi).

Viewed from the perspective of Veblen's analysis of universities' behavior, the emergence of the 'entrepreneurial university' can be recognized as a logical development in the continuation of the evolutionary process of change that was underway in the early 1900s. In that process, business values, principles, and practices gain ever more influence within 'university corporations,' altering the nature and character of the 'academic academy' ever more toward the 'academic enterprise.' The modern 'entrepreneurial university' is simply the latest manifestation of Veblen's 'educational enterprises' (1918 [1993, p. 140]). What does it suggest about the 'discretionary officials?' Namely, they still seek to maximize their personal reputation through the prestige of the university. Only now, prestige measures include patents, Initial Purchase Offerings (IPOs) of university-developed firms, credit ratings, and externally-funded research.

The increasing engagement by universities in a variety of commercial activities that are unrelated to research and teaching is being encouraged by university administrators and education ministers. The university as a revenue-maximizer is simply a managerial institution, with administrators and trustees as the 'discretionary officials.' This represents the logical continuation of the influence of business mentality through the types of individuals who become trustees and administrators, especially the latter. Veblen viewed the large 'educational enterprises' of the early 1900s as being organized in part to simulate the precedents of large modern business coalitions. This was partly explained by the administrators, their staffs, and the boards of trustees being attracted by the glamour of the exploits of trustmakers (1918 [1993, p. 141]). The boards, committees, chiefs of bureaus, and so forth that make up the bureaucracies of the modern 'university corporation' are chosen for their 'business-like efficiency' – they are good office men with executive ability. The animus of these academic businessmen becomes the driving spirit of the corporation of learning under their control (1918 [1993, p. 142]). As the 'university corporations' evolved through the 20th century, there were more and more opportunities for 'academic businessmen' to pursue commercial-like activities. Until the late 1900s, such commercial opportunities were largely in the management of endowments, which include real properties as well as financial assets, the marketing of football-related products and activities, and the competitive efforts to enhance endowments. Changes in external environments in the waning decades of the 20th century created new opportunities for the 'academic businessmen' to easily expanded their role, with the strong support of the boards of trustees who largely had similar values. While most of the non-research commercial activities only generate revenue that is largely used to continue and expand those activities, the role of the universities in such activities could easily be justified under the traditional view of the functions of the university as an academy of higher learning by asserting that funds will be generated that support research and teaching.

But the 'entrepreneurial university' refers to commercialization of faculty research, and the consequent effects on the nature and character of the university, especially on the graduate programs. Here Veblen's analysis points to the larger influence of social values on universities' behavior and the particular influence of business values on those social values. The emphasis on research that generates innovations is simply the latest manifestation of Veblen's observation that the primary mover in the evolutionary changes occurring in 'university grade' schools in the early 1900s was an unreflecting tendency to make much of all things that have 'practical value,' which meant useful for private gain in a business enterprise society (1918 [1993, p. 141]). Veblen's comments on vocational education apply equally to research efforts to generate innovations. It is viewed as conducive in a special degree to good citizenship (which means proficiency in competitive business) and the material welfare of the community (1918 [1993, p. 143]). The administrators of universities and their 'faculty gnomes' seek funds from external sources, and are eager to please by providing outputs that are viewed as worthwhile by those sources. They simply respond to the current drift (1918 [1993, p. 149]). For those sources, universities should produce things of value, and value is pecuniary value. What is good for business is felt to be serviceable to the common good (1918 [1993, pp. 144–146]). Warwick's registrar, Mr. Shattock, notes: 'The best businesses know where the best research is. They would not be the best if they didn't. The best researchers know where the best businesses are.' The recent announcement that software giant Microsoft was planning to set up a research base in Cambridge is a high-profile example of 'discretionary officials (vice chancellors) welcoming high tech industries to their university communities.'

Essentially, universities subject to the evolutionary drift are still caught in the conflict between what Veblen termed the influence of the 'current common-sense award of the vulgar,' to whom the advocacy of practical education is an self-evident principle, and the 'award of civilized common sense,' which recognizes that, in the long-run, knowledge is more desirable than things of price (1918 [1993, p. 145]). To the former, the advocacy of practical education is a self-evident principle. The 'snap-judgement' formed under the workday reality of making a living in a competitive market environment tends to exert an increasing influence, producing demands on universities to provide practical services that lead to employments and incomes. An associated influence is reflected in an increasing habitual inclination of the same uncritical character among academic men to value all academic work in terms of livelihood or of earning capacity (1918 [1993, p. 145]). Even the seasoned scientists and scholars have taken to heart this question of the use of the higher learning in the pursuit of pecuniary gain (1918 [1993, p. 146]).

At the time Veblen was writing *The Higher Learning in America*, the impact of the 'animus of these academic businessmen' was most immediately on undergraduate instruction. But he noted that it was permeating into the graduate programs, and that the trend could be expected to continue. That is precisely what is happening with the emergence of the 'entrepreneurial universities.' Veblen noted that the trend would go farthest and fastest in the professional schools, and found considerable justification for the medical and technological schools utilizing scientific knowledge generated in the university proper to do work that is of substantial use to the community at large (1918 [1993, p. 152]).

SMITH AND VEBLEN ON 'ENTREPRENEURIAL UNIVERSITIES'

There can be no doubt that Veblen would view 'entrepreneurial universities' in a harsh negative light. While he had no problem with medical and technological schools making innovative use of knowledge generated by the pure research of university scientists to do things that contributed to the community, he was opposed to commercial activities that were aimed simply at generating pecuniary values. Veblen would view the 'commoditization of instructional materials' for profit-oriented online distribution as the logical extension of the influence of the principles of business enterprise into higher education. To him it would be simply the modern version of the extension courses and correspondence course offered by the University of Chicago in his time. That EDUCOM, the academic-corporate consortium, is doing detailed studies of what professors do, breaking the faculty job down in classical Tayloristic (time-motion studies) fashion into discrete task, determining what parts can be automated or outsourced, believing that course design, lectures, and even evaluation of students can all be standardized, mechanized, and consigned to outside commercial vendors, would more clearly validate the encroaching role Veblen envisioned for business practices. The most untenable university activities to Veblen would be University attempts to protect and exploit the intellectual property created through research in patents and licensing deals.

Veblen would also perhaps argue that the 'entrepreneurial universities' will suffer the same basic failure as the research institutes. Because the latter did not train graduate students to become the scientists and scholars of tomorrow, they were not self-perpetuating. He warned that the growing influence of business principles on universities' academic programs would result in a failure of the universities to produce those who will do the pure research. The 'entrepreneurial universities,' like the research institutes, depend upon a supply of trained scientists for the production of pure research that only the true universities can provide. The trend, then, is toward sterile institutions so far as the higher learning is concerned.

How would Adam Smith regard the 'entrepreneurial universities?' Here we may have to draw more heavily on Smith's experiences as a faculty member and administrator at Glasgow University as described in Rae (1965) and Scott (1937 [1965]) than on his commentary in *Wealth of Nations*. The latter was directed toward universities whose function was to teach what were essentially undergraduate students. Ortmann (1997) has argued that Smith would regard with approval some of the recent developments in higher education, including the for-profit universities, the re-orientation of many colleges and universities toward vocationalism, and the dramatic increase of part-time and piece-rate contract instructors. Ortmann claimed that Smith gave useful advice to modern universities under pressure to adjust to post-industrial environments that are characterized by scarcer resources, increased competitiveness, and a more turbulent, less predictable environment. As modern information technologies reduce the cost of coordination, universities will become less dependent on physical facilities and collections of students and faculty members in a given place. For-profit universities offering distance-learning degree programs are supposed to compete with traditional universities and force changes in the latter. Given Smith's skepticism toward the merit of degrees as opposed to becoming educated, he might well view most of those programs as equivalent to 'sham lectures.' (As predicted, change is being effected as smaller universities that are vulnerable to competition from large-scale online educational providers have had their credit ratings downgraded and are having a more difficult time raising money in the credit markets.)

Ortmann's argument concerning universities' use of part-time instructors and piece-rate payments has special connotations from both Smith's and Veblen's perspectives. Smith observed that subsidized university education had produced so many men of letters that their incomes as teachers were extremely low. That is precisely what has happened in recent time, and continues unabated to happen. Universities' doctoral programs have produced so many Ph.D.s in fields such as the humanities that a buyer's market has emerged. If Smith's argument against the various types of subsidies was implemented into practice, the supply of Ph.D.s would then shrink, creating a market price for full time professors that offered incomes commensurate with ordinary rates of return on investment for those with the degrees. A consequence would be fewer students taught in aggregate. With respect to the 'piece-rate pay' of the numerous part-time faculty members, Smith argued that such a pay system was detrimental to the health of workers because they will tend to overwork themselves. As we noted in Chapter Three, his failure to address how professors would tend to behave if their incomes could be enhanced by fees from more students is a serious weakness in his economic analysis.

Veblen would regard the current situation of part-time employment and piece-rate pay as simply the modern version of the business-like management of universities in which faculty are treated as 'hired-hands.' But he would also argue that the fundamental problem is that there too many people are attending too many colleges and universities, creating an artificial demand for teachers of courses that only generate credit hours and degrees based on those credit hours. He would not regard the loss of those 'students' and the part-time teachers as detrimental to a genuine college education that prepared bona fide students for graduate study.

Ortmann did not address the more fundamental institutional changes leading to the 'entrepreneurial universities,' namely, research activities aimed at market innovations, funded by industry and commercially exploited by universities and industry together. If the teaching mission of the universities was not impacted in a negative manner, Smith might view these developments with some approval in view of his support of embryeonic activities in that direction by the University of Glasgow during the late 18th century. The College's support of the work of Watts, the innovator of steam engines, may not be that different from the academic entrepreneurs of the modern research universities. Certainly, Smith's own efforts to maximize the revenues from the various properties and rights held by Glasgow College would suggest that he would have little problem with modern universities attempting to maximize revenues from their various properties in commercial operations and contracts. But the bottom line for Smith would be the university's function to teach the youth what they needed to know.

How Smith would view online courses seem quite evident. He placed great emphasis on the personal involvement of the teacher with the students. Undoubtedly, he would view the 'commoditization of instruction' in much the same light as he did the giving of 'sham lectures' by Oxford dons.

Entrepreneurial universities mirror the Veblenian image that institutions evolve after patterns of behavior are established. In the case of higher education, universities have become eager to pursue and exploit commercial relationships that bring revenue from vendable educational products. Such institutional behavior merely follows the best-business-practices of the trustees who influence modern academic policy. To advance their personal reputations, University presidents and discretionary officials encourage the pursuit of third-stream (non-government) revenue to further the appearance of a forward-looking University, to buy more 'official scholars' and meet foundation expectations for research grants.

Assuming the demand for higher education is adequate to support the entrepreneurial university, one wonders if the future impact of the financial chicanery of corporate heads and their trustees will ultimately manifest itself in the boardrooms of higher education.

Bibliography

Allen, L. (1991), *Opening Doors: The Life and Work of Joseph Schumpeter, Vol. II*, New Brunswick: Transaction Publishers.

Australian National University, The (1999), *The Australian National University Intellectual Property Guidelines*, Australia Council of the University (electronic version), accessed March 25, 2003 at http://www.anu.edu.au/admin/chairbtf/documents/ippol2.htm.

Balderston, F. E. (1990), 'Organization, Funding, Incentives, and Initiatives for University Research: A University Management Perspective', in S. A. Hoenack and E. L. Collins (eds), *The Economics of American Universities*, Albany: State University of New York Press, pp. 33–52.

Barber, W. J. (1988), *Breaking the Academic Mould*, Middletown: Wesleyan University Press.

Barker, N. (1978), *The Oxford University Press and the Spread of Learning, 1478–1978*, Oxford: Clarendon Press.

Becker, W. E. (1990), 'The Demand for Higher Education,' in S. A. Hoenack and E. L. Collins (eds), *The Economics of American Universities*, Albany: Albany State University of New York Press, pp. 155–188.

Brennan, H. G. and R. D. Tollison (1980), 'Rent Seeking in Academia,' in J. M. Buchanan, R. D. Tollison and G. Tullock (eds), *Toward a Theory of the Rent-Seeking Society*, College Station: Texas A & M Press, pp. 344–356.

Brinkman, P. T. (1990a), 'Higher Education Cost Functions,' in S.A. Hoenack and E.L. Collins (eds), *The Economics of American Universities*, Albany: Albany State University of New York Press, pp. 107–128.

Brinkman, P. T. (1990b), 'College and University Adjustments to a Changing Financial Environment,' in S. A. Hoenack and E. L. Collins (eds), *The Economics of American Universities*, Albany: Albany State University of New York Press, pp. 215–232.

Brown, R. W. (1993), 'An Estimate of the Rent Generated by a Premium College Football Player', *Economic Inquiry*, **31**(4), 671–684.

Brown, W. O. Jr. (1997), 'University Governance and Academic Tenure: A Property Rights Explanation', *Journal of Institutional and Theoretical Economics*, **47**(3), 441–461.

Buchanan, J. M. and N. E. Devletoglou (1970), *Academia in Anarchy, An Economic Diagnosis*, New York: Basic Books, Inc.

Carmichael, H. L. (1988), 'Incentives in Academia: Why Is There Tenure?' *Journal of Political Economy*, **96**(3), 453–472.

Carter, H. (1975), *A History of the Oxford University Press*, Oxford: Clarendon Press.

Clotfelter, C. T. (1991), 'Demand for Undergraduate Education', in C. T. Clotfelter (ed.), *Economic Challenges in Higher Education*, Chicago: University of Chicago Press, pp. 19–139.

Clotfelter, C. T., R. G. Ehrenberg, M. Getz, and J. J. Siegfried (1991), *Economic Challenges in Higher Education*, Chicago: University of Chicago Press.

Clotfelter, C. T. and M. Rothschild (1993), 'Introduction', in C. T. Clotfelter and M. Rothschild (eds), *Studies of Supply and Demand in Higher Education*, Chicago: University of Chicago Press, pp. 1–10.

Clotfelter, C. T. (1999), 'The Familiar But Curious Economics of Higher Education: Introduction to a Symposium', *Journal of Economic Perspectives*, **13**(1), 3–12.

Cobban, A. B. (1988), *The Medieval English Universities: Oxford and Cambridge*, Berkeley: University of California Press.

Cobban, A. B. (1999), *English University Life in the Middle Ages*, Columbus: Ohio State University Press. Berkeley: University of California Press.

Cordasco, F. (1960), *Daniel Coit Gilman and the Protean Ph.D.*, Leiden, Netherlands: E. J. Brill.

Creedy, J. (1995), *The Economics of Higher Education*, Aldershot, UK: Edward Elgar.

Dresch, S. P. (1995), 'The Economics of Fundamental Research', in John W. Summer (ed.), *The Academy in Crisis*, New Brunswick, NJ: Transaction Publisher, pp. 171–196.

Ehrenberg, R. G. (1991), 'Academic Labor Supply', in C. T. Clotfelter (ed.), *Economic Challenges in Higher Education*, Chicago: University of Chicago Press, pp. 143–258.

Ehrenberg, R. G. (ed.) (1997), *The American University: National Treasure or Endangered Species?* Ithaca: Cornell University Press.

Ehrenberg, R. G., D. I. Rees, and D. J. Brewer (1993), 'How Would Universities Respond to Increased Federal Support for Graduate Students?' in C. T. Clotfelter and M. Rothschild (eds), *Studies of Supply and Demand in Higher Education*, Chicago: University of Chicago Press, pp. 183–210.

Ehrenberg, R. G. (1999), 'Adam Smith Goes to College: An Economist Becomes an Academic Administrator', *Journal of Economic Perspectives*, **13**(1), 99–116.

Etzkowitz, H. H., A. Webster, and P. Healey (eds) (1998), *Capitalizing Knowledge*, Albany: State University of New York Press.

Fleisher, A. A. III, B. Goff, and R. D. Tollison (1992), *The National Collegiate Athletic Association: A Study in Cartel Behavior*, Chicago: University of Chicago Press.

Flexner, A. (1930), *Universities: American, English, German*, New York: Oxford University Press.

Froomkin, J. (1990), 'The Impact of Changing Levels of Financial Resources on the Structure of Colleges and Universities', in S. A. Hoenack and E. L. Collins (eds), *The Economics of American Universities*, Albany: Albany State University of New York Press, pp. 189–214.

Galbraith, J. K. (1971), *The New Industrial State, 2nd edn. Revised*, Boston: Houghton Mifflin.

Garforth, F. W. (1980), *Educative Democracy: John Stuart Mill on Education in Society*, Oxford: Oxford University Press.

Garvin, D. A. (1980), *The Economics of University Behavior*, New York: Academic Press.

Getz, M. and J. J. Siegfried (1991), 'Costs and Productivity in American Colleges and Universities', in S. A. Hoenack and E. L. Collins (eds), *Economic Challenges in Higher Education*, Albany: Albany State University of New York Press, pp. 261–392.

Goldin, C. and L. F. Katz (1999), 'The Shaping of Higher Education: The Formative Years in the United States, 1890 to 1940', *Journal of Economic Perspectives*, Winter, pp. 37–62.

Goodspeed, T. W. (1916), *A History of the University of Chicago*, Chicago: University of Chicago Press.

Green, J. R. (1993), 'Future Graduate Study and Academic Careers', in C. T. Clotfelter and M. Rothschild (eds), *Studies in the Supply and Demand in Higher Education*, Chicago: University of Chicago Press, pp. 145–182.

Gribble, F. (1910), *The Romance of the Oxford Colleges*, London: Mills & Boon, Limited.

Haskins, C. H. (1923), *The Rise of Universities*, New York: Henry Holt and Company.

Hawkins, H. (1960), *Pioneer: A History of the Johns Hopkins University, 1874–1889*, Ithaca: Cornell University Press.

Hayden, F. G. and K. Stephenson (1992), 'Corporate Transorganization and Veblen's Thesis on Higher Education', *Journal of Economic Issues*, **26**(1), 53–85.

Hobhouse, C. (1946), *Oxford*, New York: Oxford University Press.

Hoenack, S. A. (1990), 'An Economist's Perspective on Costs Within Higher Education Institutions', in S. A. Hoenack and E. L. Collins (eds), *The Economics of American Universities*, Albany: Albany State University of New York Press, pp. 129–154.

Hoenack, S. A. and E. L. Collins (eds) (1990), *The Economics of American Universities*, Albany: State University of New York Press.

Hopkins, D. S. P. (1990), 'The Higher Education Production Function: Theoretical Foundations and Empirical Findings', in S. A. Hoenack and E. L. Collins (eds), *The Economics of American Universities*, Albany: Albany State University of New York Press, pp. 11–32.

James, E. (1990), 'Decision Processes and Priorities in Higher Education', in S. A. Hoenack and E. L. Collins (eds), *The Economics of American Universities*, Albany: Albany State University of New York Press, pp. 77–128.

Jencks, C. and D. Riesman (1968), *The Academic Revolution*, New York: Doubleday.

Kemp, D. A. (1999), 'Research and Research Training: a National Investment', in *Knowledge and Innovation: A Policy Statement on Research and Research Training*, Australia: Commonwealth of Australia,' (electronic version), retrieved March 25, 2003, from http://www.dest.gov.au/archive/highered/whitepaper/1.htm.

Kimberling, C. R. (1995), 'Federal Student Aid: A History and Critical Analysis', in J. W. Sommer (ed.), *The Academy in Crisis*, New Brunswick, NJ: Transaction Publishers, pp. 69–93.

Koch, J. V. (1983), 'Intercollegiate Athletics: An Economic Explanation', *Social Science Quarterly*, **64**(2), 360–374.

Leathers, C. G. (1971), 'Intellectual Activism: A Schumpeterian Threat to The New Industrial State', *Nebraska Journal of Economics and Business*, Summer, pp. 3–11.

Lee, M. L. (1971), 'A Conspicuous Production Theory of Hospital Behavior', *Southern Economic Journal*, **37**(1), 48–58.

Lindsay, C. (1976), 'A Theory of Government Enterprise', *Journal of Political Economy*, **84**(5), 1061–1077.

Lindsay, C. (1995), 'Universities and the Training of Scientists', in J. W. Sommer (ed.), *The Academy in Crisis*, New Brunswick, NJ: Transaction Publishers, pp. 287–303.

Lucas, C. J. (1994), *American Higher Education*, New York: St. Martin's Press.

Mackie, J. D. (1954), *University of Glasgow, 1451–1951: A Short History*, Glasgow: Jackson.

Mallet, C. E. (1924, 1928), *A History of the University of Oxford, Vol. II–III*, New York: Longmans, Green and Co.

Manne, G. G. (1978), 'The Political Economy of Modern Universities', in A. H. Burleigh, *Education in a Free Society*, Indianapolis: Liberty Press, pp. 165–205.

Masten, S. E. (1995), 'Old School Ties: Financial Aid Coordination and the Governance of Higher Education', *Journal of Economic Behavior and Organization*, **28**(1), 23–47.

McCormick, R. and R. Meiners (1988), 'University Governance: A Property Rights Perspective', *Journal of Law and Economics*, October, 423–442.

McCormick, R. E. and M. Tinsley (1987), 'Athletic versus Academics? Evidence from SAT Scores', *Journal of Political Economy*, **95**(5), 1103–1116.

McCormick, R. E. and M. Tinsley (1990), 'Athletics and Academics: A Model of University Contributions', in B. L. Goff and R. D. Tollison (eds), *Sportometrics*, College Park: Texas A & M Press, pp. 193–204.

McMahan, W. W. (1974), *Investment in Higher Education*, Lexington: Lexington Books.

Meiners, R. E. (1995), 'The Evolution of American Higher Education', in *The Academy in Crisis*, New Brunswick, NJ: Transaction Publishers, pp. 21–43.

Meiners, R. E. and R. J. Staaf (1995), 'Property Rights in Academe', in John W. Sommer (ed.), *The Academy in Crisis*, New Brunswick, NJ: Transaction Publishers, pp. 197–216.

Merton, R. C. (1993), 'Optimal Investment Strategies for University Endowment Funds', in C. T. Clotfelter and M. Rothschild (eds), *Studies of Supply and Demand in Higher Education*, Chicago: University of Chicago Press, pp. 211–242.

Mill, J. S. (1882), *Dissertations and Discussions, Vol. 1*, New York: Henry Holt and Company.

Mill, J. S. (1961), *Principles of Political Economy*, New York: Augustus M. Kelley.

Mill, J. S. (1963), *Collected Works, Vols. 4, 5, 18, 21*, Toronto: University of Toronto Press.

Newhouse, J. P. (1970), 'Toward a Theory of Non-Profit Institutions: An Economic Model of a Hospital', *American Economic Review*, **60**(1), 64–74.

Noble, D. F. (1988), 'Digital Diploma Mills: The Automation of Higher Education', *First Monday* (online), **3**(1), January, 1–13.

Noll, R. G. (ed.) (1998), *Challenges to Research Universities*, Washington, DC: The Brookings Institution.

Ortmann, A. (1997), 'How to Survive in Postindustrial Environments: Adam Smith's Advice for Today's Colleges and Universities', *Journal of Higher Education*, Sep./Oct., pp. 483–501.

Pacey, P. L. and E. D. Wickham (1985), 'College Football Telecasts: Where Are They Going?' *Economic Inquiry*, **23**(1), 93–113.

Powell, W. W. and J. Owen-Smith (1998), 'Universities and the Market for Intellectual Property in the Life Sciences,' *Journal of Policy Analysis and Management*, **17**(2), 253-277.

Press, E. and J. Washburn (2000), 'The Kept University', *The Atlantic Monthly*, March (online).

Rae, J. (1965), *Life of Adam Smith*, New York: A. M. Kelley.

Riesman, D. (1953), *Thorstein Veblen, A Critical Interpretation*, New York: The Seabury Press.

Riesman, D. (1980), *On Higher Education, The Academic Enterprise in the Age of Rising Student Consumerism*, San Francisco: Jossey-Bass Publishers.

Rosen, S. (1987), 'Some Economics of Teaching', *Journal of Labor Economics*, **5**(4), 561–575.

Rosenberg, N. (1960), 'Some Institutional Aspects of the *Wealth of Nations*', *Journal of Political Economy*, **68**(6), 557–570.

Rothschild, M. and L. J. White (1993), 'The University in the Marketplace: Some Insights and Some Puzzles', in C. T. Clotfelter and M. Rothschild (eds), *Studies of Supply and Demand in Higher Education*, Chicago: University of Chicago Press, pp. 11–42.

Russell, B. (1998), 'Turning Bright Ideas into Pound Notes', *The Independent* (London) 26 March 1998.

Schultz, T. W. (1968), 'Resources for Higher Education: An Economist's View', *Journal of Political Economy*, **76**(3), 327–347.

Schumpeter, J. A. (1950), *Capitalism, Socialism and Democracy, 3rd edn*, New York: Harper.

Scott, W. R. (1965), *Adam Smith as Student and Professor*, New York: Augustus M. Kelley (original work published 1937).

Skinner, A. S. (1996), *A System of Social Science*, Oxford: Clarendon Press.

Slaughter, S. and L. L. Leslie (1997), *Academic Capitalism*, Baltimore: The Johns Hopkins University Press.

Smith, A. (1976), *An Inquiry into the Nature and Wealth of Nations*, Indianapolis: Liberty Press (original work published 1776).

Smyth, D. J. (1991), 'A Model of Quality Changes in Higher Education', *Journal of Economic Behavior and Organization*, **15**(1), 151–157.

Sommer, J. W. (ed.) (1995), *The Academy in Crisis: The Political Economy of Higher Education*, New Brunswick, NJ: Transactions Publishers.

Sowell, T. (1969), 'Veblen's Higher Learning After Fifty Years', *Journal of Economic Issues*, December, pp. 66–78.

Stigler, G. (1963), *The Intellectual and the Market Place*, London: The Free Press of Glencoe.

Sweet, P. R. (1980), *Wilhelm von Humboldt: A Biography*, Columbus, OH: State University Press.

Tollison, R. and T. Willett (1976), 'The University and the Price System', in R. C. Amacher, R. D. Tollison, and T. D. Willett (eds), *The Economic Approach to Public Policy*, Ithaca: Cornell University Press, pp. 153–165.

Tuckman, H. P. and C. F. Chang (1990), 'Participant Goals, Institutional Goals, and University Resource Allocation Decisions', in S. A. Hoenack and E. L. Collins (eds), *The Economics of American Universities*, Albany: Albany State University of New York Press, pp. 53–76.

Veblen, T. (1961), 'Why Is Economics Not An Evolutionary Science?' in *The Place of Science in Modern Civilization*, New York: Russell and Russell, pp. 56–81.

Veblen, T. (1993), *The Higher Learning in America*, New Brunswick, NJ: Transaction Publishers (original work published 1918).

West, E. G. (1965), *Education and the State*, London: The Institute of Economic Affairs.

West, E. G. (1976), *Adam Smith*, Indianapolis: Liberty Press.

West, E. G. (1995), 'The Economics of Higher Education', in J. W. Sommer (ed.), *The Academy in Crisis*, New Brunswick, NJ: Transaction Publishers, pp. 135–170.

Winston, G. C. (1999), 'Subsidies, Hierarchy and Peers: The Awkward Economics of Higher Education', *Journal of Economic Perspectives*, Winter, pp. 13–37.

Index

Aberdeen, Bishop of 30
Aberdeen University 30, 58
'academic capitalism' 210, 212
academic freedom 42, 52, 76, 79–80, 95, 129
Academy of Sciences 40
accounting systems 52
accrediting agencies 178
administrators 9, 47
  budgets controlled by 125, 129–30, 153, 192, 194, 196, 197, 206–8
  competitive pressures on 181
  consensus relationship with faculty 169, 174, 192
  in 'entrepreneurial universities' 217–18, 219–21, 223
  negative dealings with faculty members 150–51
  in Smith's analysis 63, 69
  values and motives of 12, 127–31, 134–8, 144, 149, 188, 191–7, 201, 206, 207–8, 223
  Veblen's proposal for abolition of 140
admissions policies 173, 175, 176, 177, 178, 184, 204
aggregate demand, regulation of 157
aggregative behavioral tendencies 199–201
agricultural and mechanical programs 48
AIDS 211
All Soul's College, Oxford 27
Allen, L. 167
'amateurs', competition from 81, 83, 133
American Civil War 15, 46, 48, 101
American universities
  Buchanan–Devletoglou model of 13, 163–4, 168–85
  control of universities by faculties who do not sell 173–5

crisis on campuses 181–3
economic model of university behavior 12, 92, 120–43, 224–7
  endowed universities 122
  identities and motives of discretionary officials 12, 105, 120–22 passim, 123–34, 144, 149, 213, 214, 224, 225–6
  institutional drift and 'proposals' for reform 138–43
  modeling institutional behavior 134–8
  universities and non-profit corporations 121–2
evolutionary development of modern 'university corporations' 96–101, 147
  American colleges, universities and 'university corporations' 100–101
  historical development of European universities 97–100
financing by taxpayers who do not control 169–71
governing boards as taxpayers' representatives 171–2
historical development of 15–16, 44–53, 100–101
  colleges 44–7, 100–101, 135, 140
  governance 12, 52–3
  graduate/research universities 47–52
lack of competition 180–81
nature and causes of universities' failures 175–80
  economic effects of free tuition 176–8
  effects of behavioral characteristics of faculties 178–80

reasons for failures 102–19
   institutional contamination from
      business values and practices
      91, 92, 93, 110–19, 228
   institutional contamination from
      'lower schools' 102–10, 112,
      113
remedies for universities' failures
   184–5
Riesman's analysis of 151–62
Riesman's critique of 12, 144–51
   defense of university presidents and
      competitive publicity 146–50
   effects of Veblen's 'legend' 150–51
   subjective attacks on Veblen's
      personal character 145–6,
      149–50, 162
social functions of universities 11–12,
   91, 94–6, 120, 128, 147, 150
social importance of knowledge 92–4
students as consumers who do not pay
   172–3
university education as an economic
   good 169, 185
Veblen's views on 90–119
see also 'entrepreneurial universities'
apprenticeship, statutes of 64
Arizona Board of Regents 217
assets, universities' 1
astronomy 39
athletics programs 2, 5, 49, 51, 108–9
   football 51, 53, 106, 148, 159, 216,
   225
Australian National University 216–17
authorship 216

Bachelor of Arts degrees 22, 28, 32, 33,
   50
Balderston, F.E. 5
Balliol, John de 23
Balliol College, Oxford 23, 69
Baptist Church 44
Barber, W.J. 9, 135
bargaining models 9
baseball 51
Becker, W.E. 5
behavioral tendencies, evolutionary
   social theory of 123
Bentham, Jeremy 28, 81
Berg, I. 144

Berlin University 40–42
Bildung 40
black and ethnic studies 161
Bologna University 19–20, 31
Brennan, H.G. 6
Brinkman, P.T. 5
Brown, R.W. 5
Brown, W.O. Jr. 5, 6
Brown University 44
Buchanan, J.M.
   *Academia in anarchy: an economic
      diagnosis* (with Devletoglou) 13,
      163–4, 168–85
   Nobel prize awarded to 164
   see also Buchanan–Devletoglou
      model
Buchanan–Devletoglou model 13,
   163–4, 168–85
   control of universities by faculties
      who do not sell 173–5
   crisis on campuses 181–3
   financing by taxpayers who do not
      control 169–71
   governing boards as taxpayers'
      representatives 171–2
   lack of competition 180–81
   nature and causes of universities'
      failures 175–80
      economic effects of free tuition
         176–8
      effects of behavioral characteristics
         of faculties 178–80
   remedies for universities' failures
      184–5
   students as consumers who do not pay
      172–3
   university education as an economic
      good 169, 185
budget control 125–6, 129–30, 153, 192,
   194, 196, 197, 206–8
budget maximization 197, 208
buildings, spending on 115, 118, 126,
   136, 148, 153
bureaucracy 108, 113, 150, 206, 225
bureaucratic models 190
business schools 51, 114–15, 118,
   218
business values and practices,
   institutional contamination from 91,
   92, 93, 110–19, 228

conflicting institutional forces 111–12
negative effects on teaching and
   research 118–19
negative influence of business habits
   on universities' behavior 112
reinforcement of contamination from
   'lower schools' 113
utilitarian and elective curricula
   113–15
Veblen's economic model of 12, 92,
   120–43, 149, 213, 214, 224–7
wasteful competition 115–18

California, University of 15, 48, 180
California state system 170
Cambridge University 20, 22, 58, 79
   colleges 15, 21, 90
canon law 26, 30, 31, 33, 171
capitalization of knowledge 215
Carmichael, H.L. 5
Carnegie Institution 141
cartel agreements 180
cathedral schools 17, 20
Catholic Church 17, 21, 22, 23–4, 25,
   26, 29, 31–4, 58
celibacy 24
Chairs 26, 35, 37, 38–9, 43, 61
chancellors 18, 20, 22, 24, 31, 34–8
   passim
Chang, C.F. 6
charitable giving 171
charity schools 58
charter, Dartmouth College 45
Chicago, University of 7, 15, 16, 44, 48,
   49, 50–52, 121, 138–9, 144, 147,
   148, 227
Church, influence of 17, 21–7 *passim*,
   29–38 *passim*, 44–5, 58, 74, 78–80,
   112, 125, 170, 171
   *see also under names of individual
   churches*, e.g. Catholic Church;
   Church of England
Church of England 21, 25, 27, 29, 31,
   36, 74, 78–80
Church of Scotland 31, 34–8
Cisco Systems 210
citizenry 170–71, 226
Clark University 15, 48, 49
Clement III, Pope 19
Clotfelter, C.T. 5

*Economic challenges in higher
   education* (with Ehrenberg, Getz
   and Siegfried) 4
*Studies of supply and demand in
   higher education* (with
   Rothschild) 4
Cobban, A.B. 22, 23, 24
college system 15, 20, 21, 23–4, 33–4,
   59, 90
collegial models 189–90
Collins, E.L.
   *The economics of American
   universities* (ed., with Hoenack) 4
committees
   faculty 179, 189
   legislative 207, 208
'commoditization of instruction' 219–21,
   227, 228, 229
competition by universities 2
   for faculty members 180–81
   market segmentation 197–8
   Mill and 11, 83–4
   for prestige 112, 116–19, 136, 148,
      151, 162, 186
   Smith and 8, 57, 67, 68–9, 71, 91,
      163, 164
   student consumerism and 57, 68–9,
      91, 160–61, 163, 164, 184–5
   studies of 5
   wasteful 115–18, 130, 141
computer-based teaching 212–13,
   219–21, 227, 228, 229
congregation 24
Congregational Church 44
conspicuous consumption 189
conspicuous production 189
consumers, students as 12–13, 57, 68,
   70, 72–3, 75, 91, 113, 133, 145,
   158–62, 163, 164, 172–3, 177–8,
   184–5, 187–8
Convocation 24
Cordasco, F. 49, 50
correspondence courses 227
cost efficiency 192, 196
cost functions 5, 202
Councils 51
counterculture 158–60
credit ratings 223, 225, 228
Creedy, J. 5
Cromwell, Oliver 21, 25

Crown, influence of 17, 21, 22, 34, 35,
    36–7, 38
curricula
    Aberdeen University 30
    American universities 45, 48, 90–91,
        113–15, 153, 160–61, 163
    Buchanan–Devletoglou view on 176
    English universities 22, 24–6, 29, 62,
        90
    faculty control of 62–3, 153, 167,
        178–9, 192
    Glasgow University 31, 35
    medieval universities 17, 18
    Mill's views on 77
    Smith's views on 58, 59–61, 62–3, 66,
        91
    student consumerism and 160–61, 163
    Veblen's views on 95, 113–15

Dartmouth College 44, 45
Dartmouth University 45
deacons 32
deans 18, 20, 32, 34, 35, 36, 38, 42, 51,
    52, 128, 149
    Veblen's influence on behavior of 144,
        150–51
demand functions 5
demographic changes 158
departmental prestige 192, 194–6,
    199–205
design, schools of 39
Devletoglou, N.E.
    *Academia in anarchy: an economic
        diagnosis* (with Buchanan) 13,
        163–4, 168–85
    see also Buchanan–Devletoglou
        model
digitized courseware 212–13, 219–21,
    227, 228, 229
directors, divisional 51
disciplinary improvements in prestige
    199–201
discipulorum 18
'discretionary officials', identities and
    motives of 12, 105, 120–22 *passim*,
    123–34, 144, 149, 152, 163–4, 186,
    191, 213, 214, 224, 225–6, 230
distance-learning programs 228
divinity schools 30, 115
division of labor 55

doctoral-degree universities 15, 16,
    49–52, 209, 210
doctoral degrees 20, 32, 40, 42, 44, 49,
    50, 152, 158, 194, 195, 198,
    200–201, 229
Dresch, S.P. 5
Durham, Archdeacon of 23
Durham, Bishop of 23
Dutch Reformed Church 44

ecclesiastical revenues, universities
    supported by 23–4, 31, 32, 34, 36,
    37
economic analysis, applicability of 3–4
economic benefits of education 55–6,
    59–60, 75
economic models of universities
    Buchanan–Devletoglou 13, 163–4,
        168–85
    see also Buchanan–Devletoglou
        model
    recent 6–7, 13–14, 186–209
        economic model of public
            universities 187, 205–9
        Garvin 6, 7, 8, 13–14, 186–7,
            189–205
        property rights approach 197
    Veblen 12, 92, 120–43, 149, 213, 214,
        224–7
    see also American universities
    see also non-profit organizations
economic perspectives on universities'
    behavior 5–6
Economist 9–10
economists 167
Edinburgh University 30–31, 58
education ministries 42, 43, 225
educational estate 145, 157
educational maintenance organizations
    212, 219
Educational Testing Service 161
EDUCOM 221, 227
efficiency, institutional 94, 102, 168,
    169, 176, 186, 196–7
Ehrenberg, R.G. 5, 7, 9
electives 48, 51, 113–14, 133, 188
elementary education 77, 80
    government role in 74, 85–6
Elizabeth I 24, 22
Ely, Richard T. 48

endowments
  competition for 116, 118, 122, 148, 225
  government regulation of use of 82, 86, 87–9
  Harvard University 1, 46
  property rights claimed by governing boards 88
  teachers' incomes financed from 65–8, 70–71, 72, 75, 80, 81–3, 89, 118
Engels, F. 214
engineering 48, 50, 75, 96, 196, 215, 218
  see also technical schools
English universities
  historical development of 15–16, 21–9
  incompleteness, weaknesses and contradictions 69–73
  institutional nature of universities 57–9
    endowments 58–9
    governance 59
    students
  Mill's views on 74–89
    economic analysis of failures 11, 75, 80–84
    applicability of market principle in education 83–4
    effect of educational subsidies on teachers' incomes 80–81
    effects of paying fixed faculty incomes from endowments 81–3
    government regulation of endowments 82, 86, 87–9
    government schools vs. private schools 85–6
    reforms 79, 86–9
    sectarian control contributing to failure 74, 78–80
    social functions of universities 11, 74, 75–7
  normative questions 54–6
  number of 46
  positive analysis 56–7
  proposals for reform 68–9, 91, 163
  Smith on failure of 54–73
    criticism of universities 59–68
    faculty control of curriculum 62–3
    faculty incomes from endowments 65–8

reasons for failure 61–2
rules and practices 63–5
see also Cambridge University; Oxford University
Enlightenment 31
'entrepreneurial universities'
  alternative view 218–19
  challenge for economic models of universities' behavior 213
  'commoditization of instruction' 219–21, 227, 228, 229
  consequence of 'entrepreneurial' research by universities 215–18
  emergence of 214–15
  explaining emergence of 222–4
  first transformation phase 210–12
  missions 211, 213, 214, 218, 222, 223, 229
  overview 213–14
  second transformation phase 212–13
  Smith and Veblen on 227–30
  Veblenian perspective on 214, 224–7
episcopacy 36–7
equity considerations 194–6
esoteric knowledge 92–4
Etzkowitz, H.H. 211, 213, 214, 215, 222, 224–5
European universities
  historical development of 97–100
  see also French universities; German universities; medieval universities
examinations 28–9, 32, 33, 36, 42, 43, 50, 161
  as condition for entering a trade or profession 55–6, 63–4, 70
  teachers' pay based on students' success in 75, 83
examiners 51
extension education 39, 49, 50, 97, 227

faculty
  administrators' consensus relationship with 169, 174, 192
  administrators' negative dealings with 150–51
  athletics coaches as 51, 109
  changing role of 181, 183
  committees 179, 189
  competition for 180–81

curriculum controlled by 62–3, 153,
   167, 178–9, 192
demand for 201–5
as government advisors 49
hierarchical ranking of 52
houses of 38
incomes of *see* incomes, teachers'
internal disputes among 69
meetings 37, 167
part-time members 221, 228–9
powers of 12, 34, 36, 37, 38, 47, 70,
   144–5, 148, 152–8, 173–5, 176,
   178–81, 189–90, 219–21
professionalization of 152
values and motives of 12, 125, 131–3,
   137–8, 144, 148–9, 188, 191–6,
   201, 216, 218, 223–4
fees
   determination of level of 70, 71, 117
   revenues from 5, 22, 46, 49, 53, 193,
      202, 218–19
      increases resulting from increased
         prestige 203
      teachers' incomes dependent on 9,
         10, 19, 21–2, 26, 29, 33, 34–5,
         39, 43–4, 57, 65–7, 68, 70, 71–2,
         73, 82–3, 229
      students' expense on 32, 33, 35, 36,
         39, 46, 117–18, 170, 187, 221
   see also free tuition
fellows 24, 27, 29
fellowships 50, 117, 184, 195
financial aspects, studies of 5
fines 33
fiscal officers 125
Fleisher, A.A. III 5
Flexner, A. 41, 42
football 51, 53, 106, 148, 159, 216, 225
foreign tours 61–2, 73
Franklin, Benjamin 45
fraternities 47, 51–2, 108, 148, 159
Frederick I, Barbarossa 19
Frederick William III, king of Prussia
   41
free good, university education as 169
free-rider problem 170
free trade, conditions for 84
free tuition 164, 169, 172–8, 184–5
freedom, academic 42, 52, 76, 79–80,
   95, 129

French universities 59, 63, 79–80, 82
   see also Paris, University of
Froomkin, J. 5

Galbraith, J.K.
   The new industrial state 12, 145, 149,
      157–8
Garvin, D.A.
   The economics of university behavior
      6, 7, 8, 13–14, 186–7, 189–205,
      208, 213
      aggregate behavioral tendencies
         199–201
      competition in the higher education
         market 197–8
      formal model 201–5
      formal model of prestige
         improvement 205
      internal organization 193–7
      market for prestige 198–9
      non-economic vs. economic models
         189–91
German universities
   academic freedom in 79–80
   American universities influenced by
      15, 40, 49
   government control of endowments in
      82
   historical development of 15, 16,
      40–44
      Berlin 40–42
      special features of German
         university life 42–4
Getz, M. 5
Gibbon, Edward 28
Gilman, Daniel Coit 49
Glasgow, Archbishop of 30, 31, 32, 33,
   35, 36
Glasgow University 58
   Adam Smith at 8, 30, 37, 39, 58, 66,
      228, 229
   historical development of 30, 31–9
      in eighteenth century 37–9
      post-Reformation 34–7
goal consensus 192
Goldin, C. 187
Goodspeed, T.W. 50, 51, 52
governing boards 5, 9, 58, 91, 205
   common characteristics of 172
   Dartmouth College 45

diminished role of 152–3, 169
fraternities accepted by 51–2
Johns Hopkins University 49
property rights to endowments
    claimed by 88
as taxpayers' representatives 171–2
values and motives of members of 12,
    123, 125–7, 134–8, 188, 190,
    191, 197, 225, 226
Veblen's proposal for abolition of 140,
    149
governments
endowments regulated by 82, 86, 87–9
influence of 17, 21, 34, 112
role in provision of education 74,
    85–6
graduate programs 15, 40, 48
in 'entrepreneurial universities' 227
faculty dominance leading to build-up
    of 154
international students in 218
market segmentation for 198
prestige of 137, 138, 148, 194–201
    passim
undergraduate education coupled with
    90, 101, 102, 110
undergraduate education influenced by
    155–6
grammar schools 25
Greek 24–5, 30
Greek-letter societies *see* fraternities
Green, J.R. 5
guilds, medieval 17–18, 19, 32
gymnasium 41

habits of thought 111, 114
halls of residence 21, 23, 47
halo effect 200
Harper, William Rainey 50, 51, 147–8
Harvard Law School 144, 159
Harvard University 44, 45, 48, 144, 167
commercial research funding for 222
endowments received by 1, 46
Haskins, C.H. 18, 19, 20, 23
Hawkins, H. 49
Hayden, F.G. 9
health maintenance organizations
    (HMOs) 212, 219
Hebdominal Board 24
Henry VIII 25

heresy 79
high school counseling 161
Hobhouse, C. 22, 23, 25
Hoenack, S.A. 5
    *The economics of American
    universities* (ed., with Collins) 4
honorary degrees 39
Hopkins, D.S.P. 5
hospitals 6, 49, 186, 187, 188–9, 193,
    206
household production function 201–2
human capital 4, 5, 55, 169, 171
Humboldt, Karl Wilhelm von 40–41, 43
Hutchins, Robert M. 148

income effect 203–4
incomes, teachers'
dependent on students' examination
    results 75, 83
dependent on students' fees 9, 10, 19,
    21–2, 26, 29, 33, 34–5, 39, 43–4,
    57, 65–7, 68, 70, 71–2, 73, 82–3,
    229
educational subsidies and 80–81,
    228–9
financed from tax revenues 179
fixed, from endowments 65–8, 70–71,
    72, 75, 80, 81–3, 98, 118
negative effect of business values on
    118–19
Independent 224
indifference curves 204
Initial Purchase Offerings (IPOs) 225
institution, definition of 98
institutional drift 138–9, 226
institutional efficiency 94, 102, 168, 169,
    176, 186, 196–7
institutional failures 3, 7, 8–9, 12, 16
efficiency failures 102, 168, 176, 186
'entrepreneurial universities' 228
see also American universities;
    English universities
institutional forces, conflicting 111–12
institutional nature of universities 55–7
institutional specialization 94–6, 102,
    147
intellectual properties 2, 3, 210–11,
    214–21, 224, 227–8
intellectuals, radical 164–8, 182
internal conflicts 190

internal resource allocation 138, 190,
    194–7, 208, 217
Internet 210–11, 222

James, E. 6
Jencks, C.
    The academic revolution (with
        Riesman) 12, 144–5, 152–7,
        158–9, 189–90, 192
Johns Hopkins University 15, 16, 44, 47,
    49–50, 138
Journal of Economic Perspectives 5
Journal of Political Economy 149
journals, learned 50, 152
judges 82

Katz, L.F. 187
Kemp, David 211–12
Kimberling, C.R. 5
Kings's College, Aberdeen 30
knowledge
    capitalization of 215
    social importance of 92–4
Koch, J.V. 5

laboratories 48, 50
laity, influence of 133–4
land-grant programs 48
landed property 88
languages, proficiency in 50, 61
Latin 17, 18, 30, 33, 50
Laud, Archbishop 27
Laudian Statutes 26, 27
law schools 15, 30, 75, 96, 98, 117
law students 20–21, 22, 26, 117
Leathers, C.G. 182
lecture method 29, 33, 61, 105
lecturers 52
Lee, M.L. 6, 186, 188–9
legislature
    political pressure on 209
    powers of 206, 207
    values and motives of 207
Lehman Brothers 212, 219
Leslie, L.L. 6, 212, 213, 217, 218, 222–3
libraries 21, 23, 25, 36, 48, 50, 69, 118
licenses, teaching 19–20, 31, 32, 33, 43
licensing deals 228
Lindsay, C. 5, 206, 208
'literary labour', price of 81

lodgings, students' 19, 20, 21, 23, 33, 34,
    35, 38, 39, 47
Lombard Kingdom 19
'lower schools', institutional
    contamination from 102–10, 112,
    113
Lucas, C.J. 9, 18, 45, 46, 47, 48, 49, 52

M.D. degrees 37
Mackie, J.D. 31, 32, 33, 34, 35, 36, 37,
    38, 39
Mallet, C.E. 22, 24, 25, 26, 27, 28, 29
Manne, G.G. 6
Marischal College, Aberdeen 30
market failure 83, 168
market segmentation 197–8
Marx, K. 214
Master of Arts degrees 20, 22, 28, 32,
    33, 34, 36, 50, 212
mathematics 22, 26, 45, 48, 55
McCormick, R.E. 4, 5, 6
McMahan, W.W. 4
medical schools 15, 30, 50, 75, 96, 98,
    161, 218, 227
medieval universities 15, 17–18
    two models of 18–21
Meiners, R.E. 4, 6, 9, 10, 197
Merton, R.C. 5
Michigan, University of 15, 48, 211
Microsoft 226
military academies 206
Mill, J.S. 11, 16, 133
    Autobiography 77
    Civilization 75–6, 78–80
    Corporation and church property
        81–2, 83–4
    on English universities *see* English
        universities
    essay on endowments (1869) 82, 84,
        87
    inaugural address (1867) 58, 76–7, 80
    Principles of political economy 80–81,
        83, 85–6
    *Prof. Sedgwick's discourse on the
        studies of the University of
        Cambridge* 75, 78, 82, 84
    Reform in education 84
    report to the Secretary of the Schools
        Inquiry Commission (1866) 82
moderators 36

monastic schools 17, 25
monopolistic competition 161
Montrose, Dukes of 38
moral acts 171
More, Sir Thomas 25

National Bureau of Economic Research
    4
National Center for Policy Analysis
    217–18
neoclassical economic models 208
Net Perceptions 211
Newhouse, J.P. 6, 186, 188
newspaper work 81, 133
Noble, D.F. 212–13, 219, 220, 221
Noll, R.G. 6, 218
non-profit organizations
    accounting systems for 52
    models of 6, 8, 13, 120, 164, 186,
        187–9
    see also economic models of
        universities
notoriety 116, 132–3, 135–8

'official' scholars 132–3, 136, 137, 182
Ohio, higher education institutions in 46
oligopoly 198
on-line instructional materials 212–13,
    219–21, 227, 228, 229
oral examinations 50
organized anarchy models 190
Ortmann, A. 9, 59, 228, 229
Owen-Smith, J. 6
Oxford University 17, 20, 58
    academic decline of 27–9, 79
    Adam Smith at 8, 30, 69
    colleges 15, 21, 23–4, 27, 29, 90
    early development 21–3
    teaching and curriculum 22, 24–6, 29,
        62

Pacey, P.L. 5
parents, as judges of education 73, 75,
    83–4, 86, 172–3
Paris, University of 17, 19, 20, 33, 40
parish schools 57–8, 71
part-time faculty members 221, 228–9
patents 215, 225, 228
patronage 38
payment by results 75, 83

'perfected type' of executive 127–8, 134,
    136
perquisites 200, 208
Philip Augustus (Philip II), king of
    France 20
philosophy 40, 42, 44, 59, 66, 75, 77, 98
piece-rate pay 71, 118, 228–9
plant and equipment 94–5, 141
pluralism 24
political economy of higher education 4
political models 190, 194
Poor Students 34, 35, 36
Powell, W.W. 6
Presbyterians 31, 36–7, 44
presidents
    department heads appointed by 52
    faculty interests represented by 128,
        153–4
    governing boards and 45, 47
    University of Chicago 50, 51
    Veblen's views on 127, 134, 135, 140,
        146–9
    see also administrators
prestige 10
    in Buchanan–Devletoglou model 169,
        181
    in modern models 13, 186, 188–205
        departmental prestige 192, 194–6,
            199–205
        disciplinary improvements in
            prestige 199–201
        'entrepreneurial universities' and
            222, 225
        formal model of prestige
            improvement 205
        market for prestige 191, 198–9
        public universities and 206, 208
    in Veblen's model 13, 81, 110, 112,
        116–19, 129, 131, 134–8, 142–3,
        144, 148, 151, 162, 169, 186, 193
price and wage stabilization 157
pricing of university education 5, 161,
    169, 173
    see also fees
Princeton University 44
principal-agent problem 129, 130, 131
principals 34–8 *passim*
printing 39, 50
Privatdozen 43
private teachers 67–8, 70, 83–4, 85, 86

private universities
  decision-making processes for 121
  examples of 48
  funding of 53, 170
  increase in number of 45–6
  legal distinction between public
     universities and 45
  prestige considerations in 197
privileges of graduation 63–4, 67
proctors 22, 24, 27
production functions 5, 56, 194, 201–2
professional associations 37, 152
professional schools 15, 49, 50, 51, 75,
     96, 98, 101, 103, 107, 110, 117,
     118, 149, 224, 227
  see also business schools; law
     schools; medical schools
professional societies 200–201
professors
  in American colleges 46–7, 52
  at Glasgow University 31, 33, 36, 37,
     39
     appointment of 37, 38
  guilds 19–20
  incomes of 29, 39, 43–4
  teaching by 26, 29, 41, 42, 43
  see also faculty
profit maximization 121, 187, 204
'pseudo-scholars' 182
public benefits of education *see* social
     benefits of education
public choice approach 164
public lectures 26, 39
public service, universities as providers
     of 48–9
public speaking 133–4
public universities
  Buchanan–Devletoglou model of 13,
     163–4, 168–85
  economic model of 187, 205–9
  examples of 48
  features of 5–6
  funding of 53, 164, 168
  increase in number of 46
  institutional characteristics of 164
  legal distinction between private
     universities and 45
  prestige considerations in 196–7
  public service provided by 48–9
  Veblen's views on 104, 110

publication of research 50, 56, 69, 152,
     168, 188, 193, 199–200, 201,
     216–17
publishing companies 212, 219
Puritans 21, 25, 44
purposive behavior assumption 190,
     192

quaestors 36
quality changes 5
'quasi-scholars' 132–3, 136, 137,
     182

radical intellectuals 164–8, 182
Rae, J. 39, 228
rationing 173, 176, 177, 178, 184, 204
readers 52
recorders 51
rectors 18, 20, 21, 31, 32, 34–8 *passim*
Reformation 21, 26, 30, 31, 34
regents 26, 33–7 *passim*
registrars 51
Religious Tests 25, 26, 29, 44
Renaissance 21, 25
reputation 10, 57, 66, 68–9, 71, 137,
     138, 169, 192, 193, 197, 198–9,
     199–200, 208, 230
  see also notoriety; prestige
research, university
  commercialized *see* 'entrepreneurial
     universities'
  decisions on type of 156–7, 215
  function of 95
  funding 154, 156–7, 192, 196,
     200–205 *passim*
     by corporations 210–15, 217–18,
        222–6, 229–30
  intellectual properties generated by 2,
     3, 210–11, 214–21, 224, 227–8
  political economy of 4
  publication of 50, 56, 69, 152, 168,
     188, 193, 199–200, 201, 216–17
  studies analyzing 5
  teaching related to 105
research assistants 193, 195–6
research institutes 141–2, 228
research universities 3, 10, 13–14, 15,
     16, 49–52
  economic model of state research
     universities 187, 205–9

transformation to 'entrepreneurial universities' *see* 'entrepreneurial universities'
resource dependence theory 222–3
revenue maximization 204, 223, 225
revenues, sources of 193, 202, 206
Ricardo, David 81
Riesman, D. 144
  The academic revolution (with Jencks) 12, 144–5, 152–7, 158–9, 189–90, 192
  On higher education 12–13, 145, 146–7, 158–62
  on modern universities 151–7
  and student consumerism 145, 158–62
  Thorstein Veblen 12, 145–51
Rockefeller, John D. 50, 147
Rosen, S. 71
Rosenberg, N. 62, 71
Ross, E.A. 52
Rothschild, M. 4–5
Russell, B. 224
Rutgers University 44

St. Andrews University 30, 33, 58
Salerno University 20
scale economies 197
scholarships 25, 27, 36, 45, 46, 49, 58, 64, 81, 184
schools, elementary 77, 83–4
  government vs. private 85–6, 87, 88
schools of commerce 51, 114–15, 118, 218
Schultz, T.W. 4
Schumpeter, J.A. 13
  Capitalism, socialism, and democracy 164–8
science
  Academy of Sciences 40
  departmental funding 196
  teaching of 22, 26, 28, 29, 48, 50, 55, 59, 61, 62, 66, 77, 89, 90–91, 93
  university–industry collaboration in 215, 218
Scott, W.R. 228
Scottish universities
  historical development of 15, 30–39
  superiority of 66–7, 77

see also Aberdeen University; Edinburgh University; Glasgow University; St. Andrews University
Scottish Universities Act (1860) 30
sectarian control of universities *see* Church, influence of
self-interested behavior 6, 57, 62, 63, 70, 84, 92, 120, 123, 126–7, 130–31, 163, 175, 190, 192, 206, 207
  see also utility maximization
seminaries 83
Senate 38, 51
service activities, academic-related 1–2
shadow price of increased prestige 203
Shattrock, Michael 224, 226
Siegfried, J.J. 5
Skinner, A.S. 56, 66–7
Slaughter, S. 6, 212, 213, 217, 218, 222–3
Smith, Adam 27, 28, 223
  on 'entrepreneurial universities' 228–9
  on failure of English universities *see* English universities
  at Glasgow University 8, 30, 37, 39, 58, 66, 228, 229
  An inquiry into the nature and causes of the wealth of nations 7–11, 13, 21, 54–75, 81, 90, 163, 166, 210, 223, 228
  at Oxford University 8, 30, 69
Smyth, D.J. 5
social benefits of education 5, 54–6, 57, 59–60, 72, 75
social functions of universities 10
  Buchanan–Devletoglou view on 164, 168
  Mill's views on 11, 74, 75–7
  in modern models 186
  Veblen's views on 11–12, 91, 94–6, 120, 128, 147, 150
social sciences 132, 167
social skills 60
Sommer, J.W.
  The academy in crisis (ed.) 4
Sowell, T. 9
specialization, institutional 94–6, 102, 147
Staaf, R.J. 6, 10, 197
Stagg, Alonzo 51

standardized testing 161
Stanford University 7, 16, 44, 48, 49, 52,
    138–9
state universities *see* public universities
Stephenson, K. 9
stewards 35
Stigler, G. 108
student activism 163, 164, 168, 181–3
student fees *see* fees
student grants 176, 177
student loans 22, 171, 176, 177, 184,
    185, 218
student subcultures 158–60
students
    American 45, 46, 47, 133, 145, 154–5,
        158–62, 163–4, 168
    behavior of 13, 22, 27, 36, 37, 45, 47,
        104–5, 163–4, 168, 181–3
    as consumers 12–13, 57, 68–9, 70,
        72–3, 75, 91, 113, 133, 145,
        158–62, 163, 164, 172–3, 177–8,
        184–5, 187–8
    early Oxford 21–2, 25–6, 28
    expansions in number of 13, 71–2,
        80–81, 106, 117, 154–5, 165,
        166, 173, 182–3
    German 42, 43
    in medieval universities 17–21
    relation to teachers 95–6, 100, 104–5,
        107, 183, 214–16, 225
    Scottish 31–4 *passim*, 36, 37, 39
        Poor Students 34, 35, 36
    in utility maximizing model 193–7,
        202–5, 208
    Veblen's reaction to 149, 150, 160
    wasteful competition for 116–17
studium 18
studium generale 18
substitution effect 203–4
summer schools 51
survival, organizational 192
Sweet, P.R. 40, 41

tax credits 218
taxes
    education funded from 87, 164, 168,
        169–71, 179
    immunity from 32
teaching
    allocation bias towards 208

Veblen's views on 95, 104–6, 118–19,
    142, 149
teaching assistants 195–6
teaching colleges 10
teaching licenses 19–20, 31, 32, 33,
    43
technical schools 15, 49, 50, 75, 96, 103,
    107–8, 110, 149, 218, 224, 227
technological progress 170
technology transfer offices 215, 217
technostructure 149, 157–8
temporary appointments 52
tenure 5, 174, 182, 216, 221
theology 20, 22, 26, 31, 34, 35, 42, 58,
    93, 98
theses 50
'third world' studies 161
Tinsley, M. 5
Tollison, R.D. 5, 6
trade unions 134
'Trojans' 25
true scholars 132, 137–8
trustees *see* governing boards
Tuckman, H.P. 6
tutorial system 23, 26
tutors 26, 27, 46–7

UCLA 220
undergraduate education 49–50, 51,
    90–91, 96, 101, 149, 168
    demand for 5
    in 'entrepreneurial universities' 218,
        227
    influence of graduate schools over
        155–6
    institutional contamination from 10,
        102–10, 112, 113, 167
    market segmentation for 198
    prestige of 138, 156, 195–7 *passim*
    as primary function of universities 59,
        164, 168
    vocational training in 114
    see also Bachelor of Arts degrees
unemployment 166–7
United States Department of Defense
    210
United States Supreme Court 45
University Act (1854) 29
University College, Oxford 23
'university corporations'

compared with business enterprises 115, 147, 170, 185, 193–4, 225–6
evolutionary development of 96–101, 147
revenues of 206
Veblen's model of microstructure of governance of 12, 92, 120–43, 149, 213, 214, 224–7
university education as an economic good 169, 185
utility maximization
in Buchanan–Devletoglou model 168, 174–5, 177–8, 179
commercial research funding and 223, 224
criticism of utility-maximizing model 9
in economic models of non-profit institutions 188
in Garvin's model 7, 186, 191–7, 201–5
in public universities 187, 207–9

value systems, conflicting 124–5
Veblen, T. 74, 81
at Chicago University 16, 44, 92, 121
on 'entrepreneurial universities' 227–8, 229
on failures of American universities *see* American universities
The higher learning in America 7–12, 16, 90, 92–119, 189, 206, 210
'economic model' of university behavior in 12, 92, 120–43, 149, 213, 214, 224–7
Riesman's critique of 12, 144–51
at Johns Hopkins University 16, 44
at Stanford University 7, 16, 44, 92
The theory of the leisure class 12, 90, 92, 189

'Why is economics not an evolutionary science?' 223
at Yale University 16, 44
venture capital projects 214
Veterans' Administration hospitals 206
vice-chancellors 22, 24, 26, 28
Viet Nam War 13, 163
viscosity in student attitudes 161
vocational education 59–61, 91, 100–101, 113–15, 133, 148, 226, 228
voting blocks 209

'wandering' university instructors 43
Warwick University 224, 226
Watt, James 39, 229
wealth
distribution of 176–7
pursuit of 62, 71
Webster, A. 222
West, E.G. 5, 55, 58, 59
Western Governors' Virtual University Project 212, 219
White, L.J. 4–5
Wickham, E.D. 5
Willett, T. 5
William IV 37
Winston, G.C. 3
Wisconsin, University of 15, 48–9
Wissenschaft 40, 41
women, education of 60–61
women's studies 161
Woolsey, Cardinal 25
World War I 141, 152
World War II 144, 154, 170, 172, 173, 204

Yale, Elihu 44
Yale University 15, 16, 44, 48
youth, idolization of 183